selected themes in
the Study of Religions in Nigeria

selected themes in the Study of Religions in Nigeria

Edited by

S.G.A. Onibere
*Department of Religious Studies,
Obafemi Awolowo University, Ile-Ife, Nigeria*
&
M. P. Adogbo
*Department of Religious Studies,
Delta State University, Abraka, Nigeria.*

Malthouse Press Limited
Lagos, Benin, Ibadan, Jos, Port-Harcourt, Zaria

Malthouse Press Limited
43 Onitana Street, Off Stadium Hotel Road,
Surulere, Lagos, Lagos State
E-mail: malthouse_press@yahoo.com
malthouselagos@gmail.com
Tel: +234 (01) -773 53 44; 0802 600 3203

All rights reserved. No part of this publication may be reproduced, transmitted, transcribed, stored in a retrieval system or translated into any language or computer language, in any form or by any means, electronic, mechanical, magnetic, chemical, thermal, manual or otherwise, without the prior consent in writing of Malthouse Press Limited, Lagos, Nigeria.

This book is sold subject to the condition that it shall not by way of trade, or otherwise, be lent, re-sold, hired out, or otherwise circulated without the publisher's prior consent in writing, in any form of binding or cover other than in which it is published and without a similar condition, including this condition, being imposed on the subsequent purchaser.

© S.G.A. Onibere and M.P. Adogbo 2010
First Published 2010
ISBN 978-978-8422-24-2

Distributors:

African Books Collective Ltd
Oxford, United Kingdom
Email: abc@africanbookscollective.com
Website: http://www.africanbookscollective.com

Acknowledgements

We acknowledge the brilliant works by all contributors to this volume. We are particularly grateful to Malthouse Press Limited, Lagos for the prompt attention and, more, for the financial considerations which made the publication of this volume possible. We thank Mr. Obuks Adogbo who arranged and gave the typescript a thorough scrutiny.

Preface

This volume, *selected themes in the Study of Religions in Nigeria* presents comprehensive case studies of various topics in Religious Studies. It aims at bringing about the dynamics of change and innovations that characterize the study of religions in contemporary society. The guiding principle throughout the work has been to present the essential elements of all religions as simply and completely as possible. In this way it is possible to discover with remarkable precision what the religious elements are and the changes that have taken place as a result hybridization of cultural traits.

In a collection like this, it is expected that there would be variations in styles and presentation. The ideas have been harmonized so well that they do not in any way affect the thematic unity of the text. Our success in this direction is largely due to the choice of methodologies adopted by the contributors; hermeneutics, which is essentially an interpretative study of religions and exegesis, was used heuristically in this study. The contributors are renowned professors and scholars with many years of teaching experience in Universities and other tertiary institutions. We have taken great deal of time to select the materials that are relevant to the current National University Commission (NUC) Undergraduate Programmes in Religious Studies.

The work focused on Biblical Studies, Church History, Islamic Studies and African Traditional Religions. The contributors strengthened and renovated the foundations laid by previous writers. The outcome is a new movement of constructive thinking resulting in what phenomenologists call reduction, destruction and construction. In this perspective, the reduction is the redirection of the "gaze" resulting in critical re-evaluation of the traditional ideas. The destruction in this understanding is not a negative task of demolition but a positive appropriation of the traditional cosmologies in the light of contemporary socio-political and technological realities, while construction is the presentation of the materials in the light of current research efforts.

In chapter one, C.U. Manus writes on "Methods and Relevance of the Study of Religions in Nigerian Universities". He opined that whenever issues of ultimate goal and meaning of human existence are raised, mankind gropes in the dark and yearns for theological self-reflection. Here, according to him, hermeneutics and exegetic studies come to the fore. For a thorough understanding of the issues involved in African Biblical scholarship, he advocated the use of *Intercultural hermeneutics* (the mother of African Biblical methodologies). This involves the *re-reading* of the Biblical texts in terms of the categories, concepts, syntax and semantics of the African peoples. He examined the functionality and the real rationale for teaching Religious Studies in the Nigerian context. He was of the view that the future of Religious Studies as an academic discipline is quite rosy and prosperous in Nigeria in spite of the growing intellectual godlessness that is being notoriously advocated in some University campuses.

Chapters two, three and four focused on Biblical Studies. D.T. Ejenebo wrote on "Jesus the Messiah: Son of Man and Son of God". He critically examined the whole gamut of materials surrounding the concept of Jesus as Messiah and came to the conclusion that the information available in Bible and other sources show clearly that Jesus was not only the expected Messiah but was also, uniquely, the Son of Man and Son of God. The work of M.P. Adogbo focused on a critical hermeneutic survey of the resurrection stories and Christian inferences, especially among African Christians. He observed that bodily resurrection with the soul in physical form was a new innovation resulting from the death of Jesus. Although the proclamation of the physical resurrection of Jesus is an unquestionable article of faith in Christendom, much theological work still has to be done in Africa to enable the people to fully understand the intricate and incompatible issues on the resurrection of the physical body. Concluding the chapters in Biblical studies, A.O. Idamarhare wrote on Paul's address at Areopagus in African context. He examined the address as it relates to African traditional cosmologies with special reference to Bini and Yoruba kingdoms. After an exhaustive examination of the similarities between Athens and the ancient kingdoms of Bini and Yoruba he was of the view that Paul's message would have made more impact in winning more souls than it did in Athens if it was delivered in the African cities.

Chapters five and six are on Church History. The contributors, S.G.A. Onibere and D.O. Olayiwola adopted a methodology which we shall call here *Allgemeine Religionswissenschaft.* This methodology is concerned with tracing the historical development of a religious phenomenon and relating same to the social, political and economic realities of the people's cultural context. This approach applies disciplined and rigorous methods of analysis and interpretation to its subject matter. S.G.A. Onibere wrote on the emergence and development of Christianity in Isoko. He observed that religion did not arrive on the Isoko scene to meet a religious *tabula rasa* but the new religion came to a milieu that was already pervaded by the religious dimension of life. This marked the starting-point for a critical historical and interpretative study of the phenomenon in Isokoland. Olayiwola reconstructed the history of Anglican Church in Remoland. He outlined the peculiarities of the Ijebu people as a Yoruba sub-ethnic group. Using the critical historical method with hermeneutics, he evaluated the features that slowed down the missionary work in the area and proceeded to show the positive and fruitful developments of missionary enterprise in Remoland.

Chapters seven and eight are on Islamic Studies. In chapter seven S.O. Eniola examined the basic tenets of Islam with emphasis on sources of Islam and Islamic concept of religion. He opined that in Islamic concept, religion is not only a spiritual and intellectual necessity of life but also a social phenomenon. In this capacity, religion [especially Islam] unites the psychological knots and complexities of man; sublimates his instincts and aspirations and disciplines his desires and the whole course of life. Chapter eight is on the spread of Islam in Nigeria with emphasis on Ijebuland. Here T.A. Oladimeji examined the nature of religious interactions in a Yoruba ethnic group. After a thorough evaluation of the establishment and development of Islam in the area, he was of the view that the acceptance of Islam in the area was largely due to the fact that the early converts were allowed to practice their traditional religion and Islam simultaneously.

Chapters nine and ten are on African Traditional Religion. In Chapter ten Agberia focused on Urhobo traditional cosmology and the unique significance of symbolism. He explains that the vitality of symbolism is closely bound up with some form of religion. Thus most artistic works in Urhoboland are associated with religion, which pervades all aspects of the people's cosmology. He emphasized that the civilization, as well as the culture of the Urhobo, is replete with various artistic objects which symbolically represent their worldview. In chapter ten Adogbo affords us insights into the roles of clairvoyants in Urhobo traditional religion. He established that mediumship is a viable media for the explanation, prediction and control of space-time events. The Urhobo believe that success in life is anchored on the good disposition of God and the divinities towards the affairs of men, while failure or misfortune is predestined or as a result of punishment from the evil spirits. It is the quest to achieve the good things of this world that has given the mediums their prominence in the religious structure of the Urhobo.

Prof. S.G.A. Onibere
Dr. Mike .P. Adogbo

Contributors

Adogbo, Professor M.P.: Department of Religious Studies, Delta State University, Abraka, Nigeria.
Agberia, Professor J.: Department of Fine and Applied Arts, Delta State University, Abraka, Nigeria.
Ejenobo, Dr. D.T. ; Lecturer, Department of Religious Studies, Delta State University, Abraka, Nigeria.
Eniola, Dr. S.O.: Lecturer, Department of Religious Studies, University of Ado-Ekiti, Ado-Ekiti, Nigeria.
Idamarhare, Mr. A.O.: Lecturer, Department of Religious Studies, Delta State University, Abraka, Nigeria.
Manus, Professor C.U.; Department of Religious Studies, Obafemi Awolowo University, Ile-Ife, Nigeria.
Oladimeji, Dr. T.A.G.: Lecture, Federal College of Education, Oyo, Nigeria.
Olayiwola, Professor D.O..: Department of Religious Studies, Obafemi Awolowo University, Ile-Ife, Nigeria.
Onibere, Professor S.G.A.: Department of Religious Studies, Obafemi Awolowo University, Ile-Ife, Nigeria.

Contents

	Pages
Acknowledgements	
Preface	
Contributors	

Chapters

Part I   The Study of Religions

1. Methods and Relevance of the Study of Religions in Nigerian Universities - *C.U. Manus* ... 1

Part II   Biblical Studies

2. Jesus the Messiah: Son of Man and Son of God - *D.T. Ejenobo* ... 19
3. Hermeneutical Study of the Resurrection of Jesus Christ - *M.P. Adogbo* ... 33
4. To the Unknown God: Paul's Address at Areopagus in African Context - *A.O. Idamarhare* ... 45

Part III   Church History

5. Christianity and Indigenous Religion in Nigeria: the Isoko Experience - *S.G.A. Onibere* ... 59
6. Christianity in Remo Land: Prospects and Failures, the Anglican Communion as a Case Study - *D.O. Olayiwola* ... 77

Part IV   Islamic Studies

7. The Islamic Nostrum for the Understanding of Religion - *S. O. Eniola* ... 89
8. The Spread of Islam in Nigeria: the case of Ijebu Land - *T.A. Oladimeji* ... 105

Part V   African Traditional Religion

9. Cosmology and Symbolization in Urhoboland - *J. Agberia* ... 121
10. Clairvoyance in Urhobo Traditional Religion - *M.P. Adogbo* ... 139

Select bibliography ... 153
Index ... 159

Part I

The Study of Religions

Chapter 1

Methods and relevance of the study of religions in Nigerian universities

- C.U. Manus

Introduction

The chapter focuses attention on the methods and relevance of the study of religions as an academic discipline in the Nigerian universities. Unfortunately, the view that religious studies has any relevance at all quite often agitates the minds of some Nigerian intellectuals; especially those of agnostic bend. In spite of a growing intellectual godlessness that is notoriously being advocated in some of our universities, there is no doubt that the future of religious studies as an academic discipline is quite rosy and prosperous in this country. This is the thesis I strongly wish to defend in this chapter.

No one doubts that there are a few misinformed individuals who pretend ignorance of the fact that African cultures have a religious epistemology and ontology (Pobee, 391). The late Professor E. B. Idowu of the University of Ibadan, Nigeria's premier university, had illustriously defended this assertion with illustrations from the Nigerian peoples' ubiquitous acknowledgement of the presence of divine reality in the Nigerian life-world (Idowu 1962). His opinion corroborates what philosophers of religion had known, since the time of the great Dominican thinker, Thomas Aquinas (1224-1274) as the cosmological argument for God's existence; namely that "reason can proceed from an observation of the facts of experience to a conclusion about the ultimate cause of such facts" (Schmidt: 286). How many of our educated colleagues have given critical thought to the contemporary proliferation of new religious movements, African Instituted Churches and Cultic Sufism in Islam as well as the boisterous crusades, open-air revivals and the *holy noises* that bellow out of churches, mosques, temples and shrines all over Nigeria's major cities and villages? If there be no religious studies departments where critical minds are trained, who shall analyse, discuss and reflect on the tenacious manner some Christians and Muslims conduct their religious business in this country? If not, how can Idowu's premier clairvoyance be vindicated? Even in the Republic of South Africa where the theology of the Reformed Church had been used by the Afrikaner regime under P.W. Botha to fan the embers of hatred, exploitation and apartheid, still departments for the study of religions and theology are adequately staffed, supported and funded with the tax payers' money.

The functionality of Religious Studies in the Nigerian context

Old and recent research in the history of religions continues to affirm beyond reasonable doubt that human beings are religious animals: that is, that humankind is a *homo sapiens cum religioso* in one. The findings further point us up to the active role religion had played, since time immemorial, and how it continues to give meaning to the lives of human beings the world over. Ample information and dependable data now available from the studies of local scholars, anthropologists and sociologists alike attest to the fact that religion is, as language, a universal phenomenon in every human culture. Various ethnic groups in Nigeria have their own cultural expressions or conceptions of a super-empirical and non-ordinary reality that they give the names: god/s, spirits or deities. These spiritual entities are believed to influence and to rule human existence. From various human cultural histories, it is now known that the commonality of religious experience supports the fact that human beings, Nigerians not of course exempted, possess the inner capacity and inherent *desideratum* for experiencing the cosmos as sacred (Imo: 8-10). A growing *opinio consensus* among many contemporary scientists; especially physical scientists, is that religion is inherently incarnate in human nature itself. For one, Julian Huxley, a human biologist, has proclaimed to the world that religion is a way of experiencing the sense of the Holy that is innate in all human beings. According to him, "not only does the normal man have this capacity for experiencing the sense of the sacred, but he demands its satisfaction." (110). Beside this intuition offered by exact scientists, was it not Abraham H. Maslow, the American reputed psychologist, who had asserted that the naturalness and desirability of religious or "peak" experiences are necessarily part and parcel of humanity (Maslow: 19-29).

Are peak experiences lacking in Nigerians? I strongly doubt if Nigerians are excluded in this experience after all of two things Nigerians are noted for in the world, one is that "Nigerians are very religious". Visit the Prayer Sessions of one of the Charismatic Prayer Groups in many churches in the land or attend one of the many celebrated jam-packed crusades of one of the "pastors" of any African Initiated Churches or watch at a close distance any of the urban mosques, no one will tell you that Nigerians, irrespective of race, gender, class and calling do claim transcendent experiences hitherto unknown even in contemporary western religious traditions. I have recently observed and recorded experiences of this sort of spiritual linkages between humans and deity in one of Nigeria's famous crusades. Pastor Adeboye's *Divine Favour* Weekend Crusade organized to do battle with the agents of the culture of death and violence from the Nigerian campuses had kicked off at the Obafemi Awolowo University, Ile-Ife on the 19th of November, 1999. That religious jamboree attracted over 30,000 throngs of human beings cut across denominational and class lines in Ile-Ife and its environs. The rally drew many people both young and old, students and academics outside of themselves. Many of the people I interviewed that night testified that they had found themselves filled with tremendous joy and filled with a sense of rapture with the divine. Some of the students came to believe themselves as radically transformed individuals.

What I saw, heard and witnessed was far beyond ordinary experience. Is it not, perhaps, the claim of maximum achievement of spiritual satisfaction that makes tens of thousands of the Nigerian faithful to pursue the RCCG Pastor and the others of his calibre wherever they go? But with the critical mind of a religion scholar in the academy, objective questions on the phenomenon ought to be raised; namely, are these Nigerians being merely gullible? Were they just hallucinating? With such cases and the supportive empirical data, one cannot deny the fact that organized religion has become an essential ingredient to empower group life in Nigeria. On a rather critical note, I dare say, if these manifestations are not true, how may one explain why Governor Ahmed Sani, was able to be the first Nigerian administrator to have gone ahead to declare the Shari'a law to rule the conduct of Muslims in Zamfara State in an apparent defiance of the Constitution of the Federal Republic of Nigeria with the approval of the State Legislature? Or why should the Christian Association of Nigeria (CAN) be reeling under the phobia of the Islamization of Nigeria through the introduction of the Shari'a in Nigeria or why did Nigeria's membership of the Organisation of Islamic Countries (OIC) under Generals Buhari and Babangida generate such a furore in Nigeria's recent political and socio-religious history? Besides, the political implications of the undemocratic policies of some of the previous regimes in matters of religion and the dismissal of candid intellectual advice do nurture the ground for conflicts that rear their ugly heads and that haunt the nation today.

While we, as scholars of religion, agree that humans are by nature religious, Nigerian peoples' everyday life, utterances and worship patterns, in spite of the prevalence of graft, corruption in high places and other associated social pandemic, distinctively mark us out as seriously committed religious people. Senator Sunday Awoniyi's November 1999 brief speech on NTA Network News, two days after the PDP National Convention at Abuja where he claimed he was robbed through rigging of his right to win the party's chairmanship that year was regretfully lamented by him with religious oaths and aphorisms. The usual religious expressions of President Olusegun Obasanjo and many cabinet ministers such as "God being on our side", "by God's help", "God willing", "leave his death to God" are among so many such "civil religion" utterances that distinguish Nigerian politicians as perhaps innately religious. Certainly the political class resorts often to religion in order to create the impression that they are a people who know that the physical and the spiritual constitute two components of the human reality without which the existential equation would not balance (Adamolekun 1999). And often they make empty promises to the electorate concerning programmes that would promote the balance in the tilted equation.

Recent research findings on the religions in Nigeria have made scholars to be unanimous in affirming that religion is a potent force that possesses life-giving potentials for integral development of humankind and for his/her environment. Roger Schmidt, a leading American sociologist of religion has accurately and forcefully argued that religions constitute "major systems of significance for resolving ambiguities and getting a handle on life as a whole" (Schmidt: 9-10). Moreover, he admits that religion affirms that the cosmos has meaning and that human life is ultimately a significant condition. That religion addresses fundamental aspects of human existence is not in doubt when one takes stock of the contemporary Nigerian social religious and political landscape (Ibrahim 1989). Take the issue of the constant eruption of religious conflicts in the land *vis-à-vis* the social hardships that prevailed in Nigeria during the reign of terror of late General Sani Abacha. In a recent paper delivered at Harvard University Centre for the Study of World Religions (CSWR), Prof. Ogbu Kalu, a distinguished Professor of Church History and Religion formerly at the Department of Religion, University of Nigeria, Nsukka and a Visiting Scholar at the Centre in the 1998/99 school year, had drawn attention to the legitimacy crises that bedevilled the Abacha regime in Nigeria. According to Kalu, Nigeria is a land where venomous rivalries among Nigerian ethnic peoples exist. Usually, such conflicts are acerbated by the geopolitical and religious divides to the extent that Muslims claim control of the North and Christians hold sway in the south. In such a scenario, the relevance and role of Religious Studies in critiquing the situation cannot but be emphasized (Kalu: 7). The consequence of that wave of social conflict that arose from the legitimacy crisis engendered large-scale moral decadence in the wake of which an avalanche of spiritual breakdown was enthroned. In the light of such anarchic situations, Ogbu Kalu's question: "can religion be a tool of hope?" (Kalu: 7) still becomes quite *ad rem*. For me, Religious Studies programmes have been so designed that careful and well-tailored course units are offered to empower its graduates with the skill to distil the truth from what is false in religious claims and dogmas. In this light, the programmes are aimed at providing religious studies graduates the capabilities to acquire the practical and theoretical acumen to make religions fulfil their noble roles in providing meaning in times of suffering and pain in society.

The contributions of the three major religions in Nigeria and the voices and concerns of their adherents are subject-matters that must be researched, taught, appreciated and listened to. This must be admitted in the light of their experiences of life with God in the local areas and states as well as the worldviews the religions impact on the Nigerian social political institutions in general. Teaching and research in the discipline of religion are contributing, in no small measure, towards the promotion of an understanding and appreciation of a culture of life and peace in the context of human rights protection and promotion for a better society as dividends of democracy for the post-modern Nigeria (Ojo 2000). It is on this superstructure that the quest for a just society, a participatory democracy and the need to develop sustainable community development should be anchored (Abogunrin:1-4). In other words, critical thoughts generated from Religious Studies discourse would insist that our national and public policies must have a *human face*. Religious studies and theology uphold the view that every economic policy and programmes of government such as the Poverty Alleviation Programme (PAP), the Universal Basic Education (UBE), the new National Youth Employment Scheme (NYES) and the Anti-Corruption Crusade (ACC), though humanly initiated, are divinely inspired concerns that should enhance the living standards, promote happiness and wellbeing of all Nigerians. The road to heavenly bliss should begin here on earth. Besides, do I have to sound a fresh *ogene* or gong than I have recently done before our peers and nationals would come to recognize that Religious Studies enhances the promotion of human dignity and respect for Human Rights. It stimulates ideas that can benefit the programmes for national rebirth such that Nehemiah had called in the post-exilic Israel of his time. Are religious courses not empowering Nigerians so trained to engage in a permanent crusade against bribery and corruption in Nigeria? (Manus 2000: 153-172). If it has not been heard in the dailies and media in this country, let it be known now that our students and products have always been saturated with the purposes, objectives, course descriptions and lessons that religious studies exposes them to. Certainly such provisions go a long way to satisfying the quest for promoting knowledge and the acquisition of morally good virtues that religions contribute towards integral human promotion (Danfulani 1996). What I am saying is that knowledge about the Religions and the morality they impart inculcate discipline in the individuals trained under their purview who, in turn either as teachers, pastors or civil servants pass on impeccable religiously founded morals to the society. Therefore, religious and ethical studies ever remain relevant subjects for life besides academic purposes.

Social scientists like religion scholars know that human beings should live and ply their businesses in a disciplined society so that investments and economic progress are not hampered. Scholars of religion are taught to understand that societal indiscipline frustrates all genuine efforts to increase the productivity of a nation. Recent happenings are proving that Nigeria is spending a substantial amount of her scarce resources to police and checkmate the nefarious activities of the undisciplined members of the society. Religious studies scholars recognize the fact that development does not begin with goods and that it does not even begin with gigantic infrastructures. Many scholars of religion know that development and welfare do not even begin with a borrowed or erroneously copied ideology or technology. But that development, the type envisioned by New Partnership for Africa's Development (NEPAD) and disseminated by the Obasanjo administration through National Economic Empowerment Development Strategy (NEEDS) begins with discipline both within the government circle and in the larger society. religious history informs religious studies scholars that discipline, the fundamental of religious congregations and societies over the years, has been the bedrock of development that has created in part current European and Asian wealth and the respect their leaders enjoy today in the comity of nations. In-depth research in

Religious Studies is furnishing us with a growing sense and appreciation of the contribution of Christianity towards the historical success of western society despite the phenomenon of secularization and its dysfunctional consequences in the post-modern world. Besides, religious studies specifically devoted to Christianity is indicating that features of western history, society and culture in the past few centuries such as growth and stability of society, respect for the rule of law and the public ethos that make for a better society are due to the intervention and role of the Christian religion. Whether this view is acceptable or not, the fact remains that Religious Studies is drawing the attention of an increasing number of scholars and intellectuals to the fact that religion is a portent force to reckon with in any society. Some of such intellectuals, often unbelievers themselves, have even come to agree that Religious Studies has much to offer society. Such persons otherwise called culture-minded Christians, and perhaps defined with a theological jargon, can be said to belong to the *anonymous Christians* of Karl Rahner's Theology of Non-Christian Religions. In sum, I dare say that research in Religious Studies is alerting the academia that issues as human rights instrinsically belong to religions and that there is an emerging view on the validity of *Religious Human Rights* in global perspective.

What after all does National Rebirth or the *Re-Awakening* which President Obasanjo had called for portend for the Nigerian society? Certainly, scholars of religions can offer realistic prognostications and answers. Religion scholars mince no words in teaching their students that when they enter government; they should recognize that, as public functionaries, they should be highly disciplined and accountable. It is such education in discipline that should discourage our mean nationals from giving and receiving bribes, accepting gratifications, encouraging injustice, overt ethnicity and engaging in other types of abuse of office rampant in our civic institutions. What about the role of religions, the churches and the mosques in peace-making, conflict prevention, its management, resolution and reconciliation in today's Nigeria where so much inter-ethnic crises and conflicts plague the people and even shake the very stability of our communities? Nigerians should not forget the relevance of Religions in view of the historic contributions of some of the churches and the mosques. Are these institutions not known to have worked together towards the sustenance of viable democracy by participating in monitoring the last elections? Have church leaders and some of the nation's Episcopal Conferences and Synods not been engaged in the provision of analytical focus on situations of severe human degradation and peoples' rights violation? (Onwu: 1984). I am strongly convinced that it is from the lessons of religious morals and ethics that the promotion of significant national values like respect for the elderly, trust, solidarity, truthfulness, marital fidelity, love and care of offspring, knowledge about the sacrosanctity of life and good neighbourliness has come to be cultivated and strengthened. Surely these values go a long way to promote national, regional and inter-state cohesion. Religion scholars spend their energies doing research for what ideally contribute towards the search for a lasting peace and the education and conscientization of people to commit themselves to programmes concerned with even development in rural areas and places that have suffered from official neglect by past dictatorial governments. Religion students are taught the art of promoting and strengthening national integration as they learn in their ethics courses that the wide disparities in economic development between the states, urban and rural regions in the country fuel many of the crises the nation witnesses today. Certainly, religious studies scholarship equips its products with the acumen to acknowledge and respect the presence of persons of other faith traditions in our society and to embrace the call to dialogue with such neighbours (Vishigh 1991). They are taught to cooperate with all Nigerians within a multi-faith society to live together in order to forge one nation and one indivisible people under one God. These values are inculcated in order to douse, as Professor Kalu advises "the dysfunctional impact of competing religious groups on the body politic" (Kalu: 7) and to promote a universal ethic that emphasizes the affirmation of human dignity. These are some of the main objectives that constitute the core content of the religious studies syllabus in Nigeria. From great minds like Hans Küng, the famous Tübingen Professor, and Director of the Institute of Ecumenal Research and Practical Theology in Germany, there can be no peace without religious peace (Küng 1991). We do know that while religion can be a decisive factor in creating conflicts as we have recurrently seen in recent times, it is also a formidable agent in promoting peace and equity. It depends on the side it is pushed. According to Professor Küng, there must be dialogue between the religions in the quest for global peace (Küng: 55-64).

While well tailored religious studies programmes do provide a window on the religious world, the courses deepen the insights of students on the trajectories of international diplomacy as religion has nowadays been used to sway the political pendulum in Northern Ireland, the Middle East: Iran, Iraq and in the continent of Asia; India and Pakistan, Afghanistan and Indonesia, just to mention a few places. Scholars of religious studies and their students are not ignorant of the current drive by the international community for *globalisation*. In fact, religion and international relations have become jolly good bedfellows in the curricula of western universities and in a few in the African continent. The global impact of Religion is tilting public policy. And the allegiance of the international community is behesting religious educators to advise governments that globalization as it is operated in the South and in its understanding as the effort towards a single global economy and one homogenous culture; the so-called *global village*, is predominantly negative and destructive of individual national values and autonomy. The employment of the term in contemporary international religious politics to denote partnership and cooperation among adherents of various religions and religious institutions around the world appears quite problematic. Without contextualization, enculturation and conscientization, I wish to agree with Fiji theologians, that globalization is disempowering and impoverishing as it demeans national sovereignty (MF 1999:64). Besides, contemporary African scholars of religion and liberation theologians have come to realize that globalisation is a process whereby wealth produces tremendous poverty for many people in the Third World while it generates a mammoth concentration of capital in the North.

Given the views expressed so far, I dare say that rationalisation of religious studies programmes or the proposal to merge the departments of religious studies with some other units in the nigerian universities must rather be seen as an idiotic and a thoughtless iconoclasm that is carefully being thrust on an irresistibly religious land. The spirits of the founding fathers who had spent the nation's meagre resources in the First Republic to establish and nurse these departments will turn and whine in their graves. Their noble work was done in the days when Nigeria had no tertiary institutions that could either adequately cater for the education of students wishing to acquire scientific knowledge about the religions of their fatherland or competently train those who intended to obtain academic qualifications necessary for appointments in the universities and service in the churches and mosques.

There is no doubt that the nation would be making a costly mistake in her already educationally backward history if departments that had creditably fulfilled those laudable objectives are allowed to atrophy into oblivion in other departments which claim the narrative approach as the epicentre of their *raison d'etre*. Religious studies as a scientific study of the phenomena of religious behaviour, belief-systems and the conduct of humankind and societies is neither a reconstructive nor a restorative science talk of being a narrative discipline as some of our colleagues who, out of sheer ignorance of the task of religious studies, tend to hold. the nigerian nation and our colleagues in the humanities must be tutored to understand that the discipline of religious studies is essentially historical, phenomenological, sociological, contextual and hermeneutical in approach and focus, that is to say, that religious studies is essentially an interpretive science. Should there be any need for religious studies to cooperate with any discipline, the closest relative in the interogative and interpretive task is philosophy despite years of bitter acrimony and controversy between some trends of atheistic philosophy and established religious institutions; namely the Church. In the next section, I wish to advance salient arguments in favour of the hermeneutical task of religious studies.

The hermeneutical task of Religious Studies

Even though Philosophy had long been recognized as not necessary for human salvation, great minds like Ludwig Wittgenstein had maintained that philosophy is a battle against the bewitchment of our intelligence by way of language, (Wittgenstein :47e). In the light of philosophy's affinity with religion, the Medieval Schoolmen had defended the principle of *philosophia perennis,* that is to say, that philosophy is a persistent wisdom that continually reworks and renews human understanding in his pursuit of basic universal concepts such as those only achievable with the aid of data accruable from religious experience and revelation. Thus both disciplines share in the hermeneutical task; that is to say, both philosophy and religious studies are hermeneutical in scope. Both are basically *interpretive*. Methodologically, both disciplines follow the hermeneutic gateway to arrive at hidden signification of "texts", "words" and "categories" otherwise couched in obscure, arcane and symbolic language. Hermeneutics-in-praxis is therefore the required art needed to decode mythic language as did Hermes from the gods to humankind in his day (Manus 2003: 30-32). And this is right because, over the years, mankind whether in Africa or beyond had had his thoughts and beliefs sapiential or religious, written or unwritten, wrapped up in deep symbolisms which require continual decoding and re-interpretation. Paul Ricoeur the celebrated French philo-linguist; and Kwesi Wiredu, a leading African philosopher of language have forcefully argued that all cultural concepts are usually encoded enigmatically, pre-philosophically in the language of myth and in symbolisms. According to them, there is need to decode them in order to manifest the universal desire for clarification and elucidation.

Nevertheless, scholarship in the science of religion recognizes that symbols are imaginary and their truths *sui generis*. Since all the symbols of man and his myths allude to the situation of mankind in the cosmos, the hermeneutical enterprise becomes an obligation for philosophers, theologians and scholars who have made Religious Studies the storm centre of their research and thought. This is because whenever the issue of the ultimate goal and meaning of human existence is raised, mankind gropes in the dark and yearns for theological self-reflection on the datum of existence. Here, hermeneutics comes into the fore. And since hermeneutics in religion is not a matter of giving in to some kind of imaginative intuition but the elaboration of concepts that can help one comprehend language that had become so intricately clothed in symbolic and proverbial garbs, it has to be recoursed to provide clarity. And in executing the transference of the richness of signification that had preceded rational elucidation in our cultures as Africans, the relevance of the relationship between Philosophy and religious studies as interpretative disciplines cannot be under-rated in any liberal arts programme in a conventional university setting. In other words, the hermeneutical frontier is the most significant *rendezvous* for both philosophy and religious Studies insofar as both disciplines are attached to their dossiersr "accumulative intentions" and are grotesquely multivalent.

The case I am urging here is not that religious studies is unmarketable but that there is a deep collaboration and operational similarity between philosophy and religion that is made evident by the science of interpretation, exegesis and hermeneutics. Religious studies and philosophy scholars evaluate, for example, nature and natural processes in moral, aesthetic in religious terms as good or evil, beautiful or ugly, hopeful or meaningless. There may arise contrasting features but these are often expressible in religious concepts. The notion, "creation" in teleological arguments is usually employed to express the fact that there is a good order underlying our cosmic reality. "Salvation" implies that our current reality is insecure. "Covenant" suggests that we are not yet mutually well bonded with the Ultimate Reality. In the perspectives of contemporary eco-theology, when humans are seen as stewards of reality, reality becomes appreciated as good. When humans are recognized as co-creators or co-redeemers, their responsibility to the Absolute

Cause becomes emphasized, and it is only then that mankind can begin to perceive the difference between the actual and the ideal.

Let me illustrate this point further with the work of those of us who teach Biblical studies in religious studies departments. African Biblical scholarship has come of age and the international community of Biblical scholars has begun to accord it a place of honour that it deserves. In the last few years, many international conferences have been organized to hear the African exegetes tell the rest of the world how they are making Biblical stories become meaningful in their own contexts (Manus 1999). *Intercultural hermeneutics*, the mother of African Biblical methodologies, involves a movement or an interaction between two languages (texts), their underlying cultures as well as their value systems and calls for a *re-reading* of the ancient texts in the receptor culture and contexts (Manus 2003). The hermeneutical principle provides the guidelines. The science of exegesis involves a transfer of meaning from a source language; namely Hebrew, Aramaic or Greek to a target language, for example, Ibibio, Efik, Yoruba, Igbo or Hausa. Doing Biblical studies in African universities' departments of religious studies involves therefore a *re-reading* of the source text in terms of the categories, concepts, syntax and semantics of a target language, that is, of a particular vernacular of the Africans or Nigerians. This would, for example, imply the interpretation of a Greek term in a passage under study from the vantage point of a local vernacular language. In Yoruba language, for example, an *oriki* text can make a good example of using the patterns of a target text to deliver the meaning of a source text. In such an exercise, the exegete is involved in the hermeneutical enterprise. Here, he/she fulfils the role of active mediator between source text and target text, source language and target language, source culture and target culture or as the mediator berween the underlying source and target value systems, worldviews, ideologies or belief systems (Gwamna 1996). Thus the role of a seasoned exegete in religious studies is an art in intercultural communication in which he/she has to be attuned to the rich insights discernible from the daily life and struggles of the target audience, in our case, the Nigerian peoples and their social-political and economic conditions in the new democratic dispensation and market-oriented economy. Even in Biblical or Qurranic exegesis, religious studies promotes an encounter between the language and culture of the people of the past in order to facilitate a rediscovery of their concepts, categories, thought-forms and systems of the narrative social world. Much of the contemporary re-validation of the scope of religious studies is the "exegetical space" currently being provided by African inculturation theology which is engaging itself in intercultural hermeneutics on the side of womenr's experiences and perspectives in African cultures and religions (Oduyoye 1995). Since the 1990s, African women scholars in Religious Studies and Theology have begun to articulate an African Womanist Theology which is attempting to create an inclusive community where women's humanity is seriously being discussed, affirmed and empowered (Njoroge: 50). The training in these hermeneutical skills in religious studies ranks our graduates far much higher than their peers in the other courses in the humanities and the social sciences.

The real rationale for teaching Religious Studies

Religious Studies programmes should be appreciated in terms of their contributions towards the awakening of public interest in the ethical re-orientation programmes initiated by some previous administrations and the current National Rebirth Campaign launched by President Olusegun Obasanjo to prosper Nigeria's fledgling democracy (Adamolekun 1999). In spite of the decline of basic infrastructures in the educational sector and the shortage of adequate staff strength required in the pursuit of academic excellence in the discipline of religious studies, it is my candid opinion that since religion is life and life is religion, what is deepest down within the Nigerian personality or what he/she feels most intimately in his/her inner self is believed to be God. This is the theistic logic. And really, few persons are atheists in the real sense of it in most societies (Howkins: 8-9). This applies to Nigeria. The departments of religious studies in the Nigerian universities are widely acknowledged throughout sister African universities, Europe, North America and Asia as great centres of excellence in the scientific study of the living religions of man in Africa. Staff membership in international associations such as the International Association for the History of Religions (IAHR), International Association for Mission Studies (IAMS), the International Society for New Testament Studies (SNTS), International Congress of Christians and Jews (ICCJ), just to name a few, is outstandingly quite impressive. And in the UNESCO in Paris and the Alexander von Humboldt Foundation in Bonn (AvH), Germany, DAAD, Germany, the Fulbright Foundation, the Ford Foundations, the Rockefeller Foundation and the Overseas Ministries Study Centre, New Haven. Connecticut, USA, many staff of Nigerian Departments of Religious Studies had won distinguished awards for research in the field of religion and had conducted their studies as solid scholars who are renowned in intercultural and contextual studies in the disciplines of religion, theology, Biblical studies and African Christian studies. This alone vindicates the reputation and the expertise of Nigerian scholars of religion and the comparability of Nigerian university religious studies education with those of other nations of the world; after all, many Nigerian scholars of religion attended the International Association for the History of Religions (IAHR) Millennium Conference that took place in July 2000 at Durban, South Africa.

Religious Studies is pre-eminently one of the human sciences engaged in the business of generating knowledge. It disseminates knowledge about Nigeria's major religious traditions and the religious experiences of Nigerians in the contemporary age. Religious studies must therefore be studied and taught for rendering such services to the Nigerian public. In a multi-faith society as Nigeria, the scope of religious studies programmes is all-inclusive, objective and ecumenical. In its syllabuses, provisions are made for critical and Talmudic expositions of Christianity, Islam, African traditional religion, other world religions and the critical and unbiased study of their sacred books: the Bible, the Qurran and the Vedas.

Sources of African traditional religions like the Ifa Literary Corpus, African cosmogonic myths and African traditional precatory texts constitute the storm-centre of critical investigation. The sacred and the secular or rather the holy and the unholy are not left out in its critical searchlight despite increasing waves of secularization in the contemporary society which is eroding the respect accorded religious personages, doctrines and creeds. The National Universities Commission (NUC) Approved Minimum Academic Standards in Arts and Education on Religious Studies for all Nigerian universities are well fine-tuned, broad-based and neatly tailored to include a wide range of courses and electives such as comparative religion, ecclesiastical history, ethics, African customs and mores, religion and human values/rights, anthropology of religion, phenomenology, sociology, philosophy of religion and contextual african theology and others (NUC 1999).

In this new millennium, there increases the need to advance the teaching and research on the three major religions in Nigeria in order to cater adequately for the peculiarities of Nigerians; namely for the spiritual and religious interests of the adherents of these religions. In the overall interest of the nation and for the general knowledge of future politicians and administrators, the nation must come to recognize the urgent need for all graduates of our universities to be well tutored on the basic tenets of these religions in the general studies curricula of the universities. This is necessary insofar as religion plays such a crucial role in the power game and politics of Nigeria (Takaya 1989). Besides, we all know that these religions have come to be used by hoodlums to wreck the peace and tranquillity associated with the religious experiences of Nigerians, and the property of the taxpayers whose money is used to fund the universities. Thus, the future of religious studies in a religiously pluralistic society as Nigeria cannot but be emphasized and by no other persons than those of us who are energetically engaged in the scientific production of a body of religious knowledge as objectively as possible in the Nigerian contexts. When religion is studied as a phenomenon in our own setting or as something that appears among the Nigerian peoples as well as among other peoples of the world then the curricula of Religious Studies education have to be seen as the peoplesr curricula (Danfulani 1996). In that light, the following critical questions become necessary to raise: Is *Allah*, the God of Islam, the same God of Christianity? If both religions insist that there is only one God, are there sound bases for disagreement? Do both the Qurran and the Bible agree on the nature of God? If both Scriptures offer different views of the deity, how may Christian and Muslim scholars and students agree that there is one God? Would they agree in part about His nature and how He is to be served, worshipped and adored or would they disagree strongly about how He is to be approached whether through a Son or through a Prophet? Is there not immense value that accrues to the Christian who studies Islam as he/she discovers that the contrasting views with his/her religion do not only disabuse his/her mind about the ugly stereotypes he/she had hitherto been led to hold about his/her Muslim neighbours. Does the exposure to the structure and tenets of other faiths not lead him/her to think more deeply about the credibility of his/her own beliefs. Would a person so educated not function, among other things, as one who can douse religious intolerance and conflicts in his/her community?

Methods and relevance of the study of religions in Nigerian universities

Recent research has shown that analytic study of African traditional religion is producing beneficial effects on non-Africans (Metuh 1991). European and North American scholars who read the publications of African scholars of religion have begun to critique their own thinking patterns (Bryant 1995). In their materialistic civilization, the westerner totally denies the existence of non-material or spiritual realities (Howkins: 11). But African traditional religion affirms the existence of supra-sensory realities. For the African traditionalists, there is a world of the mind, a spiritual world which is hidden under this physical world. It is religious studies that is specialized in describing and interpreting this phenomenon objectively. This hermeneutic exercise directs the attention of western-minded Africans to reconsider their perception of this world. Besides, it alerts the Christian of the risk involved in his/her excessive preoccupation with temporal matters. While religious studies highlights some of the similarities and dissimilarities in the different religions in Nigeria, the discipline possesses the genius to clarify the differential richness and the contributions they make on cultural values system and changes in the social ethics of our society (Imo 1991). It is through religious studies lectures and learning on *religion* and *human* values that the Nigerian youths are empowered with the need to religiously rededicate themselves, in spite of the decay in the society, to the service of God and their fatherland. I believe that it is only the falsificators of religion or the "pushers" of religion and those academics who take religion for a ride that make religion become a harbinger of hatred and violence. And we have a reasonable number of such folks in this country. In the light of this discourse, it has to be affirmed that religious studies is not an *endangered species* and can never be one in the Nigerian university system.

It is in this bid that I wish to argue that the future of religious studies in the Nigerian universities rests on the fact that the discipline is a dynamic field of study, a worthy enterprise for research, analysis and interpretation whose findings can positively sustain religion as a unifying factor in the country (Onwu 1984). Were the nation to close down these units in the universities, their identities and prestige would sink as they would no longer be recognized as departments of academic excellence in the social sciences and humanities education in Nigeria. Will the future generations not regard such governments as iconoclasts? We have been in the system for sometime now. There is no doubt that we have inherited, since some twenty eight years of military dictatorship and 'kleptocracy' nothing but the massive destruction of the nation's economic viability and an anaemic educational policy that has misguided the philosophies of our tertiary institutions. All stakeholders must agree that religious studies is as much relevant as any other university course. Relevance must be justified by the society. If we must study religion because we must train Nigerians who take care of our spiritual life and can objectively broker inter-religious dialogue in order to guarantee peaceful co-existence, then we have no choice but to augment the admissions into religious studies programmes. We appreciate the present government's commitment to education and the launch of the Universal Basic Education (UBE) for all. We salute President Olusegun Obasanjo for allocating such a staggering amount of naira in last year's budget proposal for education in the country in spite of dwindling financial resources.

Conclusion

I seize this opportunity to launch a clarion call on our new generation democrats in both the Lower and the Upper Houses not to relent on their oars to allow the evaporation of all that Nigeria has erected over the years to happen. The purported claim of quick miracles by the technological transformation of Nigeria being made by some ill-intentioned advisers and donors such as the IMF and the World Bank must be critically re-evaluated. History and dependency theorists often prognosticate wrongly on the future development of the so-called Third World nations. We have financial experts in our universities who are more than willing to proffer positive advice on cost benefit effects on funding and university fiscal management. Our universities and their authorities should not be tired of sourcing funds locally and elsewhere for the continued education in religion of our youths; for a nation that neglects teaching and research in its spiritual heritage runs on the brink of historical and cultural extinction. Europeans who gave us the idea of the university had always started their campuses with Faculties of Theology and Religious Studies with emphasis on the teaching of the sacred languages before Royal approvals were granted for the inception of other disciplines. Great minds on religion like the Dutch renaissance humanist, Erasmus of Rotterdam, the erudite Archbishop, Anselm of Canterbury, the Dominican Professor, Thomas Aquinas and Albert the Great had so enriched western thought to such an extent that European and North American scholarship still remains grossly indebted to these pathfinders.

I find nothing obtruse in our "money bags" and the rich emulating William Gladstone, the Victorian Prime Minister who, in 1889, founded the St Deiniolrs Library at Hawarden, Flintshire, England for "*the pursuit of divine learning*". The institution has, today, up-to-date working library of more than 250,000 volumes with comfortable residential facilities and holdings specialized in theology, history, philosophy, classics and literature? Finally, let us take a cue from the American Congress which has recently created and funds a United States Institute of Peace with a strong organ: religions, ethics and human rights initiative which is essentially committed to the promotion of the peaceful resolution of international conflicts. Would it not amount to a dereliction of duty on the part of our government if Nigeria so ravaged by inter-religious and ethnic clashes be ignorant of theological dimensions of conflict resolution and management?

In the light of the above submission, I urge the government, the Senate and House of Representative Committees on Education and the relevant State Ministries of Education to direct the WAEC and NECO to restore Religious Studies, that is, Nigerian traditional religion, Christian religious studies and Islamic religious studies in their syllabuses and to make them compulsory for candidates of each faith tradition. We can no longer continue to watch our society go amoral and fundamentalist because of insufficient exposure, knowledge and awareness of the essentials of the tenets of the major religions in Nigeria. Already our society has begun to pay heavy prices for this neglect of the spiritual self-transcendence and moral formation of our youth. Can any sane person tell us why the former Osun State Governor, Chief Bisi Akande dropped, among others, the teaching of religion in that state and sacked all the teachers during his administration of that state and there was no meaningful federal government intervention on the issue? But the Good Lord provided the intervention when the PDP swept him and his anti-people policies away.

Works cited

Abogunrin, S.O. 1999 "Religion and Democracy in Nigeria," *Orita, Ibadan Journal of Religious Studies*, Vol. XXXI/1-2, pp. 1-18.

Adamolekun, T. 1999, "The Role of Religion in the Political and Ethical Re-Orientation of Nigeria," *Orita, Ibadan Journal of Religious Studies*, Vol. XXXI/1-2, pp. 19-28.

Bryant, M.D. 1995, "African Wisdom and the Recovery of the Earth," *Orita, Ibadan Journal of Religious Studies*, Vol. XXVII, Nos 1-2, pp. 49-58.

Danfulani, U.H.D, 1996, "Integrating traditional African morality into contemporary Christian religious education curriculum in Nigeria," *Jos Bulletin of Religion*, Vol. 3. No. 1, pp. 48-55.

Gwamna, J.D. 1996, "Phenomenology of sacred and the profane in African traditional religions and Biblical perspective," *Jos Bulletin of Religion*, Vol. 3, No. 1, pp. 56-64.

Howkins, K.G. 1972, *The Challenge of Religious Studies*, London, Tyndale Press.

Huxley, J.S. 1950, *Religion without Revelation*, New York, Harper & Brothers.

Ibrahim, J. 1989, "The Politics of Religion in Nigeria: The Parameters of the 1987 Crisis in Kaduna State," *Review of African Political Economy*, Vols. 45-46, p. 78.

Idowu, E.B. 1962, *Olydumare. God in Yoruba Belief*, Longman, London.

Imo, C.O. 1991, "African Cultural Values and Social Change," *Bulletin of African Religion and Culture*, Vol. 3, No. 2, pp. 29-46.

Imo, C.O. 1997, "Cultural Matrix and Awareness of God: A Case Study of the Nigerian Situation," *Journal of Religion and Theology*, Vol. 2, No. 2, pp. 8-26.

Kalu, O.U. 1999, "Harsh Flutes: On the Legitimacy Crisis in Nigeria," in *NEWS, Harvard University Centre for the Study of World Religions*, No. 2, Vol. 6, pp. 7, 11.

Küng, H. 1991, *Global Responsibility: In Search of a New World Ethic*, London, SCM Press.

Manus, C.U. 1999, "Biblical-Theological Reflections on Poverty, Ethnic Inequality and Socio-Economic Injustice in Africa: The Nigerian Example," forthcoming in *Scriptura: International Journal of Bible, Religion and Theology in Southern Africa*, pp. 14.

Manus, C.U. 2000, *"Religion and Human Rights in a Pluralistic Society,"* in Prof. Ojo, A. (ed.),Protection and Promotion of Human Rights for a Better Society in Nigeria, *Leven Club International, Lagos, Federal Government Press, pp. 153-171.*

Manus, C.U. 2003, *Intercultural Hermeneutics in Africa: Methods and Approaches*, Nairobi, Acton Press.

Maslow, A.H. 1964, *Religious Values and Peak Experiences*, Columbus, Ohio State University Press.

Metuh, E.E. 1991. "Attitude to Nature in African Religions: Paradigm for Care in the Industrial Age," *Bulletin of African Religion and Culture*, Vol. 3, No. 2, pp. 1-28.

IMF 1999. "*NEWS*", in *Ministerial Formation*, WCC Geneva, Vol. 87, October, p.64.

N. A. 1989. National Universities Commission (NUC) Approved Minimum Academic Standards in Arts and Education for all Nigerian Universities, Lagos.

Njoroge, N. 1999, "The Promise and Ministry of the Holy Spirit: Empowering Africans to Search for Fullness of Life," *Ministerial Formation*, No. 87, pp. 48-56.

Oduyoye, M. A.1995, *Daughters of Anowa: African Women and Patriarchy*, New York, Maryknoll, Orbis Books.

Ojo, A. 2000. (ed.*)*, *Protection and Promotion of Human Rights for a Better Society in Nigeria*, Leven Club International, Lagos, Federal Government Press.

Onwu, N., 1984, "Religion as a Unifying Factor in Nigeria," in Babs S. Mala *et al.* (eds.), *Problems and Prospects in Religion, Peace and Unity in Nigeria*, NSR Books, pp. 155-161.

Schmidt, R. 1980, *Exploring Religion*, California, Wadsworth.

Takaya, B.J. 1989, "Religion, Poltics and Peace: Resolving the Nigerian Dilemma," Paper read at the Council for the Worldrs Religions Conference on *Religion and Peace in Multi-Faith Nigeria*, OAU, Ile-Ife, December, 4-8, pp. 1-16.

Vishigh, I.R. 1996, "Christianity and Islam in Dialogue: The Nigerian Experience," *Jos Bulletin of Religion*, Vol. 3. No. 1, pp. 8-16.

Wittgenstein, L. 1953, *Philosophical Investigations*, New York, Macmillan.

Part II

Biblical studies

Chapter 2

Jesus the Messiah: Son of Man and Son of God

- D.T. Ejenobo

Introduction

From a historical perspective we are not very sure when the word *Christ* or *Messiah* became a proper name for Jesus. Louis Berkhof (313) posits that "the name 'Christ' was first applied to the Lord as a common noun without the article, but gradually developed into a proper noun, and was used without the article." On his own part, E. Y. Mullins (155) is of the view that "the name 'Christ' designates Jesus as Messiah or anointed one." Supporting this position Berkhof (312) affirms that "if Jesus is the personal, Christ is the official name of the Messiah." Continuing, he says that the term Messiah is the equivalent of the Old Testament *mashach*, to anoint, and thus means 'the anointed one'." Berkhof's line of argument seems to be more in line with what we find in the Gospels. The title 'Christ' seems to have been conferred on Jesus when the Messianic office of Jesus became apparent to the disciples. The remainder of the chapter will focus on a critical theological evaluation of the whole gamut of materials surrounding the concept of Jesus as Messiah.

There is no doubt that the title and concept of Messiah is the most important of all the Christological concepts in New Testament theology historically, if not theologically, because it became the central way of designating the Christian understanding of Jesus. Acts 11:26 tells us that the disciples of Jesus were first called Christians at Antioch. This would suggest that the Greek word for messiah, *Kristos* probably became a proper name when the message of Jesus as the Messiah first moved into the Gentile world. This is likely because the Gentiles did not understand the Jewish background of anointing which the Jewish word *Messiah* connotes. Thus for the Gentiles, the phrase *the anointed one* meant nothing and the term "Christian" according to Kee & Young (217) was a "derisive epithet" which carried with it, ridicule and contemptuous connotations.

A critical examination of the Old Testament reveals that the word "Messiah" (*mashach*) is used to indicate a wide range of people who were anointed with oil and thereby set apart to fulfil some divinely ordained office (Lev. 4:3; 6:22; I Sam. 24:10; II Sam. 19:21; 23:1; Lam. 4:28; I Kings 19:16). In this sense, a messiah was someone ordained by God for a specific task, and as a sign of this calling, he was usually anointed with oil by the priest. This practice is in line with the Greek etymology of the word "*krisma*" from which we derive our word *Kristos*. *Krisma* means anything smeared on, especially a scented unguent" (Liddell and Scott, 1742). In spite of this generalized usage, we discover that the more direct phrase, *the messiah*, does not appear in the Old Testament literature at all. The word itself always has a qualifying genitive or suffix such as "*the Messiah of Jehovah*," or "*my Messiah*." The nearest we can come to a messianic usage in the Old Testament is the passage in I Samuel 2:10 when Hannah prayed that "*the Lord will judge the ends of the earth, he will give strength to his kings, and exalt the power of his anointed.*"

However, when we come to later Judaism we discover that the word does not occur with great frequency in inter-testamental literature, except of course in the Psalms of Solomon (17:4; 5:23, 26) and in IV Ezra. The Qumran Community also looked forward to a messiah, howbeit, in a historical sense. There seems to be no doubt that by the time of Jesus, the Jews were definitely looking forward to the advent of a messiah. Edersheim (163) is of the view that "the ancient Synagogue found references to the Messiah in many more passages of the Old Testament than those verbal predictions, to which we generally appeal." He avers further: "This is fully borne out by a detailed analysis of those passages in the Old Testament to which the ancient Synagogue referred as *Messiahanic*. Their number amounts to upwards of 456 (75 from the Pentateuch, 243 from the Prophets, and 138 from the Hagiographa) and their Messiah application is supported by more than 558 reference to the ancient Rabbinic writings."

From these observations of Edersheim, it is clear that reading back into some Old Testament passages, it is possible to see prophetic insinuations of the coming of the messiah. But it would appear that the type of messiah depicted in the Psalm of Solomon is the one the Jews of the New Testament era were expecting. He was to be a Son of David, and while he would be born in Bethlehem, there was a tradition that he would suddenly appear among the people from an obscure origin (Mt. 21:9; 22:42; Jn. 7:40-42; Mt. 2:5; Jn. 7:26-27). The idea of a kingly Son of David who would be anointed by God to bring to Israel her lost political glory is prevalent in these expectations. This is also evident in the messianic prophecy of Isaiah when he said,

> For to us a child is born, to us a son is given; and the government will be upon his shoulder, and his name will be called "Wonderful Counsellor, Mighty God, Everlasting Father, Prince of Peace." Of the increase of his government and of peace there will be no end, upon the throne of

David, and over his kingdom, to establish it, and to uphold it with justice and with righteousness from this time forth and for evermore. The zeal of the Lord of hosts will do this. (Is. 9: 6-7 R.S.V).

There are two passages which compel our attention at this point. The first is Peter's confession at Philippi, (Mk. 8:27-29) while the second is the trial before the Sanhedrin (Mk. 14:56). Critics are not unanimous on what Peter meant by messiah, but it seems clear that he had in mind the one who is to fulfil the Old Testament messianic hope, even though it is not in terms of a conquering king. In the case of the second passage, the High Priest addressed a direct question to Jesus: *"Are you the Christ, the son of the Blessed?"* (Mk. 14:61). According to Mark, Jesus answered with an unqualified *I am*. But He does opt to define the nature of this messiahship: it is of the heavenly son of Man and not the messianic king. Matthew's variant of *"you have said so"* (26:64) only calls attention to a difference of interpretation. We can then summarize our findings by saying that Jesus made no overt claim to be messiah, yet he did not reject Messiahship when it was attributed to him; and before the Sanhedrin, when directly accused of claiming Messiahship, he assented, but gave his own definition of the term.

From the brief analysis above, it becomes obvious that there is an element of obscurity in determining the precise meaning of the term messiah in the Gospels. We shall need to examine this question in some detail when we come to talk about what is referred to as the *messianic secret* in New Testament studies. But for now, let us note that two conflicting understandings of the Messiah is found in the Gospels. On the one hand, the Jewish understanding of the word carried a political undertone, in which a Davidic king was expected to appear to deliver the people from the bondage of the Gentiles. On the other hand, we have a clear cut attempt by Jesus to disassociate himself from this concept and give a spiritual redefinition of this term. It would appear then that in his attempt to avoid the use of this term, Jesus used another, *"the Son of Man"*.

Jesus the Son of Man

Theologically, one of the most important messianic designations in the Gospels is the term *Son of Man*. Mullins (156) believes that the term Son of Man "was probably based on the passage in Daniel 7:13, and was intended by Jesus as a Messianic title pointing to His universal relations to men." Furthermore, Berkhof (313) observes that "in the Old Testament this name is found in Ps. 8:4; Dan. 7:13, and frequently in the Prophecy of Ezekiel. It is also found in the apocrypha, Enoch 46 and 62, and II Esdras 13." From these observations, it is obvious that the term Son of Man was neither new to Old Testament writings nor to the apocalyptic literature which developed in later Judaism.

In attempting a critical review of this term, three facts are of importance which should be underscored:

i) In the Gospel tradition, the Son of Man was Jesus favourite way of designating

Himself. In fact, it is the only title He freely used. "It was the most frequent self-designation of Jesus. He applied the name to Himself on more than forty occasions." (Berkhof, 313).

ii) The title is never used by anyone else to designate Jesus. Berkhof believes that in the Gospel narratives, "others all but refrained from employing" this term in their reference to Jesus.

iii) There is no evidence in Acts or the Epistles that the Early Church called Jesus the Son of Man.

While the Gospels placed this title on the lips of Jesus over 65 times, it is striking to note that the title never became a messianic designation for Jesus in the Early Church. The Church Fathers understood the phrase to refer primarily to the *humanity* of the incarnate Son of God. Jesus was the God-man, the Son of God, and Son of Man. However, according to Berkhof (313), "the dependence of the New Testament usage of it on the passage in Daniel is now generally admitted, though in the prophecy it is merely a descriptive phrase, and not yet a title. The transition from the one to the other was made later on, and was apparently already an accomplished fact when the book of Enoch was written."

In trying to look for a historical background for this phrase, therefore, we discover that though it is used as a phrase to simply designate man, it appears that Ezekiel's usage corresponds to how Jesus used it. Also the Book of Daniel seems to provide ample background for the apocalyptic application of this term in the Gospels. In the similitude of Enoch, the Son of Man has become a messianic title of a pre-existent heavenly figure who descends to earth to sit upon the throne of judgment to destroy the wicked of the earth, to deliver the righteous and to reign in a kingdom of glory when the righteous will be clothed with garments of glory and of life and enter into a blessed fellowship with the Son of Man forever.

A more detailed study of the Gospels reveals that the use of the title Son of Man falls into three distinct categories: the Son of Man as a serving earthly man; the Son of Man as a suffering man and the apocalyptic Son of Man. It is not possible within the limits of our study here to give a detailed study of all the passages in each of these three categories. What we shall do here is to call attention these passages and give a general summary at the end:

1. The Earthly Son of Man

a. He has authority to forgive sins: Mk. 2:10; Mt. 9:6; Lk. 5:24.
b. He is Lord of the Sabbath: Mk. 2:27; Mt. 12:8; Lk. 6:5.
c. He socializes: Mk. 11:19; Lk. 7:34.
d. He has no where to lay His head: Mk. 8:20; Lk. 9:58.
e. A word against Him will be forgiven: Mk. 12:32; Lk. 12:10.
f. Seeks the opinion of others about Himself: Mt. 16:13.
g. He sowed good seeds: Mt. 13:37.

h. Some will be persecuted on His account: Lk. 6:22.
i. He came to seek and save the lost: Lk. 19:10.
j. Judas betrays Him with a kiss: Lk. 22:48.

2. The Suffering Son of Man

a. He would suffer and die: Mk. 8:31; 9:12; Lk. 9:22; Mt. 17:12).
b. He will rise from the dead: Mk. 9:9; Mt. 17:9.
c. Will be delivered into the hands of men: Mk. 9:31; Mt. 17:22; Mk. 9:44).
d. Will be delivered to Chief Priests, condemned to death, and rise again: (Mk. 10:33; Mt. 20:18; Lk. 18:31.
e. He came to give His life; Mk. 10:45; Mt. 20:28.
f. Woe be to His betrayer: Mk. 14:21; Mt. 26:24; Lk. 22:22.
g. He is betrayed to sinners: Mk. 14:41; Mt. 26:45.
h. Will be three days in the earth: Mt. 12:40; Lk. 11:30.

3. The Apocalyptic Son of Man

The following passages make general, and sometimes specific references to the second coming of the Son of Man: Mt. 8:38; 14:26, 62; 16:27; 24:30; 26:64; 24:44; 13:41; 15:28; 24:30; 25:31; Lk. 9:26; 21:27; 22:69; 12:40; 17:24, 26, 30; 18:8; 21:36.

From the way the term is used in the Gospels, it is clear that Jesus laid claim both to messianic dignity and to a messianic role by His use of the term Son of Man to designate Himself. In fact, the claim involved implicitly more than mere messianic dignity, for it commanded overtones of essential supernatural character and origin. While He did not call Himself the messiah, since His mission was utterly different from that connoted to the popular mind by this term, there is no doubt that His use of the phrase Son of Man laid claim to all that is expected of the messiah. He called Himself the Son of Man because this title made an exalted claim and yet permitted Jesus to fill it with new meaning.

Jesus the Son of God

There is no doubt that in New Testament theology, the most important messianic phrase in the study of the self-disclosure of Jesus is the phrase *Son of God.* In the history of theological thought, this expression connotes the essential deity of Jesus. He is the Son of God, that is, God the Son, the Second Person of the Triune Godhead. However, as we approach the study of this expression in the Gospels, we ought not to conclude without careful study that the expression conveyed such lofty connotations, for it is a matter of historical fact that this expression was used in the religious literature of Judaism and in the Old Testament with different meanings from that which we customarily recognise (Edersheim 160-179). In order therefore to get a balanced conception of the phrase, it is necessary first to examine the history and the use of this expression in its several meanings and then come to the Gospels to attempt to determine how high a concept is conveyed by the use of the phrase

Son of God in the Old Testament

There are at least three ways in which we can define this expression:

a) A creature of God may be called the son of God in a nativistic sense because he owes his existence to the immediate creative activity of God. Thus Adam is called the son of God in approximately the same way that Seth is the son of Adam (Lk. 3:38). This definition falls within the range of the theology of creation.
b) The expression can be used to describe the relationship men may sustain to God as the peculiar objects of His loving care. This is the moral-religious usage and may be applied both to man and to the nation of Israel (Ex. 4:22; Deut. 14:1; Jer. 3:19; Hos. 11:1). In the New Testament this concept is filled with deeper significance as Christians are described in terms of sonship to God, whether by birth (Jn. 3:3; 1:12) or by adoption (Rom. 8:14, 19; Gal. 3:26; 4:5).
c) The third meaning is messianic. The Davidic king is designated the son of God (II Sam. 7:14). This usage involves no necessary implication as to the divine nature of the messianic personage; it has reference to the official position of messiahship.

a) Messianic Son of God in Judaism

The idea of the messianic Son of God goes back to the promise to David with reference to his descendants who would succeed him on the throne of Israel, and it looks beyond the immediate descendants of David to that greater descendant who should be the messianic son of God in the fullest sense of the word (II Sam. 7:14ff). This concept is further enlarged in Psalm 2 and in the literature of later Judaism. However, it is of great importance that while there is an Old Testament background for messianic sonship, the expression *Son of God* never became a familiar messianic designation. It appears in only one passage before the first century. In the 5th Book of Enoch, God says: *"For I and my son will be united with them forever"* (105:2):

i) **Greek Concept of Divine Men:** In looking for a historical precedence for the expression *Son of God*, we cannot avoid the Greek literature of the New Testament era. In oriental religions, all kings were thought to be begotten of the gods. In Hellenism, there were men who were believed to possess divine power and the ability to work miracles. Even the Greek concept of immortality of man has within it the idea that when a man is great here on earth and demonstrates some measure of supernatural powers, the gods could deify such a person at his death. Thus the idea of sons of God and daughters of God was not strange in the Greek thought.

ii) Son of God in the Gospels: It is interesting to note that in the Synoptic gospels, Jesus never uses the full title to designate Himself, though He frequently refers to Himself as the Son. In fact, there are only seven passages in which Jesus is called, or calls Himself the Son of God: Mk. 1:11; Mt. 4:1-11; 25-27; Mk. 13:32; 12:1-12; 37 and Mt. 26:63.

The paucity of the passages in which Jesus is called or calls Himself Son of God is the more striking in view of the fact that in the Epistles Son of God is a favourite designation for Jesus. In the Gospels there is not the exalted use of this expression for Jesus as we find in the Epistles. It is obvious from the passages in the Gospels that Son of God is not the equivalent of Messiah. While the messiah is the Son of David, divinely anointed to establish the kingdom of God in power, Jesus is hailed by later theological development as the Son of God because of His power over the spirit world. Berkhof (1981: 317) is of the opinion that "for those who accept the Gospel testimony there can be no doubt as to the fact that Jesus was conscious of being the very Son of God. The following passages bear witness to this: Matt. 11:27; Lk 10:22; 21:37, 38; Mk 12:6; Lk 20:13; Matt. 22:41-46; Mk. 13:35-37; Lk. 20:41-44; 24:36; Mk. 13:32; Matt. 28:19." Thus we can conclude that Jesus thought of Himself as the Son of God in a unique way, that He was set apart from all other men in that He shared a oneness with God whish is impossible to ordinary men. It is in this sense that it was used in the early Church and later Christian theology.

From the above survey, it then becomes obvious that the Christological expression Son of God does not find a high degree of support in the Gospels as a messianic designation for Jesus like the expression Son of Man. There is no doubt that in later Christian theological development, the more exalted expression Son of God overshadowed the more frequently used expression Son of Man. At the end of the day, however, we are not left in any doubt that both expressions are found in the Gospels as messianic designations. It is only the degree of usage that differs. According to Walter Connor (84), when the title Son of God was used in reference to Jesus, he was portrayed as "the primal, archetypal son of God. His relation to God as Son was fundamental to all other aspects of His being and causative relation to all phases of His mission."

However, a combination of the two expressions, Son of Man and Son of God, gives to Jesus, a uniqueness among the prophets and leaders of religious movements that is peculiar to Him. This point needs to be spelt out because no other prophet of religion ever had the effrontery to refer to himself as the Son of God. If Jesus was not convinced of the unique relationship which he enjoyed with God, He could not have made such claims. In addition, if the Church did not have ample empirical evidence to convince themselves of the validity of this claim, it would not have come down to us. Thus the authenticity of these messianic titles is not in doubt.

The Messianic Secret

There is another important line of evidence appearing in the Gospels concerning the question of Jesus' messiahship that goes along with His reluctance to use the title. Mullins (155), has noted that New Testament criticism has expanded much labour, to prove that this sense of vocation was wanting in Jesus, but it is impossible to expunge it from the record without violence." On a number of occasions, when Jesus had performed some miracles that would gain Him great public attention, He warned the persons healed to keep the matter quiet and to avoid publicity (Mk. 1:43f; 3:11f; 5:43; 7:36; 8:30; 9:9f. This command to secrecy is what is referred to in theological circles as the messianic secret.

We have tried earlier to show that Jesus' own understanding of the term messiah was quite different from the popular understanding of that time. There is ample evidence to suggest that Jesus possessed a messianic consciousness, and that He accepted the designation messiah when applied to Him. He even pronounced beatitude upon the disciples when they began to apprehend the character of His messiahship. He went further to affirm His messiahship when challenged by the Sanhedrin. However, there is equal evidence that Jesus did not widely and publicly proclaim his messiahship, and he frequently enjoined secrecy upon those who recognized it.

This tension can be accounted for by the recognition that Jesus knew Himself to be the messiah but not the sort of messiah popularly expected. Mullins (156) confirms this viewpoint by observing that "the reserve of Jesus in announcing his messiahship in the early stages of his ministry was probably owing to the danger of abruptly thrusting the idea of his own spiritual kingdom upon a people looking for a kingdom of temporal power, and to the desire that the disciples might grow spiritually into an appreciation of him and his work." This point is worthy of repetition. Jesus did not lay claim to being the Messiah because He wanted the disciples themselves to make the discovery by themselves. His mission was to bring the kingdom of God, but not the kind of kingdom the people were expecting. Thus the Messianic consciousness of Jesus must be distinguished from the Messianic revelation. The Gospels unquestionably portray Jesus as possessing a Messianic consciousness. His infrequent public affirmations of this fact and His emphasis upon secrecy must be understood against the setting of the popular expectations of the Messiah and Jesus' self-revelation of a radically different function for the expected Messiah. His Messianic self-revelation therefore involves the re-education of His disciples to a new interpretation of the Messianic mission as it was actually embodied in His person and ministry.

The Historical Jesus and the Messianic problem

Until now we have studied the portrait of Jesus as found in the Gospels. We have found objective grounds for believing that this is fundamentally an accurate portrayal that the portrait basically corresponds to the facts of the history of Jesus. But in recent times some scholars have raised the question as to whether the portrayal of Jesus which we find in the Gospels is not a creation of the Church, a Christ of faith and not a historical Jesus. According to these scholars, the essential issue in this question is that of transcendence. They argue that in the Gospels Jesus is pictured as a transcendent being who is conscious of transcendent dimension. It is because He knows Himself to be uniquely the Son of God that He brings to man the immediate presence of God.

However, the questions we should ask at this point are: *why has the historical accuracy of the Gospel portrait of Jesus been so widely rejected in modern critical study? Have the Gospels been proved untrustworthy? Has new archaeological and historical evidences come to light that has undermined their reliability in reporting history?* The problem seems to lie in the modern interpretation and understanding of the nature of history. The rejection of the Gospel portrait does not arise from an objective, open-minded, inductive study of the Gospels, but from philosophical presuppositions about the nature of history and the nature of the Gospels.

History, it is claimed, is exhaustively the study of man in his experiences. The Gospels, on the other hand, are witnesses to faith in God and what this faith believed that God has done in Jesus. Since God is not a historical character but a transcendent being, history cannot deal with the claim of faith that God was actually revealing Himself in Jesus of Nazareth. Therefore historical study of the Gospels must lay aside the postulate of faith and re-create the story of Jesus of Nazareth in purely historical, non-supernatural terms. It is the attempt to re-construct such a Jesus of history that is referred to as the quest for the historical Jesus in New Testament studies.

There are two observations to be made on this problem here:

1. **The Nature of the Gospels**: There is no doubt that the Gospels were written by men of faith who belonged to a believing community. But this does not mean that they distorted the facts of history. Many studies about Jesus have tended to place faith and history in antithetical categories. However, most historians today admit that all good history is interpreted history. History that is not interpreted is not real history. It is only a dry meaningless chronicle of people, places, events, and dates. History always tries to understand the *meaning* of the events it reports; and the fact that a man has a view point does not mean that he is a poor historian and distorts facts to support his interpretation. In other words, the fact that the authors of the books of the New Testament were men of faith did not make them incapable of writing objectively. Our observation above that the title of Son

of Man more frequently found in the Gospels did not taller with the title of Son of God more favoured by the Church but less frequently used in the Gospels is a pointer to this fact. In addition, Luke tells us at the beginning of his two-part book that he carried out some amount of objective research during the compilation of his work. In all therefore, we must see the Gospels as authentic records of history, even though such history might have been interpreted with the eye of faith.

2. **The Historicity of the Gospels**: Based on what has been said above, let us note that as a matter of fact, the Gospels contain many evidences that the traditions about Jesus were not completely recast by the faith of the primitive community. There is, on the contrary, evidence to show that the Gospel narratives are grounded on a sound historical sense. Two examples will suffice. First, Jesus avoided the title messiah, but later we find the Church using the title Christ as a proper name for Him. If the Gospel narratives were based purely on faith, then messianic secret would have been avoided completely. Second, the Church rejected the popular phrase by which Jesus referred to Himself (Son of Man) for another, Son of God. There is no doubt that the church and her chroniclers did possess a sound memory in reporting the words of Jesus and we have no reason to doubt their records. If in such matters as the messianic titles, there are apparent historical contradictions, then we have no reason to believe that the writers of the New Testament distorted historical facts. The case of obvious harsh historical materials found in the Gospel of Mark also attest to the sound historical basis of the Gospels.

We can therefore conclude that the problem of the historical Jesus stems from a modern understanding of history. The attempt to create a Jesus who is purely historical has not succeeded. In this context, the historical Jesus is a technical phrase, designating a hypothetical Jesus who could be interpreted exclusively in human, ordinary historical categories. But if we wish to be faithful to the objective evidences presented to us in the Gospels and in the later developments in the Christian world, we have no way by which we can avoid the conclusion that the Jesus of the Gospels was both the Son of Man and the Son of God. Our attempt to use modern historical analytical tools to interpret the historical materials presented in the Gospels must not becloud our minds from carrying out an objective assessment of the facts presented to us about the man Jesus.

The Gospels leave no one in doubt that the mission of Jesus was to bring men into a new understanding of the kingdom of God. Ample historical evidences are presented to us to show that the peoples of His time rejected His interpretation of the kingdom of God because this contradicted their messianic expectations. But in spite of this rejection, Jesus continued with His mission and eventually built His followership among a small group of people who accepted His teachings. The historicity of the later development of this small group into a gigantic institution called the Church is not in doubt. If the might oaks from little acorns grow, why should we doubt the historical developments which led to the growth of that nucleus of Jesus' disciples? The Gospels tell us that in the man Jesus, both human and divine dimensions met in perfect harmony. The message of the Gospels is thus simple: just as Jesus typifies the meeting of the human and the divine in one man, so it happens to all those who receive and appropriate the message of the kingdom in their individual lives. A profession of faith in Jesus is thus the catalyst required for the re-enactment of the meeting of the human and the divine in every man.

Son of Man and Son of God: the African perspective

The African concepts of Son of Man and Son of God are radically different from the ones we have examined above. Thus it is fitting that we should discuss these concepts with a view to providing a clearer understanding of the terms in African context. There is no parallelism between the biblical and African concepts of the Son of Man and Son of God. In African traditional religion, there is the concept of ancestral world. This concept is based in the understanding that when a man grows very old and dies, he joins the body of the ancestors of his particular society. This ancestral status is conferred on those who lived good and fruitful life while on earth. It is only after death that a man is assumed to have acquired some degree of divinity. Thus the ancestors are credited with spiritual functions in the affairs of the living members of the community. This concept is not in line with the concepts of Son of Man and Son of God as recorded in the Bible.

Africans do not have a biological Son of God in the manner of the Christians, rather all human beings are sons of God by virtue of creation. It is, however, clear from African theogonic and cosmogonic myths that the primordial divinities were with God in the heavens but there is no evidence that they were self-existent as the biblical Son of God. These categories of divinities served as functionaries of God in the theocratic government of the world. It is also true that in African traditional religion, the status of divinity could be conferred on a living member of the community. This happens when the individual displays extraordinary spiritual or supernatural skills. This is true of Sango, the Thunder divinity of Yorubaland. While Sango was on earth, he was a very powerful hunter and fighter. When he wants to display his spiritual powers, he spits fire out of his mouth which consumed his enemies. When he died, he was deified and acquired the attributes of *Jakuta*, the Yoruba divinity of thunder.

Again, this concept is not the same as that of the Son of Man/Son of God as we have in the Bible. Jesus is believed to be the Son of God from the beginning. He was an incarnate Son of God who came into the world through the agency of a woman (Mary) to enable him perform His earthly ministry. In the case of Sango, he lived purely as man. It was only after his death that the status of divinity was conferred on him. Even then, Sango was just one among the several divinities found in the Yoruba pantheon. Jesus Christ, as the Son of God, stands alone in Christianity. Thus while all over Africa certain individuals were conferred with divinity after their death or while living, they do not fall into the category that we find in the Bible.

We shall now focus on how the concept of Son of Man/Son of God influenced the growth and development of Christianity in Africa. It is pertinent to observe that in Nigeria the average Christian does not even understand, in explicit terms the concept that Jesus is the Son of man and Son of God. As we have shown above, the concept has been fraught with controversy from inception. Most Christians in Nigeria, and indeed Africa, do not really understand how a living man can be both man and God at the same time. It is against this background that we cannot quantify the degree of the acceptance of the Son of God in the religious life of the people.

While Christendom upholds and propagates the concept of the divinity of Christ, most African Christians are confused as to its relevance in the lives. This is compounded by the fact that even within Christianity itself, there are disagreements as to the status of Jesus Christ. For example, early Christianity witnessed several heretical statements on this issue; the Docetists hold that Christ during his life had only a phantasmal body and not real one. In this capacity, the sufferings of Jesus were only illusory. Arainism insisted that the Son is not self-existent and, therefore, there was when the Son was not. In contemporary Christianity, the members of the Jehovah Witness are not keen on the concept as other Christians. Although they accept that Jesus Christ is divine, they do not totally accept the fact that He was the Son of God. Controversies like this have made it very difficult to totally accept the view that Jesus, the son of Mary, was an exclusive Son of God. For this concept to be internalized in the African Christian, concerted effort must be made to evolve a theology that will enhance a deeper understanding of the Son of God in African categories.

Conclusion

Our study of the concept of Jesus as Son of Man and Son of God took us in a round trip to examining the whole gamut of materials surrounding the concept of Jesus as Messiah. Borchert (23) rightly observes that "when the Saviour came among His people He was far from being unexpected. On the contrary, no people either before or since have cherished such hopes of the advent of any man. A whole literature in the so-called Jewish Apocalyptic had been built up, the object of which was to think out the future world, and the days of the Messiah were like the hinges of the door on which the whole turned." In other words, the concept of the Messiah was not new to Israel before the advent of Jesus. Baxter (146) cautions that "we must not give the impression, however, that the Messianic hope appears only from royal David onwards. Certainly the Davidic covenant introduces a new phase, but the Messianic hope itself is found right from Genesis to Malachi, and then links on, through the four hundred years hiatus of the inter-testamental period, to the sudden appearance of John the Baptist."

It is clear from these observations that the Messianic consciousness was very strong in Jesus. Thus, according to Berkhof (1918:317), Jesus was very conscious of His being the Son of Man and Son of God right from the inception of His ministry. Though the conception of the Messiah by the Jewish rabbis differed totally from what was presented by the Prophet of Nazareth." We are not left in any doubt as we go through the biblical materials that Jesus was not only the expected Messiah, but He was in a unique way both Son of Man and Son of God.

Works cited

Barnhouse, D. C., *God's Glory,* Michigan: Wm. B. Eerdmans Publishing Company, 1964.
Baxter, J. S., *The Strategic Grasp of the Bible,* Michigan: Zondervan Publishing House, 1974.
Berkhof, L., *Systematic Theology,* Edinburgh: The Banner of Truth Trust, 1981.
Brown, C., (ed.), *The New International Dictionary of New Testament Theology,* Michigan: Zondervan Publishing House, Three Volumes, 1982.
Borchert, O., *The Original Jesus.* London: Pickering & Inglis Ltd., 1968.
Conner, W. T., *The Gospel of Redemption.* Nashville: Broadman Press, 1945.
Edersheim, A., *The Life and Times of Jesus the Messiah.* New York: Longman's, Green, & Co., Volumes I & II, 1917.
Ejenobo, D. T., *Jesus Christ Our Saviour.* Warri: Jonokase Publishing House, 2001.
Kee, H.C. & Young, F.W., *The Living World of the New Testament,* London: Darton, Longman & Todd, 1960.
Mullins, E. Y., *The Christian Religion In Its Doctrinal Expression.* Valley Forge: Judson Press, 1974.
Stott, J., *Men With a Message.* England: Evangelical Literature Trust, 1994.

Chapter 3

Hermemeutical study of the resurrection of Jesus Christ

- M. P. Adogbo

Introduction

Several explanations have been given in support and refutation of the resurrection stories as contained in the gospels. In Hebrew mythology, as well as their traditional cosmology, the body of man was created first and then the breath of life was breathed into him (Gen.2:7). Just as the breath was essential to life, so the body was indispensable if there was to be a living person. Death did not bring release for the soul, rather it transported man to a shadowy half-existence in Sheol, or Hades; the subterranean realm to which all the dead descend, and from which man could only escape when his soul and body were reunited in the resurrection day. This notion became a central element in the eschatological hope cherished by most of the Jewish race.

The issue of bodily resurrection with the soul in physical form was a new innovation resulting from the death of Jesus. This development has since been a marvellous and unique phenomenon in Christendom. The church has insisted that the Risen Lord was no other person than Jesus of Nazareth who was crucified. In this context, the Christ who was raised from the dead was a risen man, not just a spirit assuming human form. In this way, the resurrection was looked upon as a proof that through Jesus, a new kind of human existence had become a reality. This belief provides a living example of the life of the new age; this became the well-spring of the earliest Christian proclamation of the *kerygma*.

The proclamation of the physical resurrection of Jesus has generated several controversies, especially, from atheists and adherents of other religious traditions. The more nearly convincing of the arguments is that the theory of the resurrection was presented by the early church to make external and concrete the inner experiences that had come to the apostles and other witnesses of the Risen

Lord. Some who follow this line of thought are convinced that the appearances were wholly subjective, and that they arose out of the conviction that God's justice would not permit such an exemplary and important career as that of Jesus to come to such an ignominious and fruitless end.

The hallmark of this work is not to enter into this disputation but to attempt a hermeneutical study of the phenomenon as it is presented in the gospels of Matthew, Mark, Luke and John. In consonance with the application of hermeneutics, the work will depend largely on interpretative and comparative study of the narratives as they were circulated in the Greco-Roman (Hellenistic) world before they were documented as we have them in the New Testament today.

Critical hermeneutic survey of the resurrection narratives

The four gospels agree on the day of the women's visit to the tomb; this was after Sabbath, that is, the first day of the week. There was however, a disagreement on the time of the visit. Mark wrote that it was early when the sun had not risen. Luke and Matthew agreed that it was early dawn while John added that it was still dark. On the number of personalities involved in the visit, Matthew named two; Mary Magdalene and the other Mary while Mark named three; Mary Magdalene, Mary mother of James and Salome. Luke who continued to use the pronoun, "them" later named three; Mary Magdalene, Joanna, Mary the mother of James and then referred to the rest as "other women with them". From Luke's point of view, many women were involved in the visit to the tomb. John, however, named only one, Mary Magdalene.

On the motive for this early morning visit to the tomb, Matthew simply puts it that the women went to see the sepulchre. Mark says that they brought spices so that they might anoint the body of Jesus. Luke agreed with Mark but emphasized that the spices were prepared by the women themselves. In the gospel of John, no reason was given for the visit. Mark states that the women expressed doubt about their ability to remove the stone. However, when they got to the tomb, they found that the stone had been rolled back. This was also the account in Luke and John, but Matthew gave an account of how the stone was removed; "there was an earthquake, for an angel of the Lord descended from heaven and came and rolled back the stone and sat upon it. His appearance was like lightening...And for fear of him the guards trembled and became like dead men". (Mt. 28:2-4).

Matthew claimed that the news of the Risen Christ was given to the women by an angel. This view was similar to the account in Luke which says that two men passed the information to the women. Mark simply puts it, "And entering the tomb, they saw a young man sitting on the right side, dressed in a white robe; and they were amazed." (Mk.16:5). In the gospel of John the story was radically different; the woman could not find the body of Christ and she returned to inform the disciples. As soon as the report was given by Mary Magdalene, the disciples raced to the tomb and found it empty as reported. By this addition, John has achieved one objective, that is, both men and women witnessed the empty tomb. It was when the tomb was certified empty that two angels appeared to Mary who stood weeping after the others had gone back. Mark singled out Peter who must be informed about the risen Christ even after the generality of the other disciples have been told.

After what seemed to be the end of the drama at the tomb, the story opened again with the physical appearance of Jesus to "them" (the women). In Matthew, 28:8, Jesus told them to go and inform the disciples to go to Galilee where he would see them. A very important point to note from the forgoing is that Matthew has moved the scene of events from Jerusalem to Galilee, while other writers were still in Judea.

A comprehensive account of the appearance of Jesus to the two men on the way to Emmaus is found in Luke. It is significant to note that in this account, Cleopas, one of the two, was certainly not one of the twelve disciples. Luke made it clear that the visitor was not known to the two and that the visitor expressed absolute ignorance about the crucifixion of Jesus. To make for an earlier omission in the sequence of events, Luke fused the story of the visit of the women to the tomb into this event. The visitor, who later was identified as Christ proved to be vast in the *kerygma*.

The climax of the visit to Emmaus was that a dead man who had risen took part in the customary breaking of bread before he disappeared. In response to this unusual occurrence, the disciples exclaimed, "Did not our hearts burn within us while he talked to us on the road, while he opened to us the scriptures?" (Lk.24:32). Jesus did not introduce himself in this story; he appeared both as spirit and human. As a human being, he participated in the eating of bread, and as a spirit, he was not recognized before he vanished. Mark only referred to the story in brief, "After this he appeared in another form to two of them, as they were walking into the country" (Mk.16:12-13).

The effort of Luke to present Jesus as both spirit and human did not end with the above narrative. He gave another account in which Jesus appeared to the disciples while they were in Jerusalem after the events in Emmaus. As they were discussing the resurrection and how Jesus appeared to Simon and physically participated in the breaking of bread, Jesus stood among them. They were not only startled and frightened but supposed that they had seen a spirit. Then Jesus queried,

> Why are you troubled, and why questionings rise in your hearts? See my hands and my feet that it is myself; handle me, and see; for a spirit has not flesh and bones as you see that I have. And while they still disbelieved for joy, and wondered, he said to them, "Have you anything here to eat?" They gave him a piece of broiled fish, and he took it and ate before them (Lk.24:38-43).

In the gospel of John, the disciples shut themselves up in the evening for fear of the Jews. Then Jesus came, stood among them and greeted, "Peace be with you". He showed them his hands that were nailed and his side that was pierced. The disciples were glad when they realized that what they saw was the Lord. After Jesus had given them the Holy Spirit, he disappeared. In another encounter, John records that Thomas, one of the twelve, who was not with them when Jesus appeared, doubted the story and said, "Unless I see in his hands the print of the nails, and place my finger in the mark of the nails, and place my hand in his side, I will not believe" (Jn.20:25).

In the characteristic style of Johannine narratives, he stayed action for eight days before Jesus appeared again to the disciples. This time, Thomas was with them when Jesus appeared. Jesus told Thomas to physically examine him to authenticate the marks made by the nail and sword. It was after the examination that Thomas believed that Jesus was his Lord and God (Jn.20:28). Jesus' remark was remarkable, "Have you believed because you have seen me? Blessed are those who have not seen and yet believed" (Jn.20: 29). By this narrative, John has made a theological point; Jesus has commanded all adherents to believe, even if on no other reason but faith. The door had been slammed against all others who may wish to have a physical examination of Jesus. In this context, the early believers of the faith and subsequent converts do not have to see Jesus in body or spirit as demanded by Thomas before they believe. This became a fundamental doctrine in Christendom.

The appearance of Jesus at the sea of Tiberias (Jn.21:1-4) is a continuation of the author's effort to prove that the risen Christ was still a worker of miracles. The disciples had toiled all the night without success. At Jesus' command, they cast the net on the right side of the boat and there was a great catch which they could not haul into their boat. The stage was now set for the disciple to be given a formal authority and commission to carry out the job Jesus had left behind.

Then the day of the great commission came after the various manifestations and appearances of Jesus to the disciples have been accomplished. In the gospel of Mark, the events took place in Jerusalem while the eleven disciples were at table. This was the situation in John 20:19-23, but Matthew moved the scene from Jerusalem to a "particular mountain" in Galilee. However, one thing is clear from the various accounts; the disciples still doubted the resurrection even after Jesus had upbraided them for their unbelief and faithlessness.

In the final address, Mark records that Jesus commanded that the gospel be preached to the whole creation and those who believed should be baptized. The disciples were given authority to cast out demons, speak in tongues; they will pick up serpents, and if they drink any deadly thing, it will not hurt them, etc. Matthew agreed with Mark but added that the baptism should be in the name of the Father and the Son and of the Holy Spirit. Jesus then assured his disciples of his continued presence until the close of the ages (Mt.28:19-20). In John, the ceremony was brief; Jesus told them, "Receive the Holy Spirit. If you forgive the sins of any, they are forgiven, and if you retain the sins of any, they are retained" (Jn.20:22-23).

St. Paul and the Resurrection

The idea of resurrection in the Epistle of Paul to the Corinthians was due to the skepticism in the church of Corinth. The belief in life after death and the immortality of the soul were generally acknowledged in the Hellenistic world. The *kerygma* that Jesus was raised with his human body was not in agreement with the thinking of the Greek. The point in dispute was not the soul or spirit of Jesus but the idea that Jesus rose with his physical body. During this early period, wherever there were early Christian witnesses and communities, and however varied their massages and theology, they were all united in believing and acknowledging the risen Lord. But as the church developed, there arose a controversy in the Church of Corinth over the resurrection of the body. It was in response to this disagreement that Paul wrote,

For I delivered to you as of first importance what I also received, that Christ died for our sins in accordance with the scriptures, that he was buried, that he was raised on the third day in accordance with the scriptures, and that he appeared to Cephas, then to the twelve. Then he appeared to more than five hundred brethren at one time, most of whom are still alive, though some have fallen asleep...Last of all, as to one untimely born, he appeared also to me...Now if Christ is preached as raised from the dead, how can some of you say that there is no resurrection of the dead? (1 Cor. 15:3-12)

Paul has expressed this message with the greatest emphasis not only to the Corinthians but also to the whole of "primitive Christianity", "Whether then it was I or they [i.e. the other apostles] so we preach and so you believed" (1 Cor. 15:11).

Paul also says in this chapter that faith absolutely stands or falls with this message of Christ's resurrection: "If Christ has not been raised, then our preaching is in vain and your faith is in vain. We are even found to misrepresenting God, because we testify of God that he raised Christ, whom he did not raise" (1Cor.15:14-15). In this passage, Paul pours forth a terrible chain of consequences upon his hearers; he prefers to face them squarely rather than stand on shifting ground, "If Christ has not been raised, your faith is futile and you are still in your sins" (1 Cor. 15:17).

Paul was of the view that it was only faith that could make the faithful followers of Jesus Christ to gain immortality with him in the heavens by way of the resurrection of the dead. Apostle Paul says,

> Lo! I tell you a mystery. We shall not all sleep, but we shall all be changed, in a moment, in the twinkling of an eye, at the last judgement. For the trumpet will sound, and the dead will be raised imperishable, and we shall be changed. For this perishable nature must put on the imperishable, and this mortal nature must put on immortality. ... then shall come to pass the saying that is written: "Death is swallowed up in victory. O death, where is thy victory? O death, where is thy sting?"...But thanks be to God, who gives us victory through our Lord Jesus Christ (I

Cor.15:51-58).

From what has been said in the view of Bornkamm (183), "it then follows that we are to understand the Easter stories too as testimonies of faith, and not as records and chronicles, and that it is a *message* of Easter we must seek in Easter *stories.*" That is not to say by any means that the massage of Jesus' resurrection is only a product of the believing community. Certainly the form in which it comes down to us in the contemporary world is stamped with this faith. What became clear and grew to be a certainty for the Church was that God himself had intervened with his almighty hand in the wicked and rebellious life of the world by the raising of Jesus of Nazareth from the power of sin and death.

Critical Evaluation of the Resurrection and Appearances

There seems to be an agreement on the date and time of the visit of the women to the tomb; this was certainly in the early hours of the morning. Mary Magdalene was named as one of the women actors in all the gospels but there were discrepancies in the names of the other women and number that visited the grave. This leads us to this important question; "Could it be that the writers got their information from different sources?" We may again add; "Why the variations in the various accounts?" What is however natural, is that the two reporters who witnessed an event cannot give a prototype account. There must certainly be differences in the presentation as each reporter would emphasize his area of interest and concern.

When the report of the guard is considered, one wonders how St. Matthew came about the tradition that the soldiers had been paid to hide the truth (Mt.28:11-15). This is certainly an important event in the entire episode. One may, therefore, be tempted to ask why only Matthew recorded this great event. There is a general feeling that Matthew, a Jew, was finding a solution to the problem of a witness of the risen Christ. Matthew did not make it clear whether the guards were Jews or Romans. The popular feeling is that the guards were Romans. Considering the integrity of the Roman army during this period, it seems doubtful to accept that a Roman soldier would accept a bribe to tell or hide an information which would not only tarnish his reputation but also that of the Roman government.

We may as well ask, "Why did the women ever venture into the tomb site when they knew it was guarded?" It may be inferred that the women attempted this venture as they posed no danger in view of the respect accorded women at this period. This is more so as the disciples were conspicuously absent during the visit. They only raced to the tomb after they had been told that Christ had risen and, therefore, the guards would not be at the grave. The possibility of this assumption stems from the fact that at the time of crucifixion, all the disciples fled while the women stood at a safe distance to watch the drama. According to this account,

There were also women looking on from afar, among whom were Mary Magdalene, and Mary the mother of James the younger and Joses, and Salome, who, when he was in Galilee, followed him. And ministered to him; and many other women who came up with him to Jerusalem (Mk.15:40-41).

We now turn to the issue of body and spiritual resurrection. As we have shown above, Luke and John made desperate efforts to present the risen Christ as both man and spirit. This was consequent on the fact that in spite of the unity of faith that bounded the worldwide Jewish community together, there were also certain differences in the interpretation of their faith. The most obvious disagreements arose between the Sadducees and the Pharisees. It was also a fact that during the period when the gospels were written, there were Hellenistic cultural traits which began to make various modifications and accommodations in the religious thought of the non-Palestinian Jews or what is often referred to as Jews in Diaspora.

The Sadducees were the most conservative segment of the Jewish population both politically and religiously. They were particularly opposed to the idea of physical resurrection as well as speculations about apocalyptic and eschatological hopes. They taught that there was no future state and no resurrection from the dead; "The same day Sadducees came to him, who say that there is no resurrection; (Mt.22:23). They also denied the existence of angel or spirit; "For the Sadducees say that there is no resurrection, nor angel nor spirit" (Acts, 23:8).

The Pharisees, in contract to the Sadducees, came to accept the doctrine of the resurrection and the eschatological concept of the kingdom of God. They believed in the existence of angels and spirits; in the resurrection of the dead and the transmigration of the soul. When Paul was confronted by the Sadducees and the Pharisee, he cried out, "Brethren, I am a Pharisee, a son of Pharisees; with respect to the hope and resurrection of the dead I am on trial. And when he had said this, a dissension arose between the Pharisees and the Sadducees; and the assembly was divided" (Acts, 23:6-7). We must be quick to say here that the resurrection which the Pharisees were anticipating is far removed from the Christian belief of physical and spiritual resurrection.

The scriptural accounts of Jesus' appearances after the resurrection are ambivalent. On the one hand, the physical reality of his reanimated body is emphasized. He eats food; he shows his wounds. On the other hand, he is elusive, like a ghost. He passes through doors that are closed and locked; he suddenly appears and suddenly vanishes. Though reanimated body is corporeal, this body is not subject to those laws of physical nature that govern the movements of ordinary mortals. This paradox which is evident in human history has become a doctrine to which every true Christian must subscribe; Christ died, Christ resurrected and Christ is coming again.

In the view of Augustine, as quoted by Kelly (478), "the resurrection of all men at the last day is an undoubted dogma of the Christian faith; this identical flesh will be raised which is buried, which dies, which is seen and touched, which must eat and drink if it is to go on existing, which is sick and subject to pain." Notwithstanding this identity, however, "the bodies of the elect and the dammed alike will be clothed with incorruptibility, in the case of the latter that their chastisement may be everlasting." The resurrection bodies of the saints will be perfect and entire, with all theirs organs, and only what is ugly or deformed will have disappeared, and when children are raised, they will have mature bodies of adults. What this implies is that the resurrection body will be exempted from all the consequences of sin, such as death, infirmity, deformity and differences of age.

Christian inferences from the Resurrection narratives

Christendom has consistently maintained that the resurrection is an unquestioned article of faith. The most important thing about the Christian idea of the resurrection is that Jesus certainly died and resurrected after three days in the grave. This event has brought God's salvation to all believers. In this context, the body which every Christian anticipates is distinctively different, in that resurrection body is imperishable, glorious, powerful and spiritual. This body will be exempted from all the consequences of sin, such as death, infirmity, deformity, differences of age and so human nature, while remaining true to itself, will ascend to a spiritual and impassable state. This assertion becomes obvious when viewed against the claim of Paul that "flesh and blood cannot inherit the kingdom of God" (I Cor. 15:50).

Resurrection means that death is defeated. It also meant that the kingdom of God which was present in Jesus had also conquered death, and, therefore, the reign of God had come with power. The continued ministry of Christ has endued the disciples and all adherents of the faith with power to overcome all evils in the world. In this way, the resurrection became the manifestation of "all that Jesus began to do and teach" (Acts 1:1). In this consideration, the resurrection has come to mean the beginning of an end.

The apostles proclaimed that the death of Jesus was predestined and therefore, a divine order. He had to die; Lk.17:25, "But first he must suffer many things and be rejected by his generation"; Lk. 24: 26, "Was it not necessary that the Christ should suffer these things and enter into his glory?" to become an eschatological figure. Mk. 10:45, "For the Son of man also came not to be served but to serve, and to give his life as ransom for many." In the view of the writers of the gospels, God made the death necessary for Jesus Christ. In this understanding, the death of Jesus was a vicarious death. That is, he died for the sake of other human beings.

This idea of vicarious death is almost entirely new as it was not explicitly stated in the Old Testament except in the period between the Old and New Testaments when it was supposed that some one had to die to save others. The idea that the Messiah should suffer was not part of the Jewish tradition. We may therefore, conclude that these passages were products of early Christian reflection. The account in Isaiah 53 which Christians have often depended upon is not conclusive on the issue. This account refers to the Lord's servant and not the Son of God. The Jewish race was expecting a glorious Messiah that would come from the house of David; there is a great difference between a biological Son of God and the son of David. The accounts in Is.26:19, Ez.31:1-14, Dan.!2:2, Hos.6:2, which were reflections during the inter-Testamental period (about 3 B.C.), were essential eschatological hopes of a race under foreign domination. It is against this underlying tacit knowledge that the Jews rejected the claims of the disciples that Jesus was the expected Messiah.

The essence of the resurrection faith implies that Jesus was transferred to the existence of God. The first born among the dead; he is above death and corruption. He is comfortably seated at the right hand of power and glory. By this Jesus has become the bearer of eschatological salvation; he would soon come back in glory to accomplish what he preached on earth, namely, the Kingdom of God. All Christians believe that only the followers of Jesus would naturally benefit when he comes back. It is therefore, imperative that this gospel be proclaimed throughout the world.

Christian Resurrection and the challenges of the African traditional cosmologies

In Christianity as well as African traditional religions, there is a general belief that after death, the dead person's material body disintegrates and is re-absorbed into the inanimate component of the biosphere. Unlike a body, we do not know categorically what happens to the soul, which is the invisible and impalpable component of the living body. Several ideas and beliefs have been adduced in the history of mankind with the same degree of constancy and frequency as they relate to the fate of the soul after death.

In Christianity and African traditions, some of the beliefs and ideas are incompatible while in some instances, both traditions have given credence simultaneously to certain aspects, such as the reality of death and the ambivalent nature of the human body. This sub-section, therefore, throws insights into the incompatible concepts as they relate to the issues of eschatology and the hereafter. This quest became mandatory in consequence of the problems it has generated for converts to Christianity who are faced with the traditional religious milieu that have encapsulated their environment.

Eschatology in Christian categories refers to the irrevocable finality of the approaching world catastrophe. According to Eichrodt, this "fresh imagery is constantly found to point to utter annihilation of the whole cosmos, which is vividly described in terms of flood and fire," (470). In Jewish traditions, even the heavenly powers are affected by this retribution. For the hereafter, in this work, we shall be concerned with what happens to the soul which survives the physical destruction of the body.

The African concepts of eschatology and the hereafter are radically different from the notions shared in Christianity. African cosmological views do not point to irrevocable finality of the world. Rather, life is a cyclic process of birth – death – and rebirth. This epitomizes a belief in everlasting existence of man and the world, that is, life and world without end.

The details of African conception of the soul and life after death is available in Mbiti (1996) and Awolalu and Dopamu (1979). Suffice it to note here that in African traditional cosmologies, people share the notion that there is a constant interchange of matter; thus every living thing is discharging waste matter so long as it remains alive. At death, the material substance of man is completely discarded. The spiritual component is not annihilated simultaneously. In this regard, death is only a transition; that is, a means of passing from the physical world to the spiritual realm of the ancestors. At death, the supra-personal spiritual reality is reabsorbed into the spiritual entity that is its source. In this way, death is only a change of life.

This fundamental aspect of African belief has been a source of worry to some Christians who were groomed in the traditional environment. In Christian categories, death is the end of human existence. Those who are dead do not have a second opportunity to return to this physical world. The soul of the Christian goes to Sheol on the event of death to wait for the day of the irrevocable finality of the world. The soul would then face the judgement of God. Another area of divergent opinion is the issue of the re-embodiment of the spirits on the day of resurrection. Africans, as we have pointed out, do not cherish the hope of resurrection not to talk of a spirit being re-embodied with the physical body of his previous existence.

The adherents of Christianity believe that on the day of the final consummation, God would bring the living and the dead into judgement. Among Africans, as we have shown, life is not static. It is a cyclic process in as much as a man travels between this physical world of mortals and the ancestral world. This marks a departure from the view held in Christianity. Africans believe that every round of existence end with the judgement of the living members of the community. In this context, there are two categories of death; bad and good deaths.

Bad death, in African belief systems of thoughts, includes those who die as a result of punishment by the divinities in consequence of their evil actions. Deaths resulting from lightening, small-pox, leprosy, etc. are in this group. Also deaths during pregnancy and child birth, suicide, drowning are bad deaths. The victims of these irregular deaths do not normally receive the appropriate funeral rites as they are judged to have died as a result of their sinful actions. They are buried hurriedly in bad bush or sacred groves. In this capacity, the spirits of these irregular deaths do not find their way into the ancestral world in consequence of the judgement of the living. They become wandering or malignant spirits as they are banished from the ancestral realm.

The good death, on the other hand, is that which comes at a ripe age. There are elaborate rituals at the funeral since the people do not see anything wrong or tragic about the death. The judgement has been passed by the living members of the community. This makes it clear that the issue of the final judgement by God is alien to African people before the introduction of Christianity in the continent. The problems posed by these divergent views are extensive and multifarious in nature. They deserve a separate study which, hopeful, will be forthcoming in another work. What is urgently necessary here is the realization that African Christianity is faced with a great challenge.

The questions that come to mind are; is it really possible for an African Christian to cast away the inborn notion that ancestors live in the spirit world? What is the fate of the departed relations who were not converted to Christianity before they died? Why the prevalence of spirits that manifest in every day activities of the community? It is simple to dismiss these questions with a wave of the hand or to say that they make no sense. One thing is incontrovertible; the fact that one is born and reared in the African environment is a clear index that the traditional values and the norms have been internalized. Conversion will only create a dual personality with African values on the right hand and the foreign or acquired ones on the left. This is the hallmark of the challenge posed by adaptation and inculturation for the African Christian.

Conclusion

The study focused on resurrection in the Christian context. The adoption of hermeneutics yielded great dividend. Apart from the fact that it interpreted the beliefs of the adherents in their categories, effort was also made to establish their relevance to African traditional cosmologies. In this perspective, it was possible to discuss incompatible beliefs, such as resurrection and immortality in which hypotheses cannot be verified by physical observation or experiment.

The stories about the resurrection as they are documented in the gospels were critically examined with a view to establishing the divergent view in the accounts of the writers. The investigation revealed incoherence and inconsistencies in the various accounts. The picture that emerged is that of one author making effort to put right what others have omitted or misrepresented. In the process, the critical reader finds it difficult to put the records straight.

This was probably the reason why some non-Christians have insisted that the resurrection episode was an attempt by the disciples of Jesus who were disillusioned by the death of their master to formulate a story to transform what certainly was a shameful death to a glorious dawn. There are others who say that the appearances were wholly illusions, and that they arose out of the conviction of the disciples that God's justice would not permit such an exemplary and important career as that of Jesus to come to such an ignominious and fruitless end.

On the part of all Christians, the resurrection of Jesus is a reality that cannot be controverted. They have remained steadfast that Jesus certainly died and resurrected after three days in the grave. This is a clear assurance of God's salvation for believers of the faith. The body of all believers will not pass away; rather, they will be transformed in becoming a part of new creation. The images of this glorious creation are summed up in Christian eschatological hopes. One account reads,

> Immediately after the tribulation of those days, the sun will be darkened and the moon will not give its light and the stars will fall from heaven, and the powers of the heavens will be shaken; then will appear the sign of the Son of man in heaven, and then all tribes of the earth will mourn, and they will see the Son of man coming on the clouds of heaven with power and great glory (Mt. 24:29-31).

Those who are able to pass through the judgement ordeal will be "clothed in white robes" as "they have washed their robes and made them white in the blood of the Lamb," and in this capacity, "they shall hunger no more, neither thirst any more ... and God will wipe away every tear from their eyes" (Rev. 7:13-17). This is precisely the hope that every Christian carries along in his sojourn though this mortal life.

The Christian belief in resurrection and the immortality of the soul are not compatible with the African concepts as we have shown. But the reality is that Christianity has been firmly established in Africa. What is required to bridge the gap is that African Christian Theology should be extended in its scope of reflection on traditional and current cultural aspects of the African society. The approach to these realities includes affirmation of valid cosmologies, liberation from Euro-centric categories and transformation of the traditional ideals. In this way, there will evolve a theology that accommodates the intricate aspects of the African cultures, especially, as they relate to issues on the resurrection of the body.

Works cited

Alward, S., *African Christian Theology*, London: Geoffrey Chapman, 1975.
Awolalu, J.O. & Dopamu, P.A., *West African Traditional Religion*, Ibadan: Onibonoje Press, 1979.
Bettenson, H.(ed.) *Early Christian Church*, Oxford: University Press, 1963.
Bornkamm, G. *Jesus of Nazareth*, London: Hodder & Stoughton, 1960.
Bruce, F.F., *Jesus and the Christian Origins outside the New Testament*, London: Holder & Stoughton, 1974.
Carman, J.B., "Religion as a Problem in Christian Thought" in D.C. Dawe & Carman (eds.), *Christian Faith in Plural World*, New York: Orbits Books, 1978.
Eichrod, W., *Theology of the Old Testament*, Vol. I, London: SCM. Press, 1975.
Gwakkin, R.I., Early *Church History to AD. 313*, 2Vols, Macmillan, 1927.
Kee, H.C. & Young, F.W., *The Living World of the New Testament*, London: Dalton, Longman & Todd, 1960.
Kelly, J.N.D., *Early Christian Doctrine*, London: Adam & Charles Black, 1968.
Matthews, W.R., *God in Christian Thought and Experience*, Digswell Place; James Nisbet & Comp. Ltd., 1963.
Mbiti, J.S., *African Religions and Philosophy*, London: Heinemann, 1969.
Shorter, A. *African Christian Theology*, London: Geoffrey Chapman, 1975.

Chapter 4

To the unknown god: Paul's Address at Areopagus in African context

- A. O. Idamarhare

Introduction

Paul's memorable address at Mars Hill is the third recorded sermon of Paul. Luke makes the discourse one of the highlights of the Apostle's missionary activity. According to Paul's personal statement (I Thess. 3:1), Athens represented just a brief stay on the way to Corinth. He waited his companions there after their expulsion from Berea, before their departure to Corinth (Bornkamm, 1871: 65). Studies on the subject of Paul's address at Areopagus are not strange to scholars. Repeated attempts have been made to elucidate, analyse, and criticize or to treat the text (Acts 17: 22-34) exegetically. What is however new in this study, is the contextual relevance of this remarkable address to the African situation. This is the focus of the present study.

The Importance of Athens (Gk. Athenai)

Athens was the ancient capital of Attica (Greece) whose role had been preponderant one in the development of the ancient civilization; it had lost all its political grandeur from the 4th Century B.C. According to Leon-Dulfour, (105), by the 1st Century A.D., it had become politically insignificant in the Mediterranean world (Dillon & Fitzymer, (199), yet it was still a centre of Greek intellectual life and symbolized Hellenistic learning and piety. Athens grew up around a 520 feet-high rocky plateau called the Acropolis. Here on this elevated place lied the many-columned and beautiful temple of Parthenon, the monumental architectural wonder, clustered with other sacred edifices that were known as "the many tempted Acropolis" (Thompson, 2000:1635). To the mouth of the Acropolis stood the celebrated civic centre and market place (Gk. *agora* as it was called) where people not only carried out commercial activity but discussed questions of political and social interests, and to an extent the intellectual life of this great centre of Hellenic culture (Thompson, 1635). To the northeast on the lower plane was a rocky hill called the Areopagus (or English: Mars Hill) where the Council of the High Court met. Originally, the council made up of about thirty senior citizens met in the open-air space carved out of the rock on the top of Mars Hill, but in later years, it often met in one of the council chambers adjoining the *agora*. Luke suggests that both the "court of the Areopagus" and the *agora* were well-known places and familiar to Paul (Thompson, 1635). In the market he "reasoned...day by day with those who happened to be there" (17:17), among whom were the Stoics and the Epicureans, followers of the two Greek leading philosophical schools (Mackenzie, 67).

Athens was one of the great cities of the Roman Empire. The apostle Paul as a great strategist campaigned in such great cities where there were great influx of dwellers and foreigners. From these centres, the message would spread like wild fire far and wide. So he came from Berea to Athens, a city with 1,000 years of history, glorying in past fame. Athens, the founder of democracy was the home of many great philosophers: Aeschylus, Sophocles, Euripides, Thucydides, Plato and Socrates (Blaiklock, 352); it was thus the home of intellectualism and learning. It was therefore appropriate base to sow the seed of the gospel.

The Epicurean and Stoic Tenets

The Epicureans were the followers of Epicurus who taught that mental blessedness is the highest aim of man and that this is perfected when it is passive and completely freed from disturbance and annoyance. The worst enemy of mental bliss is baseless fears especially of the anger of the gods and of death. They held that the gods and the soul of man are material and that death terminates all and that in death there is no consciousness hence there is no resurrection. Thus Epicureanism was more of indifference and its influence was destructive and geared towards a sensual view of happiness.

Stoicism is very close to Christianity in some respects while in other ways it is very remote. Its idea of the world is materialistic. It taught that all things originated from the vital warmth by various degrees of tension and that to this vital warmth all things will return. It conceived the vital warmth as the intelligent, self-conscious, world soul, an all-in-dwelling reason, *logos* of which our reason is part. This *logos*, it held, is the God, the life and wisdom of all, which is within us. It taught about one natural law, one rule of conduct for all men and the universal brotherhood of man. Thus, the Stoics believed that one's position in life is merely an accident. Therefore the highest pursuit of man is to obey reason, the *logos* and that passions and lusts are enemies to perfect obedience to reason. Hence Stoicism encourages asceticism. Their idea of God is essentially pantheistic (Walker, (87). In their view God is a vague terrifying force which lacks traces of anthropomorphism.

To these two groups with admiration and curiosity, Paul appeared as *henon daimonion dokei kataggeleus einal* (promoter of foreign divinities) before they brought him to the Court of the Areopagus to expound his message (Guthrie *et al.*, 1970: 996).

The universality of Paul's Address

After an introduction of his observation that the Athenians are scrupulously religious (*deisidaimon*) (lit. "demon-fearing" sometimes interpreted as superstitious). Paul delivers his great speech on the renowned Areopagus above the *agora* market place and facing the Acropolis, which rises from it. Like a trained Pastor, he takes up an inscription on an altar to "the unknown God" (*Agnosto Theou*) as his text and expounded a number of ideas and motifs which have prototype of post classical philosophy of religion and criticism of religion (Bornkamm, (65). He argued that God should not be worshipped after the idolatrous fashion of Athens and the pagan world in general. He stated the general relationship of God to that of the world. God is the creator and sustainer. The nature of God was again described in terms borrowed from the Old Testament (Psalm 147:6; Isaiah 42:5) and the Hellenistic philosophy; "He made the world and all that is in it." The God of whom he speaks is not just the Creator; He needs nothing least of all shrines. He does not really need temple and cannot be contained in any tangible form of idols made by man (an allusion to Stephen's speech)? He has in fact determined the periods and boundaries of the whole cosmos and has given the empires of the past "allotted periods". He gives all men life and breath and ordained that men who live and have being in Him should seek him and find him. Paul stresses the essential unity and destiny of mankind, for basically the human race is of one stock (Dillon & Fytzymer, 200), *ex henos*. These truths Paul substantiates with quotations from Greek conceptions: "In him we live and move" was the pantheistic belief of the Stoics which may be modelled on that of Epimenides of Knossos a popular semi legendary figure of ancient Greece (Kee & Young, 248) and the idea that men are God's offspring is further illustrated by a quotation from a Greek Stoic poet, Cleathes found also in the work of Artic the Cilician poet (Marshall, 321). These were points Paul's audience would easily agreed with but the next are much more difficult. Paul concludes his sermon by saying that whereas God has in time past overlooked, the ignorance of men ("overlooked by-gone periods" R.J. Dillon and J.A. Fitzmyer) a change has now become imperative for all men for God is commanding all men everywhere to repent in anticipation of the eschatological judgement of the world which would be carried out by God's appointed agent, Jesus whom he had raised from the dead (Guthrie, 996).

In this speech, scholars have pointed out that neither the style nor the approach of Paul is quite like what we find in his letters. For example,

Bornkamm maintained: "Its content is a first-rate witness to post-apostolic preaching and theology, but not up to historical Paul, its distinctive feature is that of Luke's 'Paul'..." (Bornkamm, 65). The aim of this chapter is not to reconcile the indifference because of the limitation of time and scope of the chapter. Rather we shall concern ourselves here with the universal application of the sermon, which immediately touches on the African situation.

Obviously, Paul's attack is against idolatry and polytheism with its notion of representing God with tangible objects. He was really advocating Christian monotheism as an indispensable emphasis of Gospel proclaimers thus he elaborates on the spiritual nature of God, who is active in creation and providence and who is the true goal of those who have erected an altar dedicated to this "Unknown God" (*Agnosto Theuo*) of which they admit ignorance. His mission was to declare to them that the god whom they worship without knowing is the God who orders events and fulfils his purpose in his creation (Kee & Young, 248). Indisputably a direct attack on idolatry and polytheism tends to hinder the prospect of the Christian message rather than help it. It is the advocating of monotheism in religion that does not make meaning to polytheists. Thus Paul emphasised the fact that God overlooked the idolatry of the past and now demands repentance of all nations. Paul's polemic message contains a logical approach, which is encouraged among preachers today. He adapted his message to his audience as was done by Jesus who took into account the people's background and so developed themes that were familiar to his audience. This background became the basis from where he proceeded to deal with the spiritual or theological issues. For instance, in his discourse with the woman of Samaria, he talked about ordinary water but later shifted to the living water (John 4: 6-23) thus moving from the known to the unknown.

In the Areopagus sermon, there is the sense in which God is shown to be the Father of all. The religious world believes that he sustains our lives for every moment; "for in him we live and move and have our being" (Acts 17: 28). On account of this we may be said to be "God's offspring" (17 v 29). In Africa, "God is believed to be the absolute controller of the universe", that is, he is the "creator and sustainer". Unfortunately there are privileges attached to this more general "fatherhood". The relationship, which the word properly connotes, is missing (Boice, 321). Moreover Paul's address gives a proper background approach to adapting the Christian message to the so-called pagan world. It shows that no nation, people or community is devoid of the knowledge of God. The poor and rude approach of the early missionaries in condemning African traditional religion as fetishism, paganism, diabolism and so on contributed to their failures in many places, sometimes even inciting opposition or persecution. If we also, take the sermon along with Pauline arguments in Romans 1: 8– 2: 16, it shows us the proper function of "*natura revelation*" of God to all and sundry as a "*preparatio evangelica*" in propagating Christ to the pagan world (Guthrie, 991). Thus, the accusation that the so-called primitive peoples of the world have no concept of God is contrary to Paul's massage.

The idea of *Agnosto Theuo* is not strange but has its parallel among African people notably the Yoruba. The numerical strength of their divinities is put at 201, 401 and so forth (Idowu, 22). But, the remarkable point is that the number of 1 added to 200, 400 or 500 as the case may be, represents the Unknown God, divinity or divinities. It is a common belief among the Africans that the divinities are very many; sometimes they say they are innumerable so that the *Agnosto Theuo* cannot be an inconceivable phenomenon.

An overview of the Areopagite Address

Silas and Timothy joined Paul at Athens, although this information is not recorded in the Acts. However, it was clear from the records that Paul sent Timothy back to encourage the new converts at Thessalonica while Silas was probably sent on a similar mission to some other churches in Macedonia; either Berea or Philippi. By this time, Paul was not idle but did two things (Acts 17:16-18). He carried on active preaching and discussion in the synagogue with Jews and "devout Gentiles" (proselytes). The Acts does not tell us the results (Filson, 234).

Meanwhile he also was stirred by the idolatrous life of the Athenians and got into discussion with persons he met in the *agora*. Paul, with keen discerning eyes, looked at the scores or hundreds of statues of gods and goddesses; he became provoked as he spoke against such visible denial of his monotheistic faith and his loyalty to Christ. The sophisticated Greeks (the Epicurean and Stoic philosophers) became curious, took him aside from the bustle of the *agora* to the Areopagus and asked him to share his views (Acts 17: 19-21). Perhaps, when they heard Paul preaching about Christ and Resurrection (the Greek word for "resurrection" is *Anastasis*, a feminine noun), they thought that Paul, following a recurring ancient pattern was talking of a pair of deities, the male god Jesus and the female goddess *Anastasis* (Filson, 234-235).

The ten verses of Paul's memorable speech at Areopagus given in Acts 17:22-31, is best a brief summary of Paul's own words made to a Gentile audience unacquainted with the Jewish religion. Paul began by saying: "Men of Athens, I perceive that in every way you are very religious. For I passed along and observed the objects of your worship, I found also an altar with the inscription 'To an unknown god" (v. 22).

Paul said that the Athenians were very superstitious; they were concerned and active in religion, but they were miserably misguided as they dedicated an altar to an unknown god. This God, according to Paul, had given revelation of himself to all men, therefore, the Athenians cannot speak of God as being unknown to them and that this creator God is the Lord of heaven and earth. He does not live in shrines made by man. Nor should they serve him by human hands as men serve idols, bringing him sacrifices and food of various kinds as though he needs anything. He is self-sufficient (Dickson, 103-104).

Paul then emphasised God's revelation of himself by reference to the idea of common humanity of all men, the granting of territories to nations and the historical epochs of their life on earth. These are avenues given to men "to seek after him and find him" (v.27). In fact God is not far from man: 'In him we live and more and here our being' 'For we are indeed his offspring' (v. 28).

The source of the first quotation is unknown but certainly derived from Judaism while the second comes from the works of their own poet Aratus. This Paul argued that God is present everywhere, therefore he being creator, cannot be made into a creature represented as an idol, made into inanimate objects such as metal or wood.

Finally Paul appealed to his Athenian audience to repent because the time God overlooked the ignorance of men had past. God is now "commanding all men everywhere to repent" (whether Jews or Gentiles) in anticipation of an appointed time Jesus Christ would judge the world as had been attested to by his resurrection from the dead. The reference to the resurrection of the dead puzzled some and they mocked Paul (most probably the Epicureans who do not believe in bodily resurrection) while others (perhaps the Stoics) wished to hear him again. Nevertheless Paul made some converts among who were Dionysius the Areopagite and a woman named Damaris.

It may be noted in passing that Paul's speech at Areopagus followed the pattern of the recurring theme of what C. H. Dodd described as the *"kerygma"* or "proclamation". In it, Paul drew attention of the Athenians to their wrong allegiance in worship to the "Unknown God" (*Agnosto Theou*) instead to the Lord the creator of the world and all things therein. He revealed to them that it was wrong for them to have reduced God to graven images. Thus he appealed to the Athenian audience to repent as the dawn of the messianic age was at hand in the appearance of Jesus whom God had ordained to judge the world.

Some scholars have opined that the speech is Luke's own artistic embellishment or free composition with the results varying from complete acceptance to complete rejection of its historicity (Dillon & Fitzmyer, 366). Certainly the argument is beyond the scope of this study. Suffice to conclude this introduction that Luke makes his position clear that he adopted the same principles and methods of a trained Greek historian (Guthrie, 360-361; see Falusi, 6) in writing his theological history (Lk. 1: 1-4) & Acts 1: 1-4). No doubt, Paul's speech is re-casted by Luke to depict the open confrontation of the Christian proclamation with the representatives of Greek culture and philosophy but it has a universal relevance and application. Thus, this paper is presented to highlight the importance of Athens in Paul's days and to show that the scrupulous religious life of the Athenians has a considerable resemblance with some old cosmopolitan towns in Africa with particular reference to Nigeria. It also points out that the cold reception of the Greeks to Paul's expository message is nothing strange in comparison to the emergence of the Christian proclamation in Nigerian soil. The two specified comparisons with Old Warri and Benin, two important ancient towns in Nigeria are treated to illustrate our position.

Comparison of the religious life of the Athenians and Africans

As already mentioned, Athens had lost its political fame by the first century A.D. but retained its past glorious history and cultural heritage. The name Athens (*Athenai*) is derived from the city's patron goddess, *Athene* (Guthrie et *al.*, 1970: 996). It was reputed for its religiosity, a centre of pagan religion and Hellenistic philosophy. Of importance to note is that Athens, no doubt prototypes some of the old cosmopolitan towns in Africa such as ancient Benin and Warri in Nigeria. For example, Benin was the capital of the ancient Bini kingdom with the *Oba* as the traditional and political head with powerful chiefs as his subordinates. It has preserved its past cultural influence and to a large extent its political importance. Today it is the capital of Edo State of Nigeria and the traditional and cultural home of the entire Edo speaking peoples of Nigeria. The first recorded contact of the *Oba* with European missionaries C. 1472 was reputed to be highly remarkable. *Oba* Ewuare (C. 1440 – 1473) was said to have received the Catholic missionaries, the Capuchin, warmly as Paul and his companions were initially received in Athens. The contact of the missionaries with *Oba* symbolises the confrontation of the Christian faith versus the Bini cultic religion, the European culture versus the African culture. One of the *Obas,* Esegie (C. 1504 - 1550) permitted one of his sons and some chiefs to be baptised and be taught to read. He sent his son to Portugal to learn first-hand religion and the ways of the Portuguese. But during this period, the *Oba* was engaged in the Idah war (Erivwo 1978: 22), and the effort of the Catholic missionaries to effect massive conversion was ineffective. The failure of the missionaries could be accounted for by their mistaken methods of evangelism employed to plant Christianity in Benin. Among other factors, the Bini cultic religion, we are told, was an institutionalised force (again a prototype of the beliefs of Greek philosophical sects) that could not be brushed aside by the erroneous notion of missionaries which equated it to diabolism (Makozi & Afolabi, 6). To ask the *oba* and his traditional chiefs, as the missionaries did, to abandon their worship of the divinities was tantamount to an insult and show of sheer arrogance. When in August 1651, they tried to restrain a religious festival involving human sacrifice, they were beaten up by an angry mob and subsequently deported (Ajayi, 223). Therefore, other attempts by the missionaries were unfruitful and the Christian faith failed completely to displace the traditional religion. The reminiscent product of these soul-winning endeavours led to the emergence of the syncretistic Aruosa Church still found in Benin City today.

Some scholars have suggested that the results of Paul's address at Areopagus yielded little or no fruit. According to Borkamm "if Paul actually did preach in Athens – while there is no mention of this in his letters, it is nevertheless very probable and may form the historical core of Luke's picture – we may certainly suppose that he failed. But the reason for the failure was hardly an attempt to adapt his messages to Greek culture and philosophy."(65) In the opinion of Howard Clark Kee and Franklin W. Young, Luke makes a tantalising twist of the account by mentioning that Paul converted Dionysius, one of the judges in Athens. But as they maintained:

> Actually, nothing further is known of this Dionysius, although this name was a favourite non-de-plume for quasi-philosophers in the fifth century and later. As enigmatic as Dionysius is the subsequent history of the community of Christians in Athens we know nothing more about the Athenian church in the apostolic age (251).

However, Kwesi Dickson (107) revealed that Dionysius (one of the converts), was probably a member of the council of the Areopagus (hence he was described as the Areopagite). Legend has it that this Dionysius eventually became bishop of Athens.

It has also been observed that a body of Neoplatonic literature attributed to this Dionysius appeared several centuries later than his age (Guthrie, *et al.*, 997). All these views strongly suggest that Paul's missionary impact did not last long in Athens. It is therefore probable that he encountered stiff oppositions, escaped the threats (Barrett, 707), but won at least a few converts that never stood firm for the faith, and this probably accounts for Paul's hasty departure to Corinth.

The cold reception of the Greeks to Paul's address can also be compared with what happened during the planting of Christianity in Old Warri town of the Niger Delta of Nigeria in the 15th and 16th centuries. Then, Old Warri was the seat of government of the Itsekiri kingdom with the *Olu* as the political and traditional head. Today, the *Olu* has lost much of his power to the Federal Government of Nigeria but the present Warri remains the headquarters of Warri Local Government Area of Delta State. In Old Warri, the earliest recorded contacts with European missionaries dated as far back as C. 1477. Here also frantic efforts made by the representatives of the Christian faith proved abortive. The results were similar to those of Paul's missionary effort to evangelise Athens. The Augustinian Monks came and laboured indefatigably in the Warri area 1556–1574 and persuaded the *Olu of the Itsekiri* and his people to embrace Christianity. The *Olu* allowed his crown prince to be baptised, christened Sebastian. True, as *Olu*, Sebastian encouraged the acceptance of Christianity, he sent one of his sons Domingos in 1600 to Portugal to be trained as a priest but all these attempts failed (Erivwo 1978: 3). The Prince Domingos came back from Portugal with a wife and so broke the oath of priesthood. Even the form of shaky Christianity practised at the moment was confined to the royal court and so the gospel did not take root (Ajayi, 3). By the beginning of the nineteenth century, there was nothing to show for all the labours of the earlier missionaries except a few relics like the huge cross at the centre of Old Warri, a few church decorations among the cultic shrines (Ajayi, 3). Thus, the traditional religion reasserted itself and obliterated the earliest attempt to plant Christianity in the western Delta of Nigeria until its later reappearance in the late nineteenth century.

The uniqueness of Paul's Message to Africans

In order to determine the impression, which Paul's message would create in Africans and their reactions, whether positive or negative, it is pertinent to summarise the African belief system. The Africans believe that there is a Supreme Being who created the world and as well sustains it. He is the giver of the people's morality. He is the determiner of the people's destiny. Hence Ifesiah (44) remarks:

> In fact this pivotal belief in *Chineke*, the Creator, is something one knows without being taught. One only needs to come to the age of reason and observe the world around one; the belief in the Supreme Being in Igbo religion as well as African religions is simply axiomatic because he is the focal point of Igbo theology.

To assist Him in His theocratic government, the Supreme Being created the divinities and in conjunction with the ancestors they watch zealously over the people's morality. This indicates that man is imbued with conscience to guide him in his ethical living, as the Yoruba say, "In order to aid man in ethical living, *Olodumare* has put in him *Ifa aya* (The Oracle of the Heart or The Oracle which is in the Heart). "It is this Oracle of the Heart that guides man and determines his ethical life." (Idowu: 154). The implication of this is that the Africans do not believe like the Epicureans and Stoics that the world was created by chance nor are they materialistic. Paul's message to the Africans would have met with positive reaction since most of the themes are familiar with them. Paul mentioned God as the creator and sustainer of the universe and all that is in it. This is merely an affirmation of the African religious beliefs and practices. In verses 30–31 of our text, Paul talked about the judgement of the world by God. The Africans through the cult of the ancestors emphasise the need for everybody to live in accordance with the normal code as given by the Supreme Being. To be qualified for an ancestor, one has to give a moral life as dictated by the society. Amponsah's remarks (101) about the Ghanaians also apply to all Africans:

> Relatives who are regarded as ancestors might have led a good moral life... The names of wicked people are not mentioned during libation... Drunkards, adulterers, an extravagant person, a coward, a lazy person are considered to be evil. A thief is a nuisance to society and therefore cannot be regarded as an ancestor.

The idea of judgement as indicated by Paul is eschatological and will be executed by a particular person – Jesus Christ. The Africans no doubt have the idea of judgement which is here and now and those found worthy enter into the ancestorhood while those found guilty are not rewarded with ancestorhood. It could be said that the Africans have the concept of reward and punishment. It is in consonance with his idea that Ezeanya (44) remarks: "And so, the cult (of ancestors) is a great incentive to good living."

The resurrection of the dead (verse 32) which caused much dissension among the Epicureans and the Stoics should have created much curiosity to hear more on the Africans since they have the belief that "death does not write finish to life" (Idowu, 186), and to see the possibility of reconciling their belief system with what Paul was preaching. They would even accept that God could raise the dead in order to bring their ancestors back to the physical world since they believe in a functional religion. As S. U. Erivwo (12) puts it, many of those who embraced Christianity did so because of a desire to be free to eat food they could not eat before conversion." The Africans in religious matters could be described as existentialists.

Since the religious and philosophical background of a people determines their reaction to situations, it is no surprise to read that some of Paul's audience mocked him while others wanted to hear him again. Although Luke does not state categorically the group that mocked Paul, but based on their philosophical tenets, the Epicureans who believed that there was no consciousness in death and that death ended everything should be suspected of the mockery because Paul's statement must have sounded cacophonous in their ears. On the other hand, the Stoics who had certain tenets very similar to those of Christianity the *Logos* which is God, the life and wisdom of all which is within us and thus the universal brotherhood of man – should be those who showed willingness to hear Paul again and it must have been from amongst them Paul made his converts – Dionysius, the Areopagite, Damaris and others with them (verse 34).

It is appropriate to conclude here that Paul made many of his converts from among the Stoics whose philosophical ideas corroborate with Christian tenets. No doubt, he would have met with less dissension and made more converts if Paul had preached to the Africans. This is because his approach and strategy of preaching were not of total condemnation of the so-called pagan religious beliefs and practices as did the missionaries who came to Africa and branded everything African as heathenish.

Conclusion

As noted above, much scholarship has been expended on the Lukan account of Paul's address at Areopagus and the substantial historical value has sometimes been seriously questioned. Numerous attempts have also been made in modern times to judge Luke in terms of the categories of modern historiography. But one thing is certain. Luke conformed in his work to the norms of ancient historiography characteristics of contemporary Greek historians. It is therefore far from being an invention or a mere artistic embellishment.

We have seen that there are many similarities between Athens and the ancient Nigerian towns of Warri and Benin. Three outstanding facts are clear in Paul's message:

(i) The universality of God as the Creator and sustainer of the universe or the idea of natural revelation of God to all nations.
(ii) The brotherhood of all mankind
(iii) The concept of retribution and judgement of evil people (although the Africans do not believe in physical resurrection of the dead as Paul proclaimed).

These three ideas are predominant in the religious beliefs and practices of the Africans. Therefore Paul's message would have made more impact in winning more souls than he did in Athens. These ideas are embedded in African cosmology but unfortunately the early missionaries who came to Africa failed to take into account these important facts in the evangelisation of Africa. They condemned the people as devoid of the concept of God. They also condemned their religion and culture. The Christianity they preached was therefore looked upon as a foreign religion. It is of paramount importance therefore that in these days that the church in Africa is concerned with indigenisation and contextualisation of the Christian message, the latter should be properly adapted to the religious beliefs and cultural background of the people for effective evangelization.

Works cited

Ajayi, J.F.A., *Christian Missions in Nigeria 1841-1891*, Ibadan: Longman, 1977.
Amponsah, K., *Topics on West African Traditional Religion*, Vol. 1, Ghana Adwinsa, 1977
Barrett, C.K., Paul's Speech in the Areopagus, *New Testament Christianity for Africa and the World*, London: SPCK, 1985.
Boice, J.M., *Foundation of the Christian Faith*, England: Inter Varsity Press, 1981
Dillon, R.J. & J. A. Fitzmyer, Acts of the Apostles. *The Jerome Biblical Commentary*, New York, Geoffrey Chapman, 1974.
Bornkamm,G., *Paul* London, Hodder & Stoughton, 1871.
Ezeanya, S.N., A Critical Review of Ancestral Cults in Nigeria, *Ife Journal of Religions*, Vol. 1, December 1980.
Erivwo, S.U., *A History of Christianity in Nigeria: The Urhobo, The Isoko and The Itsekiri*, Ibadan: Daystar, 1979.
--------"The Delay of the Evangelisation of the Western Delta of Nigeria," *West Africa Religion*, Nsukka, Department of Religion, vol. 17, 2, 1978
Falusi G. K, Lecture Note to Master's Students, May 1987.
Floyd, V. F., *A New Testament History*, London: SCM. Press Ltd., 1977.
Guthrie, D., *New Testament Introduction*, England, Inter Varsity Press, 1968.
Guthrie, D., et al., *The New Bible Commentary Revised*, Inter Varsity Press, 1970.
Idowu, E.B., *African Traditional Religion: A Definition*, London: S. C. M., 1975.
-------- *Olodumare God of the Yoruba*, London: Longman, 1977.
Ifesieh, E.I., The Concept of Chineke as Reflected in Igbo Names and Proverbs: *Communic Viatorun*, No. XXVI, 1983.
Kee, H.C. & F. W. Young, *The Living World of the New Testament*, London, Longman & Todd, 1974.
Kwesi, A. D., *The Story of the Early Church*, London: Darton, Longman & Todd, 1977.
Marshall, L.M., *The Challenge of New Testament Ethics*, London, Macmillan, 1966.

Makozi, A.O., & G. J. Afolabi Ojo (Ed); *The History of the Catholic Church in Nigeria,* Lagos: Macmillan, 1985.

McKenzie, J.L., *Dictionary of the Bible,* New York, Geoffrey Chapman, 1968.

Thompson, F.C. (ed.), *The Thompson Chain-Reference Bible, New International Version,* Michigan, Zondervan, 2000.

X Leon-Duffour, *Dictionary of the New Testament,* London, Geoffrey Chapman 1980.

Walker, W., *A History of the Christian Church, Edinburgh,* T. T. Clark, 1968.

Part III

Church history

Chapter 5

Christianity in Isokoland: a study of religious traditions in contact and change

- S. G. A. Onibere

The Christian presence

Isokoland, comprising sixteen polities, has two of the twenty-five local government areas in Delta State of Nigeria. It is located between longitudes 6^0 and 6^0 60^1 East and latitude 4^0 10^1 and 5^0 10^1 North. Thus the Isoko people are boarded on the north and west by the Urhobo, on the north and east by the Kwale-Igbo, and on the south by the western Ijo. It was to this area that Christianity came in the beginning of the twentieth century; and our task is to unveil the arrival and growth of this phenomenon, spanning a period of approximately forty years.

The wider context into which we must fit the arrival of Christianity is to be traced to the Iteskiri kingdom with headquarters at Warri (Ryder, 1-24). Warri, located on the coast, was naturally suited to receive the Christian faith. Hence strenuous efforts were made by various missionaries between the fifteenth and early nineteenth centuries to plant the new religion in that kingdom. This venture was initiated by the Portuguese, missionaries of Roman Catholic persuasion, as from the fifteenth century and ended in the early part of the 19th century without any appreciable results (Ikime, 206ff). The missionary enterprise was thus abandoned as abortive. In other to capture the Itsekiri for the kingdom of God, there were renewed efforts in the latter part of the nineteenth century by Bishop Ajayi Crowther in 1892 (Ikime, 1968: 38f), Captain Harper (Acting Vice-Consul for Warri District) in 1893 and Bishop Tugwell in 1894 (Erivwo, 21f). And, like the Portuguese, it was a futile adventure. It was Bishop James Johnson of the Niger Delta Pastorate, as from 1901 (Ayandele, 268), in collaboration with C. M. S. through the Niger Mission, who embraced success in the Christianization of the Itsekiri and other peoples (Dike 1957 cf. Erivwo, 120).

It is worthy of note that Christianity which arrived on the Isoko scene in 1911 was preceded by the formal establishment of colonial government and came through two channels (Ikime, 63ff). As regards the first entry point, the Warri-Urhobo route, it may be necessary to discuss a tradition; a certain Mary Omado went to Kwokori in Urhoboland for commercial purposes. In the course of this, however, she encountered the Christian religion for the first time, embraced it and brought it to Ilue-Ologbo from where it spread to what is known as *Isoko-Eru* (Upper Isoko), which includes Otibio Owhe, Emevor, Iyede, etc. And the influence of Bishop James Johnson as related to this channel of Christianity to Isokoland must not be underestimated (Erivwo, 137).

The second entry point is to be sited at Patani in Ijawland, where the Niger Mission, accredited agent of the C.M.S., had been operating. It is believed among the Isoko that Christianity was brought from Patani to Isoko-Ame (Waterside Isoko) through the agency of an Ijo woman known as Bribina. The specifics of the tradition are as follows. Bribina had been Christianized in the home town, Patani, and H. Proctor of the Niger Mission was instrumental in one way or the other. In the course of time, she gave birth to twins which were regarded as an abomination to the traditio-religious milieu. But she was unwilling to have them liquidated on account of her new religion. Hence she was banished to a small Island opposite Patani. Sooner or later an Igbide man, Ebiegbe, who had commercial contracts with Patani, chanced to see her in the pitiable condition on one of his trips. He showed kindness to her and it worked out that both of them became husband and wife before long. Bribina, now permanently settled at Igbide in Isokoland, with the husband embarked on the task of Christianizing the Igbide with considerable success:

> Twenty or thirty persons soon joined her (in her husband's town) at meetings for prayers on Sundays...and now the inquirers have moved out of the town, built a little village with room set apart for Christian worship and begged for a teacher (*C.M.S. Report*, 1912-1913:42).

And from her base at Igbide, as stated in the preceding quotation, Christianity spread to Owodokpokpo, Enhwe, Emede, etc.

The dual entry of Christianity dictated the form the early organization of the church did take. Hence the onus for administering Isoko-Eru rested on Warri where Rev. Cole was in full control; whereas for Isoko-Ame, it was Patani's responsibility, the jurisdiction of Rev. Proctor with Rev. J.D. Aitken. Politically, however, both segments of Isokoland were under Warri District and the name of one Commissioner Douglas was associated with the Warri jurisdiction. It is worthy of note, however, that our sources, both oral and written, reflect the fact that the Patani headquarters were more dynamic in the evangelization of the Isoko people. Thus in 1911, Proctor with Aitken toured the Isoko country for purposes of evangelization. Proctor, as recorded in the *Niger Mission*, G3, 1911, was very convinced of the need to have the C.M.S. commit itself irrevocably to the task of Christianizing the Isoko; and so he appealed to Salisbury Square but in vain. J.D. Aitken was also relentless in his appeal. Again it fell on deaf ears.

In 1913, however, the importunity of Reverends Proctor and Aitken bore some fruits as the latter was commissioned by the Executive Committee of the Niger Mission to tour the "Igbabo country with a view to the formation of a new district" (*Niger Mission*, G.3. 1913). In view of this recommendation, J.D. Aitken undertook the tour of *Isoko-Ame*, visiting such places as Ovwodokpokpo, Igbide, Emede and Oleh. Aitken eventually made Igbide his headquarters instead of Patani in Ijawland.

The tour of the Isoko country, as recorded by Ikime (64), was again undertaken in 1914 by Aitken, a time when the territory could boast of 500 converts. But what worried Aitken was that these converts were standing on a precarious ground since the rudiments of the new religion had not been inculcated in them. Consequently, Aitken "pressed the Niger Mission to commit itself irrevocably to work among the Isoko" (Ikime, 64). As a result of this recommendation, the Niger Mission committed itself to missionary work among the Isoko people. In 1914, there emerged an Isoko District of the Niger Mission. With this turn of events, there was occasioned a synthesis of the segments of Isoko country in consequence of which it was decided to have the headquarters at Patani (Niger Mission, G.3. 1914).

In 1918 Roman Catholicism, as I gathered from personal interview with Ven. B.P. Apena, made some contacts with the Isoko people at Ozoro. It was from there that the R.C.M. spread to some other parts of Isokoland. It is pertinent to point out that there was no resident missionary until 1954. The missionary help received before that time was in terms of "occasional visits for the purpose of saying mass and administering baptism (Ikime, 71). One of the missionaries to visit Isokoland in connection with Catholic Christianity was one Father Cavagnera, an Italian (Bane, 157). All things considered, however, the success that attended Protestant Missionary enterprise is no way comparable to that of the Roman Catholic.

Perhaps it may be judicious to consider how the church, especially the Protestant version, ran its services of worship. When Sunday arrived, Christians in particular locality repaired to the house of the founder for worship purposes. They were all clad in white, a symbol of purity and innocence (Ukenu 7). Primitive Christianity in Isokoland had no stereo-typed liturgy and it was characterized by much emotionalism. Hence there was much drumming, dancing and singing. Surely, this sort of set-up was a continuation of the traditio-religious milieu and a traditionalist who got converted did not feel any sense of loss liturgically. At the end of the choruses there could be prayers and words of encouragement from members in terms of visions, dreams and the mighty saving acts of God. The leader could round up the exhortation time (Ononeme, 3).

It was during the worship service also that new members were welcome into the church. At a convenient point, all new members were required to stand and come forward; whereupon the leader asked them whether they would be able to renounce in totality the worship of traditional deities. If the answer was in the affirmative, as it usually was, they were then required to pay the fee of three pence to ensure official administration in the church. At the close of the service, all members would repair to the house of the new convert to have the emblems of his divinities burnt. All of them were collected, brought outside and set on fire amidst dancing and singing. Thus converts to pristine Christianity in Isokoland parted with their past by destroying *in toto* the emblems of their former worship. It may be, and has been, argued that such destruction has deprived the Isoko of valuable works of art and so the advent of Christianity to the area should be regarded as an unfortunate event (Ikime: 63f). But we may have to demur from that vein of thinking by giving the following submission. Acceptance of Christ required a clean break with the past. Consequently, the divinities to whom they pay allegiance prior to their conversion had to be totally renounced, even if this meant parting with the images that represented them. Indeed, the sincerity of their conversion could not have been better demonstrated than by the liquidation of these emblems. To the new converts, it is true, the images were not acquired for aesthetic reasons, although many of them displayed aesthetic excellence. Rather they were means of comprehending and concentrating on the invisible – the extraterrestrial beings. It is most probable that the continued presence of the images might have spelt a spiritual crisis of no small gravity for the converts; and the lack of them, as was the case, was to relieve them of such a temptation.

It is pertinent to note that evangelism was taken very seriously by nascent Christianity in Isokoland. The missionary took off from the headquarters at Ole accompanied by a sizeable number of Christians who had come from the various churches to carry his luggage – a task they did with all interest and enthusiasm. We may illustrate this by having recourse to a story told about one such visit. The present writer was told by Archdeacon B.P. Apena that when he was the headmaster and church-teacher at Uzere, the church met to select those to carry the luggage of one of the visiting missionaries. After the selection, one of the members of the church raised his hand and protested in these words;

When you picked Christians to carry the luggage of Rev Garrard, I was not among those selected. When at another time, you went to Ozoro for another clergyman, I was also left out. When do you think I shall play my part in God's work, when I am dead? Today, whether you pick me or not I must go to carry the luggage.

This protest caused much laughter; and of course the issue was resolved in his favour. It is very evident that much enthusiasm characterized evangelism in this primitive stage of Christianity. And since there was no means of transport, the missionary was carried in a hammock amidst singing, drumming and dancing. Gunshots were fired at convenient intervals between Ole and the agreed destination! Before the missionary entered the town, he was received by his hosts who came out in large numbers to welcome him. There is no doubt that it was an occasion of much joy. At the arrival of the missionary, all repaired to the church building for a short service, "followed by an open-air campaign for converts by preaching the good news of Jesus" (Ononeme, 9). At the conclusion of all, the missionary would repair to the rest house provided by the hosting town. And should any convert be made their images were burnt immediately (Erivwo, 141).

By now it must be clear that the Christian presence had become a reality and not a fiction.

The tension line

It must not be supposed that Christianity arrived on the Isoko scene to meet a religious *tabula rasa*. On the contrary, the new religion came to a milieu that was already pervaded by the religious dimension of life. And it is of supreme importance to note that there were points of contact between the indigenous religion and the Christian faith. To be sure, both religions professed a belief in a super-sensible world in which dwelled extra-terrestrial-beings, viz, Deity, divinities and other spirits. In the language of Christianity, the divinities and spirits constitute the principalities and powers in the heavenly places. (Eph. 6:12).

Perhaps it may be judicious to single out the Deity to demonstrate in some detail the convergence of doctrine between the two religious traditions. God, whom the Isoko call Oghene, is regarded as the Creator of the universe and all the things in it, including human beings. It is in this sense that all mortals are regarded as sons of God, bringing the Fatherhood of God to a sharp expression. It is thus indubitable that the Isoko have a concept of God, though they might not be able to articulate it as much as the Christians, nor might it be as detailed as does occur in Christianity. Besides, the Isoko, as I have pointed out elsewhere, accord worship in various forms to the Supreme God. With this background, it is little wonder that the people had no difficulty in embracing Christianity, particularly as related to the concept of God. The dimension, and very important for that matter, that was missing was the uniqueness of the new religion. Christianity is the *only* way to eternal bliss: Isoko religion can be at best regarded as a *praeparatio evangelica*. The summary of our contention here is that God had gone to Isokoland before the missionaries; and it was now left for the missionaries to direct, in the power of the Holy Spirit, the misguided zeal of the Isoko to the path of truth, the path of the only saviour of humanity, even Jesus Christ.

That pre-Christian Isokoland was theologically fertile to receive the new religion is not in any doubt. The situation was, however, stimulated by the fact that there were many factors which conspired to attract the non-Christian elements in the area. The first is the issue of liturgical adaptation. In the traditional religion, the liturgy was characterized by the dynamic participation of members and it is by means of this that the Isokoman emerged very religious! Nascent Christianity in the area maintained this continuity with the result that their worship sessions were marked by emotional outbursts, the joy of the Lord, a feeling of fellowship and a much-cherished intimacy. The structural contact between the two religions must not be underrated.

Secondly, the potency of nascent Christianity was a very important source of attraction for pre-Christian Isoko population; and here we shall consider four components to Christianity's potency. There was the element of prophetic fulfilment. Ukuenu (10) narrated that a certain Usikpedo of Otie-Owhe was one of the leaders of the church there who displayed prophetic powers. He prophesized that plantains would wither and they withered. He also prophesized that there would be the invasion of locusts to destroy food-crops and this happened *verbatim et literatim*. A much more convincing prophecy of Usikpedo was related to his death. He was sure of the time of his death. In view of this, Agbada, one of the church members who was a carpenter, prepared his coffin beforehand. When the day arrived, ha had his bath, got dressed up and sat down, discussing with his Christian friends until ha passed away. He was the first Christian to be given a Christian burial in that village.

There was the miraculous element as regards Christianity's potency. In a personal communication with Madam Marioghae of Araya in Aviara polity, she told the present writer that a copy of the Bible miraculously appeared in the area. The tradition maintains that there was an Arayaman, a farmer by profession, known as Esievo. He was not a Christian. One day Esievo discovered to his dismay that a book was lying open on his yams in his farm. The most stupendous aspect was that despite the rains (because it was the rainy season) the book was not touched by any drop of water. However, he took the book to Isara who was the leader of Araya Christianity since it was suspected that the book might be a copy of the Bible. Isara confirmed what they had thought it was. The news of the discovery of the Bible spread everywhere and not a few came from other towns to see it. It was decided that the Bible be taken to Patani where Rev. Henry Proctor had his headquarters. When it reached Proctor's hands, he confirmed that it was a copy of the Bible.

The potency of nascent Christianity was also demonstrated by its healing aspect. There is a tradition (*Church Records,* 7 September, 1970:1) in Otibio-Owhe church which credits the founding of that church with a certain man, Ologbo. This man was unfortunately a leper who came to know that at Kwokori in Urhoboland all diseases were healed through the power of Christianity. Thither he went and as expected he was cured of his much dreaded disease of leprosy. Obviously, he was so raptured by Christianity's potency that he gave himself to the new religion with all zest. The fire that had been kindled was taken back to his village of Otibio. And before long a reasonable number has joined him, being particularly impressed by the healing power of Christianity. Indeed there are traditions of how the insane were healed besides granting fertility to barren women by the divine initiative. There was much power in the blood of the Lamb!

In the area of witchcraft, Christianity was also able to demonstrate its potency. To all intents and purposes, witchcraft is a belief that no Isoko man can escape. It is very much with the people. Indeed the confessions of witches lend support to beliefs in the phenomenon. And any institution that claimed to deal with such a menacing phenomenon was most welcomed. And so it was when Christianity came onto the scene it shattered the power of witchcraft. Witches feared becoming church members lest their secrets be known. Should any person faint during any worship service, it was put down to witchcraft in the victim. There is a concrete example that may be worthy narrating. Isaiah Ajowhomu, one of the leading members of the Otie-Owhe church discovered through the power of God that the church there was menaced by witchcraft. One of the complaints was that the spot over which the church bell hung was constantly soiled by faeces. At another time, an owl, believed to be an incarnation of witchcraft among the Isoko, was found one morning entangled in the cloth used for dressing the altar. The church was, therefore, forced to pray to know the person who was responsible for all this. Before long it was discovered that it was Ajowhomu's wife who was responsible. She was accordingly cursed by her husband that she would be eaten by worms. One day, Amuho, so she was called, went to harvest cassava; whereupon her foot was pierced by a thorn. Gradually, as reported by Ukuemu (15) the foot got decayed despite all treatments until maggots could be seen in it. She died for this.

Surely, she was eaten by worms! Again, there was power in the blood of the Lamb! The church was thus a potent force against the evil machinations of witches. Paradoxically, however, the church became later on an asylum for witches fleeing the retribution of the community. The Isoko people had devised a means of detecting and punishing, indeed eliminating, witches in the *Eni* oracle, a potent institution in Uzere which, according to an unpublished work of Peek (1966), was proscribed by the British administration in 1905. Then there were the *Igbe* religious movements, especially *Awotchi*, which is now defunct, to which those accused of witchcraft repaired to establish their innocence or otherwise.

A third attraction for the pre-Christian community was that Christianity walked in defiance of the moral and ritual taboos that were imposed upon, and bound the votaries of traditional religion. The moral obligations were multitudinous enough for the traditionalists. Yet the indigenous worshippers, particularly the clergy, were meant to bear the burden of a host of ritual regulations. It may be interesting to note that the whole polity of Aviara was not allowed to taste the cassava tuber (*Manoic, Manihot, Exculenta*). With the advent of Christianity as recorded by Hubbard, "every single man, woman and child in the whole clan accepted the new faith gladly, defied the *edjo*, burnt the idols which represented them, and grew cassava" (277).

The priests bore the brunt of the ritual restrictions. They were forbidden to eat certain fish, particularly *obiero* (*Docmac*); they are forbidden to enter the compound of a deceased man until after a definite period; they were forbidden to have sexual intercourse with their wives at certain times; and they were forbidden to enter certain forests. The list can be multiplied *ad infinitum*. It is clear that religion such as Christianity which could liberate the adherents of traditional religion from that bondage would be most welcomed. It was no surprise, therefore that many welcomed Christianity as they sing: (a song which is a mixture of Isoko, Urhobo and Ijo words):

Emo ri Jesu wha riobo ra gha-o-Orugbele
Emo ri Oluwa wha riobo ra gha-o-Orugbele
Emo ri Jesu wha riobo ra gha-o-Orugbele
The children of Jesus eat things forbidden
The children of God eat things forbidden
The children of Jesus eat things forbidden

To sum up, the theological convergence between Christianity and indigenous religion, notwithstanding the many and various attractions, shows the continuity between the two religions. The Isokoman was thus placed in a conducive milieu for the acceptance of the gospel of Jesus Christ. It is therefore no surprise that our sources speak of a mass movement among the Isoko people. There were many converts seeking the rite of baptism. In the *C.M.S. Report* of 1921-22:25, Rev. J.D. Aitken is reported to have performed the prodigious feat of baptizing eighty persons and marrying 63 couples in one day in the year 1922! As recorded by Ikime (66), by 1925 not only did Isoko Christians receive the first confirmation – the number being put at 2,000 – but that the number of local congregations had risen to approximately 85. The summary of the situation as given by Rev. S.R. Smith, Secretary to the Niger Mission, is relevant. He articulates; "Nothing that I can say will give adequate idea of what is going on among the people who have come out of idolatry in thousands to serve the living and true God. The women in many congregations outnumbered the men, and to meet with congregations of from 500-1,000 every morning and evening consisting of the majority of the population was an experience never to be forgotten" (*C.M.S. Report*, 1921-22:25). The picture depicted above is far from discouraging. Yet the act remains that there were other opposing forces at work either to damp the virility of those already in Christianity or of those who were outside it. In a word, the tension line had been drawn: and the form this tension took will now fall for consideration.

In the first place the discontinuity between Christianity and indigenous religion was incarnated in the institution of marriage. True, marriage in Isokoland, as in Africa, was regulated by a strict principal of polygamy. To the Isokoman, a man must marry, and must marry more than one wife. There were socio-economic reasons for giving prominence to polygamy. A man's status in the society depended on the number of wives and children he was controlling. And it was most tragic to have no children to perpetuate one's name. Besides, many wives, their children help in farming, fishing and trading – a sort of economic assert. Polygamy in a word, was a time-honoured institution and well entrenched in the fabric of the society. One was considered insane to have only one wife and of course it was most unimaginable to have none.

It was to this institution that Christianity directed its attack. We may perhaps consider Christianity for being a bit clever in introducing its new value into

Isoko society. At the dawn of Christianity in the area, not much ado was made about polygamy: converts were made and even catechumenated without being bothered about the issue of polygamy. It was at baptism that the problem came into a sharp expression. The church's stand was that a Christian man *must* divorce all his wives except one, usually the most favoured among them, especially the one with potentiality for more children. The children of the man, whether their mothers were retained or not, as observed by Ajayi, could be baptized, so were the divorced wives who were the involuntary victims of the social institution (106).

Isoko Christendom realized how difficult it was to keep to the principle of monogamy. Rev. J.D. Aitken has so well indicated this problem. He ventilates:

> Polygamy is a hindrance to the spread of the Gospel, and is the cause of most troubles...Monogamy bids fair to be more dangerous than even polygamy. There are twice as many girl children as males. We have whole towns and villages where every man, woman, or child is a professed Christian It is very well to say that statistics in Lagos town show that proportions of births of males to females are equal. They are not here. And when all the people of a village are inside a church, one sees the disproportion...It seems to be natural under polygamy. There are many unengaged girls at the present time and some big girls who cannot get husbands...(*C.M.S. Report,* 1921-22:22f).

But despite the recognition of the enormity of the problem, the church was loath to relax the ramifications of monogamy. In Araya-Aviara, for instance, there were cases where non-Christian man, already a polygamist, was betrothed to a Christian girl, most probably prior to her conversion. When the time for baptism came, it was incumbent on the girl to be married to a Christian monogamist. Obviously, her relationship with the non-Christian man must be snapped should the man refuse to repudiate all his wives to marry her, an episode that was never recounted! It may be pertinent to note that there were girls who prepared to break with their fiancŭ calling them *ahwo Ijipiti* (i.e. the people of Egypt). These girls preferred being married to fellow Christians whom they designated *ahwo Izrel* (the people of Israel). What the Araya church did was to leave the problem to the committee members who arranged the marriage between a girl in that position and a member of the committee or an ordinary member in the church. If the man had no money, all the expenses were paid by the committee to whom he paid back the money instalmentally later on. In this way the problem was contained to some extent. But the non-Christian populace was very much enraged, particularly the man who was originally betrothed to her. The reason for such a collision was more than obvious. As the researcher gathered from *Church Records* at Erawha-Owhe, a Christian was to be killed for repudiating all his wives except one.

All the same, as gathered from Ven. B.P. Apena, the church in Isoko tried its best to keep to the provision of monogamy as taught by the missionaries.

However, some Christians who could not accommodate the tension had to quite the church for either the traditional religion or the African Church which had reared its head in about 1920 with branches in Anibeze, Ikpidiama, Okpe-Isoko and Owodokpokpo.

Drawing our discussion to a close as regards polygamy the following questions may be posed: how justifiable was the church in imposing monogamy on Isoko Christianity? It is a truism to maintain that the problem has exercised the minds of theologians, conferences and committees all down the centuries, even before Christianity penetrated Isokoland. Howbeit, two positions have always stood out clear in all the disputations: the strict principle of monogamy, probably appealing to the biblical practice (Ajayi, 106) and the liberal policy of polygamy (Latourette, 176). There are of course arguments on both sides, some of which may be considered. In connection with polygamy it can (and has been) argued that monogamy is not cardinal to Christianity: it is not a *sine qua non* for salvation. If anything, there are echoes of it in the Bible, apart from the clear and dogmatic injunction to the clergy to desist from the practice of polygamy. Why make so much noise about what is not central to biblical theology?

As a matter of fact, the proponents of this view continue to maintain that the enforcement of the monogamous principle is a reflection of the society of the carriers of Christianity. Why should they enforce what to them is purely a social convenience on the people who belong to a different set-up? Again it has been declared that the social situation of Isoko is such that polygamy is the natural principal that should obtain. To be specific, it would sound illogical to expect the Isoko people to change to monogamy when no attempt has been made to alter "the pattern of the people's social and economic life" (Ikime, 72). What is probably most serious, it is further claimed, is that children and wives of a polygamist are made to suffer deprivation, injustice and perils through no fault of theirs. Must one rule, granted that monogamy is the ideal, be kept at the expense of another – the principle of love?

These are penetrating and far-reaching analyses of the issues at stake. But the anti-polygamy camp has its own arguments too. True, the Bible is not probably explicit about the issue of monogamy as it applies to the lay members of the Church: there are only echoes. But echoes may be as valid as explicit statements on the issue. Again the provision of monogamy as binding on the Isoko is consequent on Euro-centric Christianity. But must the missionaries be blamed for presenting Christianity through the eyes of westernism? After all, one can only give the best to his loved one; and these missionaries thought, and are in fact convinced, that they were giving their best for the people. We cannot hold them culpable because they were functioning within their horizon of understanding. Then there is the argument that it was unnatural to force monogamy on a socio-economic milieu which was incongruous with such a strict principle of monogamy. It must not be forgotten that the advent of Christianity to the area revolutionized the socio-economic set-up. A new social class arose whose aspirations were different from those of their forebears. Besides, occupational pursuits became different. It is, therefore, not true that the socio-economic milieu remained unchanged: the old and new were juxtaposed, as it were.

Finally, it is clearly unjust to repudiate all wives except one at baptism because the victims were exposed to difficulties through no fault of theirs. A better course of action should have been to give communion to those who became polygamists before conversion. This seems a valid argument. But there are some gaps. In the first place the amendment might be open to abuse. Some might marry many wives knowing fully well that they would join the Church later on. And though it is the irresponsible who would do this, it is still a fact to reckon with. More substantial, however, is the contention that an exception to the provision of monogamy is the beginning of the demise of the rule, since there is no end to exceptions.

All told, it does appear that monogamy is the ideal. No one is unaware of the jealousies, wrangling and bitterness that occur in polygamous homes. On a lighter side, however, economic sanctions in present-day Isoko compel all to make do with one wife.

The second component of discontinuity was the ancestral cult. It was disturbing enough to wrest the power of government from the living fathers and give it to the new class – the educated class; it was disturbing enough to deprive elders of their privilege of tasting the heads of certain fish and animals; It was disturbing to see Christians treat with careless abandon their civic duties of clearing footpaths leading to the shrines; it was disturbing to see these Christians sit back during annual festivals. All this was disturbing. But most disturbing, however, was the ecclesiastical law which forbade the ancestral cult. All the others the non-Christian community might try to understand; but not the issue of ancestral cult.

Ancestral worship, it must be noted, was deeply entrenched in Isoko religion. Our sources are dogmatic in maintaining that after *Oghene*, it is the ancestor who come next because without being born by the ancestors, the Isokoman reasons, there will be no devotees for any extra-terrestrial being, including the divinities. Indeed, the Isoko man was duty bound to accord worship to the ancestors for the following reasons. Every Isoko was born into the religion particularly the cult of the ancestors. It was the eldest son who was automatically designated the priest to the cult of his dead father insofar as he had killed the animal and performed the accompanying rituals. Secondly, the Isoko family was an extended one including the ancestors who were still regarded as members of the family, though now more potent on account of a change of living situations. Thirdly, the people regarded the ancestors as bestowers of the blessings of progeny, health and longevity. They were the controllers of the destinies of the living. Hence the Isoko felt it would be ingratitude of the first order to neglect his ancestor. The non-Christian community was up in arms since Christianity was riding roughshod on a much cherished religious component such as the ancestral cult. Even many a Christian could not escape the logic of the situation, much more so when he discovered that Roman Catholicism was venerating (to them worshipping) the saints!

Perhaps we may at this juncture touch on some of the specifics of ancestral cult. When a person died, he was buried by his relatives and friends. After about three weeks, there is a second burial called *abo useho uwou* (the bringing of the hand home). It means that without this the deceased would not be accorded an ancestral status because he would not be accepted by his mates in *eri* (the afterlife). He would then constitute a nuisance to his children for neglecting the second burial rites. (These rites, to be fair to Christianity, were shot through and through with "paganism".) When all this had been done he was admitted into *eri* and thereafter accorded regular worship which takes so many forms. Here Christianity must not be held culpable because it was just being true to its ethics. There could be no iota of compromise on this issue. The Isoko convert had to choose between Christ and Satan.

The last source of friction between Christianity and indigenous religion was the issue of totemism and taboo. The issue was paradoxically an attraction and source of conflict. Upon conversion Christians defied totemism and taboos to the utter discomfort of the non-Christian members of the community. Thus sacred objects, like images of divinities, were disregarded and destroyed; sacred places, like shrines, were desecrated and sacred animals, like iguana, held in sanctity, were killed with impunity.

We have definitely not covered the whole spectrum but enough has been said to show the tension between the two religions. The situation had become very explosive. And when the traditionalists came to learn, and bitterly too, that the extra-terrestrial beings whom they thought would fight for them did not do so, they took up arms themselves in 1916 against the Christians in the society. Hearts throbbed with fear as the next minute was uncertain. Distrust was let loose in the market-place. Of course all this was incarnated in the burning of Christians' houses, the setting on fire of churches, liquidation of lives and litigations on both sides. Indeed the persecution was universal and long-drawn.

At Emevor in November of 1923 there was a harvest service, during which much produce was given to the Lord. But an unknown non-Christian set both the church and harvest proceeds on fire – nothing was recovered from the conflagration. The members of the church were very angry; whereupon Agbro, Udevu and Ogheghe complained to the *odio* of the town, Mr. Ifowe, who summoned the whole town to the marketplace for interrogation. But the culprit could not be identified. The matter should have perhaps died like that had not one Eruwedede exposed himself by shouting: "The house was burnt down by Oviethe, the town juju". Christians took up the challenge and Messrs Agbro and J. Egwejemu went to Warri to intimate Commissioner Douglas with the problem. Arrests were made on the side of the non-Christians – those involved being Ifowe, Eruwedede, Edore, Aragba, Oduwe and Agbro. But they were all released on bail.

After their return, the non-Christians burnt down the court premises so as to fasten the blame on Christians on the Day of Judgment. The Day of Judgment arrived and the non-Christians accused Obrifo and Amidi of burning down the court premises. This allegation could not be sustained because John Emu's evidence maintained that Obrifo slept with him that night of the incident. The Christians won the case and the non-Christians were ordered to rebuild the church and to pay the sum of twenty pounds to the Christians for destroying the harvest proceeds. But on return, the traditionalists did not comply with the Commissioner's order. The Commissioner was alerted by the Christians, as a result of which he came to Emevor to see things for himself. He ordered them to make reparations to the Christians. They eventually complied. What happened in Emevor happened in other Isoko churches; and so some Christians were forced to move to where they could practice their religion without interference. Hence Ovwodokpokpo emigrated from Igbide as Udhedhe from Ozoro, Kenan-Owhe from Owhe, Kenan and Ikpidiama from Iri and Bethel with Eden from Oyede.

Nor must it be supposed that the Protestant-Catholic relationship was smooth all the way. At Otibio-Owhe trouble burst out between them. The Roman Catholics had no place of worship and decided to use C.M.S. church building for the purpose without any formal permission. Apparently some of the Roman Catholics were once C.M.S. members and might explain why the Catholics seized the house of worship in that way. Be that as it may, the C.M.S. members were annoyed at their action and decided on embarrassing them. Knowing when the Roman Catholics came to worship they took up positions in the Church premises and forcibly prevented them from using the building. There was of course a physical combat and the *odio,* Mr. Agadama, was alerted. The *odio* tried to reconcile the warring factions but in vain. Consequently he sealed off the church so that neither of the denominations had access to it. The Anglican followed his action by going to Warri to lay a complaint before Commissioner Douglas, who came to see things for himself and decided the case in favour of the Anglicans. Thereafter the Anglican-Catholic hostility became non-existent.

Commissioner Douglas at the head of government at the time, it is worthy of noting, was alleged to be pro-traditionalist in the rancour between the Christians and traditionalists. Indeed he was believed to have been an adherent of Ugo, a divinity that was once famous among the contiguous peoples of Urhobo and Isoko. As a matter of fact, Archdeacon B.P. Apena reveals that Reverend Cole and Aitken appealed to Governor Lugard in Lagos against Douglas for his atrocities against Christians. A commission of inquiry was set up by Lugard; and Commissioner Douglas was found guilty and relieved of his post. Some cases were reviewed in favour of the Church and destroyed churches were rebuilt. The church was no doubt riding on the crest of ecclesiastical success. Thereafter the traditionalists held them in much honour.

But while some were waxing strong on account of the persecutions, others thought it was wise to retrace their steps. Reverend Garrard noted that where hundreds of converts were previously, the statistics fell to 60 or 70 in each congregation. The decline in church membership was facilitated by many factors. Through no fault of God, the potency that characterized primitive Christianity in the area was virtually absent: the emotional outbursts, the *glossolalia*, the healings and miracles were a comparative rarity, if not non-existent. A cold and formal religion stood in its place. Power in the blood of the Lamb did not mean much again. When Bishop Lasbery came to Isokoland he was expected to perform miracles of healing; but to no avail. He was as embarrassed as those who expected him to do so. Again, teachers who could teach the fundamentals of the new religion were few; and so when some could not reconcile some of the paradoxes of Christianity, they recanted. Then there was the complaint of the high moral demands of the new religion. It seemed to some that they had exchanged restrictions for restrictions, if not much more difficult in the case of Christianity. This was a time which showed those who were genuine Christians.

All the same, the minority that was still standing for God were concerned to have the problem of lukewarmness in the church solved by all means. Thus in God's own time, there arose various prayer groups, membership of which was virtually restricted to the womenfolk. This was in about 1940. We may note the prayer group of a certain Opelomo Omako of Ivori-Iri, as reported by Ononeme (11). He was a teacher in Lagos; and felt called by God to come back home to revive Isoko Christendom in the power of the Holy Spirit. One of the most troublesome ills plaguing the church in Isokoland at that time was the phenomenon of witchcraft. To Isokoland Opelomo came, formed the prayer group called Ole-Onweheku (prayer for tamplying on the wicked) and settled to business. With his group composed only of women, he moved from town to town praying for the eradication of evil. He succeeded to a considerable extent especially as regards witchcraft. But his days had been numbered and numbered by the witches who felt the pinch of his prayers in or outside the church. In the year 1952 he died after a prolonged illness. Was God's purpose defeated? The answer was a categorical negative. God raised others like Abire and Phillip Akpona Egburie of Ozoro to carry on the work. But like Omako they vacated the scene too soon.

God was still at work; and so he raised up a man who was to stand for a long time. He was Adamu Igbudu of Araya. His group as initially designated *Ole-Orufuo* (prayer for cleanliness) and the womenfolk dominated it. It started at the same time with others but gained prominence in c. 1946. The occasion was that Ume Church invited the group to conduct their harvest service for them. The result of this was very startling: the Ume church was able to raise one hundred and forty pounds. The news went everywhere as to attract the attention of the superintendent of Isoko churches, a certain Rev. E. Ezekwesili, an Igbo. Adam Igbudu was encouraged and he visited church after church winning converts and strengthening believers. In 1946 Rev. Garbutt left Isoko for home as Rev. E. Ezekwesili did for Igboland. Their successor, Rev. G.P. Bernard, was indifferent to the whole phenomenon. It was in the time of Venerable B.P. Apena and Bishop Agori-Iwe, however, that encouragement was given to the group. Now the group functions under a different name – Anglican Adam's Preaching Society". And one sincerely wonders what have become of Isoko Christendom had God not raised Adamu Igbudu.

Reflections

There are those who would not see anything good in Christianity except to brand it as a base and extravagant superstition aimed at disrupting the tradition-religious equilibrium of the Isoko people. Christianity, it is claimed should have adapted to local forms such as liturgy and music. The ambivalence that tore (and still tears) the church asunder is consequent on the presence of a Eurocentric Christianity. Besides, it is Christianity that is responsible for encouraging promiscuity in married and unmarried because traditional morality has been undermined. These, and many others, are the charges laid at the door of Christian missions. Are all these charges tenable?

Traditional society, it is alleged, was virtually obliterated by Christian missions which saw no good among the Isoko people. But we have to remember that at that time to allow the converts a measure of freedom in sorting out what should be incorporated into Christianity would have been to expose them to syncretism, if not indeed crass idolatry. It was necessary to let the converts know that becoming a Christian mean a revolution occasioning a total break with the past and not the reformation of the traditional religion. In fact militant evangelism as was upheld by nascent Christianity was averse to this vein of thinking, namely, accommodating of traditional forms. Indeed, some continuity was allowed by the missionaries who used *Oghene* (a pre-Christian name for Deity) to designate God in the Christian context. There were obviously harmless customs, insofar as Christianity was concerned, which the missionaries left intact. As a mater of fact, it is impossible to obliterate a people's culture – automatic contextualization is always a force to reckon with. Hence the charge of obliteration of Isoko culture and religion must be taken with a very big grain of salt.

Again, Christianity has been accused of stimulating promiscuity in the Isoko society. This, to our mind, is to romanticize the past. Surely, the past was not a Utopia. We are all aware of how the traditional culture promoted sexual laxity in some respects – perhaps unconsciously. It is common knowledge that no repercussions attended a man who violated a woman (married or unmarried) in Isoko society; but should a married woman engage in the same act she was visited with disaster from the realm of the ancestors. (An unmarried woman was also free from supernatural vengeance as well should she be found to lack sexual restraint.) The logic of the situation is that men (married or unmarried) and unmarried women have unlimited freedom to practice immorality. How utopian then was the pre-Christian milieu? As a matter of fact, it was Christianity that instilled into the society the idea of respect of persons because the freedom given to those categories in pre-Christian Isoko society to practice immorality could lead to societal chaos; and it had in fact done that, resulting in physical combat and litigations. It is Christianity which came and called the traditional culture to order. Thus the accusation should be the other way round; traditional society gives free reins to permissiveness.

And finally we may consider the issue of ambivalence. There was no doubt that some Christians trafficked between the church and the shrine when they found themselves in difficulties. But it is evident that the fault did not reside in Christianity but in the Christian who had not given his life completely to the Lord Jesus Christ. If such a believer had adopted the Christian culture *in toto* then there would have been no problem. Half-heartedness surely yielded such ambivalence. There were many who were poised for action against the devil and were able to hold their ground to the end. The fault therefore lay in the human recipient of salvation and not in the divine bestower of grace.

Thus we must discard all the charges as having no foundation. Indeed Christianity was responsible for substituting better values for superstitious ones. In the pre-Christian era the birth of twins was an abomination, a forerunner of misfortunes to come; and so they must be destroyed. Christianity has dispelled this unwarranted fear. Again, babies who did not cry at birth were left to die from neglect. Christianity has also dispelled that. Nor must we forget the evil of human sacrifices which made travel highly unsafe. Christianity was responsible for its eradication.

Indeed apart from superstitions which the new faith extirpated, it was privy to the eradication of illiteracy, disease and social bankruptcy. The C.M.S. must be credited for pioneering education in Isokoland, especially as much was accomplished by them in this field. The first vernacular literature, the translation of St. Mark into Isoko in 1918 and the remaining gospels in 1921, was possible through the C.M.S. by the instrumentality of Johnmark Eloho of Uzere town. The C.M.S. missionaries felt there was an acute need to teach the people to read the scanty literature in the vernacular. Thus Itinerary Schools were opened to be closely followed by the Vernacular Schools in 1917. But since these Vernacular Schools could not satisfy the people's desire for a much more regular education, schools of the latter category were envisaged, a task made easier by the arrival of Messrs James Welch and Hubbard in 1919. Thus in 1931 some regular schools were established by the pair while allowing some Vernacular Schools to run until more staff were available. Though finance was an obstacle, they forged ahead. A significant step was undertaken in 1936 when a central school was opened at Ole; and another significant step in 1939 when the first post-primary institution, a Preliminary Teacher Training College (later to become St. Michael's College) was established at Ole. The Roman Catholics had by now started their own regular elementary education and in 1956 established a Teacher Training College at Ozoro while the C.M.S. established a Grammar School at Emevo almost at the same time. The R.C.M. followed them by building its Grammar School at Ozoro about the same time too.

As with education, the C.M.S. was the first to initiate social, medical and economic benefits in Isokoland. The year 1930 saw the opening of a medical centre at Bethel. It was placed under the management of Miss Dorothy Jewitt. This centre consisted of a child welfare clinic, motherless babies, a maternity and dispensary. To stimulate social work a vocational training home to prepare would-be wives of mission workers was established at Ole in 1931 and a white lady, Miss Sheeth, was appointed to direct it. It aimed at making happy homes. By 1941 the whole medical centre had been moved to Ole. The Catholics joined the race as late as 1958 when they erected a maternity centre at Ozoro to be closely followed by a hospital. Perhaps we need also to be reminded that Oswald Garbutt took it upon himself to build roads connecting such towns as Oyede, Ole and Owodokpokpo. This project was possible, Venerable B.P. Apena maintained, because Oswald Garbutt had a friend back home in England who chose to preach the Gospel through giving money. There were other projects of economic advantages undertaken by the missions, particularly the C.M.S.

All in all, that the Christian missions are of immense benefit to the Isoko society is an indubitable fact. Consequently we should always be grateful to the missionaries. For the present, Christianity co-exists, and must co-exist, with the traditional religion. Howbeit, it should be a co-existence of mutual respect for each other, while Christianity with its unique message of salvation must continue to ride in its crest of evangelistic success over the indigenous religion, remembering adaptation to (and not syncretism or obliteration of) local traditions. For the future the nature of the relationship between both religions seems hidden in obscurity. It is a probable premise, however, to suppose that the indigenous religion will continue to pose a challenge to Christianity, without any suggestion that it will swamp Christianity – if anything, the contrary is likely to be the case.

Works cited

Ajayi, J.F.A., *Christian Missions in Nigeria*, 1841-1891, Longmans, 1965
Ayandele, E.A., *Holy Johnson: Pioneer of African Nationalism*, 1836-1917, Frank Cass Co. Ltd., 1970.
Bane, J. *Catholic Pioneers in West Africa*, Dublin: Clonmore & Reynolds, 1957.
C.M.S. Report, 1912-1913, West Equatorial Africa, (also,1915-1916; 1921-1922).
Dike, K.O., Origins *of the Niger Mission*, 1814-1891, Ibadan: U.P., 1957.
Erivwo, S.U., "Christianity in Urhoboland," Ph.D. *Thesis*, University of Ibadan, 1972.
Forster, W.P., "Pre-twentieth Century Isoko: It's Foundation and Later Growth" in Benneth, N.R., (ed.) *African Historical Studies*, Vol. II, No. 2, 1969.
Hubbard, J.W., *The Sobo of the Niger Delta*, Zaria: Gaskiya Corporation, 1948.
Ikime, O., "The Coming of the C.M.S. into the Itsekiri, Urhobo and Isoko Country," *Nigeria Magazine*, No. 86, 1965.
- *Merchant Prince of the Niger Delta*, Heinemann, 1968.
- *The Isoko People: A Historical Survey*, Ibadan: U.P., 1975.
Jewitt, D., "Report to the Synod" 1931, (unpublished MS. n. d.)
Latourette, K.S., *A History of Christianity*, Eyre & Spottiswoode, 1964.
Niger Mission, G. 3. A3/012: Protector to Editor, *C.M.S. Gazette*, 29th April, 1911, (also, A3/013, 1913; 1914).
Ononeme, F.E., "The Anglican Evangelistical Band in Isoko Local Government Area of Bendel State of Nigeria," (unpublished Long Essay, University of Ibadan, 1978).
Peek, P.M., "The Founding of the Isoko Clan of Uzere," (unpublished typescript, 1966).
Ryder, A.F.C., "Missionary Activities in the Kingdom of Warri to the early Nineteenth

Century," *Journal of the Historical Society of Nigeria*, Vol.II, I, 1960.
The Church Missionary Outlook II, 1974.
Ukuanu, M.O.U., *A Short History of St. Michael's Anglican Church, Otie*, Oleh: Mercury Printing Press, 1970.
Uyeri, J.E., "Development of Education in Isoko, 1910-1960," (unpublished M.A. Thesis, University of Ibadan, 1977).

Chapter Six

The Anglican Church in Remo land: failures and prospects

- D.O. Olayiwola

Introduction

The chapter intends to achieve a goal, namely to reconstruct the history of a Christian denomination, the Anglican Church, using a culture area approach. The church is chosen for our historical and theological analyses because of its age, that is, the Anglican Church was, from all available data, the first church to penetrate Remoland.

The methodologies employed were critical – historical method with hermeneutics. With these the peculiarities of the Ijebu people, as a sub-Yoruba ethnic group, were taken into consideration. The features which had long been internalized in Ijebuland constituted the major factor which slowed down the missionary work in the area. However the initial obstinacy and obstacles gave way to positive, fruitful, progressive and dynamic thinking among the Ijebu Remo people.

Historical and cultural background

What is today known and called Remo, until barely the close of the twentieth century Yoruba cultural history, was referred to as Ijebu Remo. It is logical to say then that Remoland shared in the fortunes of human excellence, genius, enthusiastic consumption of western literary education, and adoption of modern techniques of entrepreneurship of the Ijebu people generally. In the estimation of Ayandele (ix) who did a full length monographic study of the Ijebu, had said that the Ijebu (Ijebu-Ode, Ijebu Remo, Ijebu Igbo, Idowa, Odopotu, Ijebu-Ife, etc.) stand very high in Africa in general and in Nigeria in particular. On the same breath, Ayandele priced the Ijebu peoples as "the Jews of Nigeria" for the prowess they had demonstrated as prominent middlemen between the European traders on the Atlantic Seaboard and the rest of Nigeria. Meanwhile other Yoruba states were already engulfed in large-scale cataclysmic eruptions of wars in the pre-colonial era.

The nineteenth century Yoruba land was notorious for anarchy, confusion, slave-hunting, pillage and political dismemberment. All these cataclysms culminated in the Kiriji wars of 1877 to 1893. The war put the Ijebu peoples in splendid isolation. The result was that the Ijebu were in a position to retain their village communities, products and organic growth, unlike the war-torn parts of Yorubaland which were forced into accelerated urbanization for security purposes.

Economically the nineteenth century was the golden century of the Ijebu peoples. Their commercial activities extended as far as Nupeland where they sold a special kind of cloth used by slaves and plebeians north of the Niger-Benue. Within Yorubaland itself, their commercial activities carried them to Ilugun, Ketu and Ode-Ondo. Ibadan was their greatest market for the exchange of imported articles like chinaware, printed clothes, rum, guns, powder and beads for slaves. Precisely by the middle of the nineteenth century the Ijebu had become complacent and self-reliant. And as they were more prosperous than their neighbours, they were convinced that they were the master race. Corpulent and healthy looking, their houses and streets were superior to those of their neighbours; their land was well cultivated and they bred their own goats and cattle. From 1866, Lagos depended on Ijebuland for most of their timber for houses and piers. It was even said that European observers found the Ijebu peoples more intelligent than other Yoruba groups (Ayandele, 4), while "they are remarkable as a race for their integrity to a fault" (*C.M.S. Journal*, 1887).

It was not surprising that in the preceding years the impact of the Ijebu peoples at the national level was in the logic of history. Their political, economic and social achievements on the national plane by the middle of the twentieth century were nothing short of spectacular. They subscribed to Nigerian Chief Obafemi Awolowo, who hailed from Ikenne and became one of the titans of political super-rulers in the fifties; and also Chief Timothy Adeola Odutola, a heavyweight industrialist and businessman of national dimension by the fifties.

The religious background

The kingpin of the lives of the Ijebu peoples was their religion. Basically they had the same religious tradition and system as those of other Africans. It was the worship of Jehovah – Olodumare or Olorun through a plethora of divinities. Religion was elemental in every thought and action of the individual and society. Religion prescribed moral action, described the cosmos, the rights and obligations of the individuals in society, the obligations of rulers and society, the constitutional relationship between the governors and the governed. Religion determined the laws and offered protections to country and society. Institutionally the Agemo, the Osi and priests of the various divinities and the Odi who divined Ifa for the Awujale were realities for the Ijebu, no less than the executive and legislative arms of government like the "natural" rulers and Osugbos – all of whom were units within the spiritual consideration of the Ijebu cosmogonic myth and history. The point should be made that the Ijebu peoples did not see the Awujale as not only the political head, but also "a spiritual father who was never seen to eat as ordinary mortals, and automatic death awaited anyone who mentioned his name" (Ayandele, 4). The other kings in Ijebu land could not dare to visit the Awujale without his consent and proper permission for them to do so.

The tradition persists to say that Obanita (the pristine Awujale) Onipakala and Akarigbo of Ijebu Remo were brothers. The trio left Ile Ife to settle at the present abode called Ijebuland. When they reached Ijebu-Ode which was the headquarters of Ijebuland, a misunderstanding arose amongst the trio. Onipakala and Akarigbo conspired to part ways with their eldest brother, Obanita (Johnson, 4). Onipakala came to settle at Ogere Remo while Akirigbo made Sagamu (*Orisa gun amu* – the gods made pots) his debut. Ade Odumuyiwa has hinted that Remo is the name given to thirty-three towns within the conglomeration (Odumuyiwa, 2). Some of the towns in the conglomeration of Remo land are Sagamu, Iperu, Ode, Isara, Ogere, Ikenne, Ilisan, Ipera, Makun, etc.

The C.M.S. missionary activities in Remoland

Fully aware of the disastrous effects of the white man having direct access to the interior, the Ijebu peoples (including Remo) would not allow white traders a footing on their soil. The best consideration the Awujale gave was to grant German traders an offshore island, Lekkie, in 1849. Ijebus's concern about their middleman's position being undermined by direct access to the interior by the white man cannot be over-stressed. They knew that the result of that eventually would be economic suicide. However, it should be emphasized that the Ijebu had greater dread of the political and military consequences. Ijebus' fear of the danger and cunning of the white man became reinforced in 1852 when, through the intermediary of Anglophile Saro collaborators, the Awujale was hoodwinked into signing a treaty with the British in that year. It should be stressed that, unlike the situation among the Egba, or Lagos people, or the Oyo or the Ondo, and later in the century, the Ekiti and the Ijebu were the only Yoruba people who never hankered after friendship with the white man in Lagos. On the contrary it was the British who began to woo the Ijebu for friendship. It was in the process of doing so that the British examined and employed all kinds of strategies and stratagem to achieve their imperial and religious interests.

Absolutely unyielding, the Ijebu, who believed that no world could be better than their own and their culture and civilization were the very best for themselves, refused to grant repeated requests of missionaries who were allowed to pay pilgrimages to Ijebu-Ode. The conclusion of the missionaries was that the Ijebu were absolutely impervious to outside influenced. Missionaries found themselves being invariably treated with contempt, indignity and undisguised hostility by the people. According to the missionaries, they were denied the courtesy of seats at interviews and were compelled to pay for water they drink. In every village, said the missionaries, the people were horrified by a white skin and they sacrificed fowls, goats and dogs to appease the gods who were believed to be annoyed at the presence of such strange human beings in Ijebuland (Ije, 1932).

However, long before the Imagbon war of 1890s, the isolation wall around Ijebuland began to crack. Some Remos had with the Egba attempted to introduce Christianity into Ijebuland. From 1854 to 1861 Balogun Atambala of Ikorodu desired to use the British power in Lagos against his political enemies and through this, the C.M.S. were able to send two de-Ijebulised Saro as mission agents to the town – these were Puddicombe and Parkes. In Ipara, Isara and Ogere where some individuals had been exposed to neighbouring Christian Egbas, they had to practice their new faith secretly before they fled to Abeokuta or Lagos or Ibadan. The most persistent of these was one Joseph Oyegunsen of Iperu who had converted to Christianity in Egba capital in 1851, from where he returned home fifteen years later. The humiliation that awaited any ardent Ijebu who ventured to the Remo area, which missionaries believed was more receptive than the areas directly under the Awujale, was recorded in detail by James Johnson, the most energetic African Missionary to Ijebuland before the military expedition. He toured the Remo area extensively in 1876, 1882 and 1890.

Unknown to the Awujale the Ijebu monolith had begun to shake from within; the idea of Remo Division becoming independent from the capital had already begun to take shape. Some sections in Remo had secretly begun to reveal to missionaries and the Lagos government that there were serious ideological differences between themselves and the Awujale. Left to themselves, they began to say they were anxious for an end to isolation from the rest of the world. Their motive, as the British were to discover in later years, was primarily political – they were looking for the earliest and most convenient opportunity to become independent of the Awujale. To this end, the Remo had in 1878 declared to the British and missionary adversaries of the Awujale that they would welcome British protection from threats from the Egba and the Awujale. They were really anxious to have back their Saro as the Egba had done. In 1890, Dewuja, the Akarigbo of Sagamu reached an agreement with the indefatigable James Johnson for location of two missionaries in Sagamu, while Iperu, Ogere, Ode and Isara for the first time openly promised to grant permission to individuals who became converts to Christianity to worship openly (Ije, 1907).

The brain behind the incipient movement for Remo independence was a colourful character, Joseph Pythagoras Haastrup, who later in the wake of cultural renaissance changed his name Ademuyiwa Haastrup. Born in 1863 to an Ifa priest, he was converted to Christianity as an adopted child. Inducted into western education in Lagos, he entered trade on the Niger and ultimately set up a firm known as Ademuyiwa Haastrup & Sons, Merchants, Auctioneers, and became a zealous lay preacher of the Methodist church.

The few converts who remained in Iperu spread the new faith to Ogere, Isara and Ilisan. Therefore, we could safely assert that by 1856, the Christian church had been established in Iperu. Rev. James Johnson (Later Rt. Revd. James Johnson) who was regarded as the Apostle of Anglican Christianity in Remo assumed work fully on 19 May 1878. He was to water the mustered seed already planted by Daddy Joseph Oyegunsen. As it turned out to be, serious persecutions from the Ogbonis and adherents of Yoruba-Remo autochthonous religion vitiated the growth of the church. Christianity of the Anglican type took a tortuous journey in Remoland. It was only on 13 August 1892 that James Johnson and late Messr Williams were able to make a major break-through. A piece of land was ceded to James Johnson for building a church and school at 'Sewolu'. On the 19 August 1892, the first baptism took place where four male adults and some children were baptized by Revd. James Johnson. One the baptized children was said to have come from the Paseda family. Christianity therefore, gained a sound footing in Iperu with St. James' Anglican Church well built (Ellis & Johnson, 23-25). Other denominations sprang up later in Iperu such as the Methodist, the African Church, the Roman Catholic and Christ Apostolic Church. It is also significant to note that from Iperu, Christianity spread to other towns in Remo, like Ogere, Ode and Isara.

It is a fact that as far back as 1850, the late Revd. C.A. Gollmer had done some missionary work at Ofin proper – the old city and royal seat of the Akarigbo. The work died out due to Ijaye war of 1861. It was later in 1892 that Revd. James Johnson and Messr Williams replanted missionary work at Sagamu. The Akarigbo was reminded of the earlier efforts by Gollmer at Ofin, the king and his court quickly assigned a portion of land in the township of Ofin to the missionaries to begin their work. The royal accent and public allotment of a site for missionary activities in Ofin symbolized the approval and total freedom given to anyone who would embrace the new faith.

The Akarigbo was convinced that it was time for Remo to endeavour as other Yorubaland did, to gain from Christianity whatever she could gain and also put herself in a position to understand and deal propitiously with the white man – the British Government. Remo, by this time, also felt that the time had come for her to cease to suffer from ignorance of letters, put an end to misunderstanding between the Remo people and the white man. This friendly disposition of the Akarigbo helped in no small measure the spread of Christianity to other communities, apart from Ofin, in Sagamu.

Thus, Sagamu became the political as well as religious capital of Remoland. Today, Sagamu houses the headquarters of the Church of Nigeria (Anglican Communion) in Remo Diocese; the Christ Apostolic Church Mission, the Methodist Diocese and the Celestial Church (Odumuyiwa, 39). Iperu was said to have lost the game since 1944. Revd. Canon Falode was then the District Chairman who decided to remove his seat from Iperu to Sagamu on the excuse that the latter was more civilized than the former and that the political headquarters of Remoland was Sagamu. Professor Emmanuel Odumuyiwa has informed us that "Christianity spread to the whole of Remoland through the Anglican denomination" (39). It is also said that there is hardly any village or town in Remoland that is devoid of Anglican presence.

The Anglican Church in Remoland became diocessanised in 1984 with St. Paul's church as the Cathedral. The first diocesan Bishop was the Rt. Revd. Ogundana. His Episcopal Ministry was a huge success and he retired about July, 2003. Rt. Revd. Dr. Olusina who succeeded Bishop Ogundana was a round peg in a round hole.

We shall now turn to the second segment of the chapter which focuses on the failures and prospects of the Anglican Church in Remoland.

The failure aspects

Internal rancour, tenacity of the autochthonous religion and culture, the powerful challenge of the New-Age Churches and materialistic 'gospel' among others, were the problems besetting the Anglican Church particularly in Remoland and generally, Nigeria.

To begin with the internal rancour, our Lord Jesus said that when a house is divided against itself, such house cannot stand. No sooner the Remo Anglican Diocese came into being than a problem arose of almost uncontrollable proportion. The cracks on the wall of Christianity in Remo came to the fore and they nearly shattered the microcosm. The whole trouble started with the agitation from the Cathedral at Sagamu over some intolerable performance of the then Provost, Very Revd. Sokunbi. The then Bishop, Rt. Revd. Ogundana, transferred the provost of the Cathedral to Immanuel College of Theology, Ibadan as a face saving device. The Anglican Christians could not swallow the transfer as they suspected some measure of victimization of Sokunbi from the Bishop. Sokunbi, it was gathered, hailed from Ikenne and his people would not fold hands and watch Sokunbi treated like a *persona non grata*. The embers of fire of revolt began to spread from Ikenne to other parts of Remoland. Matters came to the head when it was learnt that the Very Revd. Sokunbi decided to go on hunger strike at Ibadan. Eventually he died. The news of his death reverberated the whole Diocese and it was clear to the Bishop that a battle line was drawn up. The storm was tempestuous and the whole Province of the Church of Nigeria, Anglican Communion bemoaned. It was a trying period and the host of hell was let loose. The imbroglio harvested a chain of reactions. First, hostility for the Bishop arose. Second, the Pentecostal Anglican Church emerged as a schismatic group as dismemberment grew against the Church headed by Rt. Revd. Ogundana. However, at the end of the tunnel, there appeared a shining light. Efforts were mounted by the Provincial Authorities to bring peace, love and unity back into Remo Anglican Diocese. Whether the efforts achieved desired results is a matter of conjecture. People outside the Anglican Church began to record the ugly incident as a failure of the Church.

In another dimension, the unresolved problem of African Traditional Culture and Religion also reared up its ugly head and this problem is hydra-headed. The heart of the problem had to do with the interaction of the traditional culture and Christianity. The missionaries virtually undermined all aspects of the traditional culture and the religion disparaged. This would explain why the extended family system became disrupted when converts were made. Nothing could be more catastrophic to the African community than to prevent individuality that is crystallized in the family unit. The cultural conquest also pervaded the intellectual arena as it was generally conceived that the brain of the black man is inferior to that of his white counterpart. The conquest extended to the ideological realm. Nigerians began to assume an air of inferiority complex. They could not see themselves as in anyway comparable with the white people. Even their traditional divinities could only be equal to the white man. That is why we have such names as Oguntoyinbo, Sangotoyinbo of Fatoyinbo. The big yams were *Isu-oyinbo* (white man's yams) and sweet oranges were *osan-oyinbo* (white man's oranges).

Against this backdrop, the nationalist propagandists like Edward Wilmot Blyden, James Johnson, and H. Atundaolu, Mojola Agbebi, Otunba Payne, D.B. Vincent, not to go further, stirred up African cultural nationalism. Recently, the Inculturation Theologians like Professors J.A. Upong, Chris Manus, Ogbu Kalu, J.A. Omoyajowo, David Olayiwola and others began to call attention of the people to the fact that positive elements of the traditional religion and culture could be used to decode the gospel message in clearer terms. Today, people over-react and insist that all elements of our traditional culture and religion must be baptized by the Church (Olayiwola, 253-267).

The first was the problem of cultism and nagging issue of home burial. Before the advent of Christianity in Remoland, there had existed the Ogboni Fraternity. Contumacious belief that the Yoruba indigenous Ogboni performed some political functions impressed the educated Africans to accommodate the secret societies. For instance, among the Egba and Ijebu, Ogboni fulfilled the role of the national court of appeal; tried criminals and executed them. Professor Ayandele hinted that "the institution also fulfilled a most desirable constitutional role. By the checks it placed on the monarchy it prevented absolute rule, while its power prevented the masses from being lawless" (Ayandele, 1962: 241-280). Ayandele also added that the so-called Christian Ogboni Fraternity was also formed as a result and it was said that Townsend, Faulkner and J.B. Wood were members. We only need to say here that cultism of any form and origin is a Christian deviation; it is demonic, satanic and is capable of leading to hell.

The nagging issue of home burial has been addressed squarely by the Church Authority. No more can the church continue to sit on the fence on the issue. Rt. Revd. Professor J.A. Omoyajowo, the Lord Bishop of Ijebu Anglican Diocese has articulated scriptural reasons why home burial should be discontinued. Yet, as a member of the house of clergy in that Diocese still hold tenaciously to the practice. Thus the controversy still ranges on in Ijebu. Protagonists of home burial locate examples to support their position from Remo Diocese. It is not the aim of the present study to bellicose Remo Diocese over the issue but to point out that the church has failed to take a joint biblical and constituent stand on home burial.

The challenges of the New Age Churches cannot be glossed over. One of these is the 'Prosperity Gospel'. From my research, I have come to conclude that prosperity gospel preachers will not like to preach messages that will make people to jeer or hoot at them. Such preachers bolster the prosperity message on 3 John 2. In an argument with Jim Bakker, he maintained that 3 John 2 is one of the most misunderstood chapters in the Bible. The verse reads, "Beloved, I wish above all things that you may prosper and be in health, even as your soul prospers" (Bakker, 34-39).

The word 'prosper' has various forms but has one meaning in common. From the original New Testament Greek, the word 'prosper' comes from *euodoo*, which is made up of two root-words; *eu*, which means 'good, and *hodos*, which is 'road' or 'route', ' a progress', or 'journey', to be led in a good way. Apart from 3 John 2, the word is used only two other times in the New Testament, and in no place does the word refers to vast sums of money, riches or material gain. In 1 Cor. 16:2, the word *eudoo* is used. Here Paul was encouraging the Church in Corinth to prepare an offering for the suffering saints in Jerusalem. It was a relief project. Also in Romans 1:10, the word, *eudoo* is found. Paul wrote, "if by any means now at length I might have a prosperous journey by the will of God to come unto you." This message has nothing to do with money or material possessions. On the contrary, the apostle often took special care to make sure that his motivation for preaching the gospel could not be misconstrued because of money. He was simply saying, 'please pray that I will have a good journey on the road as I travel to see you". Similarly, Apostle John, the writer of 3 John 2 was saying, "I wish you a good, safe and healthy journey throughout your Christian life, just as your soul has a good and safe journey to heaven."

What should the Church do to save her members from heretical teachings? The answer to the question is obvious. Great emphasis on the Word of God now is more urgent than ever before.

Imperishable wealth: enduring heritage

The gospel of Christ has a mission philosophy, viz: that men and women are given to God and can therefore, be made fit for eschatological banquet. This is why the Church is given the mandate to "teach all nations, baptizing them in the name of the Father, and of the Son, and of the Holy Ghost" (Mt. 28:19). This was the propelling force that pushed missionaries both white and black to make gospel expedition at different times to Iperu, Ogere, Ode-Remo, Ilisan, Sagamu, Isara, Ikpara, Gbara, Lantoro, Odelemo, Emuren and others. The gospel decoders proclaimed the Good News of the Kingdom to the forebears of Remoland; taught, baptized and nurtured them, responded to their societal needs through education, civilization, and healthcare delivery system and also sought to transform the unjust structures of the nineteenth century Remo society. What Krass (11) called "Gospel and Service" was thus fulfilled in Remoland as from the nineteenth century. The Gospel and Service consists of a triad element of *kerygma* (proclamation of the Gospel); *Koinonia* (fellowship that helps to equip and strengthen the church, by teaching, pastoral work, administration and ecclesiastical organization) and *diakonia* (which involves works of humble service to others).

More than a century ago, Christianity of the Anglican type made an inroad into Remoland and it is bouncing and waxing stronger till date. One of the great legacies bequeathed to Remoland, is the Anglican Church which has an enduring 'order' and 'form'. For a church to survive the twists and turns of history, to maintain its purity of faith, to uphold a culture of non-belligerent leadership succession in her polity – that church must have had an impeccable identity. When a church enjoys stability and not necessarily getting herself petrified into false orthodoxy, then she can express and re-express the unique life of Jesus Christ for humanity. She can conveniently hand on the faith of the Fathers from generation to generation. This is why today we can celebrate the prospect, the fortune and success of the Anglican Church in Remoland for more than one hundred years ago. The success story was in 1984 crowned when all the Anglican Churches came together in Remoland and became diocessanised. Rt. Revd. Ogundana became her first Bishop.

Both the Anglican and the Methodist denominations which path-founded the road for other denominations gave to Remo schools, colleges and a tertiary institution. Remoland is today suffused with primary and secondary schools established by the Church. And quite recently, the Adventist Church opened the Babcock University at Ilishan Remo. Hospitals, maternities and other infrastructures were also provided by the Church to give Remo people a taste of modern life.

The unity which was badly needed at a time when the entire Ijebuland was balkanized became realized by the promotion of a greater sense of good neighbourliness and intra-ethnic harmony. The church preached and taught about love, unity and peace, which filtered into the fabric of Remo society. Before then, Remoism and Ijebu-Igboism, etc., were the convulsions that shattered the Ijebu monolith as a distinct entity. In 1940 a number of super-Ijebu who had been genuinely worried about the balkanization of the fatherland began to preach, through the Ijebu National Society, the gospel of reconciliation and abandonment of the *"Egure"* designation for the Ijebu outside Ijebu-Ode District. Secondly and ironically, balkanization of the fatherland had not only removed the one source of inequality but began to forge and force equality among the people who began to matter more and more, namely the educated elite who were university graduates or professionals like lawyers, journalists and newspaper proprietors. Those from the districts like Papa Obafemi Awolowo and Adesanya, barristers respectively from Ikenne and Sagamu; J.A. Adesola and J.J. Odufuwa, journalists and proprietors respectively from Iperu and Ijebu-Igbo;

Venerable S.A. Banjo and Stephen Oluwole Awokoya, respectively from Ijebu-Igbo and Awa – both graduates and brilliant – were more than a match for their counterparts in the Ijebu capital. Their language and behaviour which were well advertised in Ijebuland left no one in doubt that they saw themselves as the leaders of Nigeria towards Canaan, the Promised Land of Independence which would belong to them more than to the traditional rulers. These educated elite leaders all over Ijebuland had one thing in common – they all shared enthusiasm for accelerated modernization and had begun to look forward to participating in the affairs of Nigeria in general and of Yorubaland in particular.

Hence the commitment of the newspapers owned by Ijebus was directed to the goal of charity beginning at home. The *Ijebu Weekly News* abandoned anti-Ijebu-Ode stance and began to adumbrate pan-Ijebuism after Remo's attainment of independence in April 1938. Thus J.J. Odufuwa, proprietor of Swann Press, Lagos and owner of *Ijebu Weekly Echo* that came into being in 1947, who for years had been a strong backer of the demand of Ijebu-Igbo for full autonomy, committed his newspaper to the task of promoting unity among the various groups of Ijebuland. The imperativeness and wisdom of the Ijebus coming together had been publicly dinned in the ears by Rt. Revd. Solomon O. Odutola. Quoting Ayandele (300), he wrote in the maiden issue of the *Ijebu Weekly Echo*, 2 August, 1947:

> Ijebuland is not an undivided whole at present, the political dismemberment of a few years ago has split it into Ijebu-Ode and Ijebu-Remo – there are some who would not like the qualifying prefix 'Ijebu' behind Remo. We need what will make us realize that in the upward march of Nigeria to nationhood it is the bride that encourages internal dissension that will lose its identity.

Conclusion

We would like to conclude this chapter with some remarks: The Anglican Diocese of Remo needs to do stock-taking. The members should count their blessing and give thanks to God for His mercies over the decades. Some of the prospects and failures we highlighted are tips of the iceberg. To remedy our shortcomings we have to listen to Apostle Paul in II Cor. 5:18 that "All things are of God, who hath reconciled us to himself by Jesus Christ, and hath given to us the ministry of reconciliation."

Having been reconciled to God through our Lord and Saviour, Jesus Christ, we ourselves are given the work of reconciliation. It means that the ministry of reconciliation is God-given and it must be done with all diligence and sincerity. It implies that we have to forget the past wrongs done against us in the spirit of love. Only then can we begin to rebuild. Spiritual rehabilitation work must now begin in Remo Diocese so as to move her forward. The ministry of reconciliation manifests in several ways namely, prayer, evangelism, healing, inter-personal and family relationships, social work, politics, trade and commerce and so on.

Works cited

Ayandele, E.A., *The Missionary Impact on Modern Nigeria, 1842-1914*, London: Longman, 1962.
- *The Ijebu of Yorubaland, 1850-1950: Politics, Economy and Society*, Ibadan: Heinemann Educational Books Nig. Plc. 1992.
Bakker, J., *Prosperity and the Coming Apocalypse*, Benin: Joint Hairs Pub. Nig. Ltd., 1998.
C.M.S. G3/A3/04, Journal Extracts for the Half Year Ending, June, 1887.
Ellis, J. & Johnson, J., *The Missionary Visits to Ijebu Country 1892*, Ibadan: Daystar Press, 1974.
Ije, Prof. 165 Vol. II, *Annual Report for 1932*, also 916, *Diary Ijebu Ode, 24 April, 1907*
Krass, A.C., *Go . . . And Make Disciples*, London: SPCK, 1974.
Odumuyiwa, E.A., "A Century of Christianity in Remoland", *M.A. Thesis,* University of Ife, Ile-Ife, 1982.
Olayiwola, D.O., "Incultural Theology: A Nigerian Pentecostal Perspective", in Olayiwola, D.O. (ed.), *Contextualization of Christianity in Nigeria,* Lagos: Derib Books Ltd., 2002.

Part IV

Islamic studies

Chapter 7

The Islamic nostrum for the understanding of religion

- S. O. Eniola

Introduction

Among the fundamental intellectual topics that concern human life, the religious question is of paramount importance. It has always been regarded actually as a primary concern for the well-being and destiny of man and has produced profound insights and extensive knowledge. Scholars and researchers have undertaken wide, varying and comprehensive studies on the origin of religion. In the same vein, they attempted to establish the motives behind man's religious concerns, pursuing their researches with a particular point of view and methodology that governs also their judgments and conclusions.

The truth of the matter is that, *ab initio*, faith and belief have always been part of the texture of human society. Neither in the past nor in the present is it possible to find a society in which religious issues have not been raised. Hence in the world of Islam, the *Holy Qur'an* declares, *inter alia*, "And we did raise among every people a messenger, preaching, worship Allah and shun the evil one…" (16 vs 37).

It may even be claimed that human endeavour in the realm of religion and belief has been more strenuous and enduring than his efforts in the area of knowledge of transcendent reality, that is the essence of those things which knowledge and art strive constantly to attain. However the subject matter of religion has attracted positive and negative analogies. Indisputably, one of the factors in the emergence of anti-religious ideas and a phalanx of deniers of God has been the false teachings, the inadequacies and the intellectual perversions of the followers of some religions.

In this context, the peculiarities and separate characteristics of each religion must, therefore, be individually examined when studying the reasons that have led men to adhere to a particular religion. At all levels of education a combined study of the introductory and basic theological components of each religions is important in order to encourage broad based intellectual development and orientation, particularly among students and generally in the globalized world.

Thus this chapter is an introductory analysis of the study of religion from the perspective of Islam. Accordingly, the paper examines the basic tenets of Islam, the sources of Islam, the Islamic concept of religion and religion as a factor in national development. The chapter is also designed to facilitate general understanding at a glance of what Islam is about.

Religion and humanity

Among the great religions of the world, Islam enjoys the distinction of bearing a significant name that points to its very essence. With the advent of Islam, religion assumed a new status. It is thenceforward to be treated not as a dogma that a man must accept in order to escape everlasting condemnation but as a science based on the universal experience of humanity. An aspect of human life, which Islam has emphasized constantly more than others is the intellectual development. It is of historical significance to recall that the first revelation runs thus:

> In the name of Allah, the Gracious, the Merciful.
> Convey thou in the name of thy Lord who created,
> Created man from a clot of blood; convey and they
> Lord is most Generous. Who taught man by the Pen,
> taught man what he knew not (*Qur'an*, 96:1-6)

This is a direct divine ordinance making it imperative upon man to search for and acquire knowledge. Thus the acquisition of knowledge by the earliest generation of Islamic scholars and the erudition of their new breed successors have spanned many centuries resulting in a wide coverage of all disciplines including religion *per se*.

It is said that it is the urge towards self-preservation that gives rise to religion. Whatever that may be, the ultimate origin of religion is found at the earliest time of human existence and civilization. It consists usually of a belief in some sort of power or powers and some form of attitude towards such powers. In essence, man-made religions and revealed religions are distinct things. Over the years, the followers of religious personalities have carried out series of distortions and innovations on the original teachings of such religious personalities in history. Consequently, the spirit departs from the revealed religions with the passage of time and it becomes corrupt and bedevilled with amorphous interpretations and intellectual fabrications.

Conversely, the question, which perturbs every mind today, is whether religion is after all necessary to humanity. A cursory glance along the corridor or the history of human civilization will show that religion has been the supreme force in the development of mankind. In this connection, Muhammad Ali remarks:

> One Abraham, one Moses, one Christ, one Krishna, one Buddha, one Muhammad has, each in his turn and his degree, changed the whole history of the human race and raised it from the depths of degradation to unprecedented moral heights. It is through the teaching of this or that great prophet that man has been able to conquer his lower nature or to set before himself the noblest ideals of selflessness and the service of humanity (7).

Over the centuries, religion has manifested itself in a number of major traditions, which, for convenience, can be classified as "monotheisms," stemming from ancient Judaism, Christianity and Islam. The religions of Indian origin such as Hinduism, Buddhism, Jainism, Sikhism, and the Far Eastern religions of Taoism, Confucianism, Shinto, etc., are either pantheistic monism or utilitarian in nature. From about the sixth century BC., as pointed out by Smart (1988), the major religions began to take shape. However, modern study of religion is largely a product of techniques of scholarship developed in the nineteenth century. The use of historical, archaeological, philological, philosophical and other related methods led to a new range of explorations into the ancient past of religion.

Islam's appraisal of these processes prompted the inference that the nature of religion and definitions of religion have a systematic inadequacy about them. Like everything of the spirit, religion cannot be described, as to make clear to the detached observer, the characteristic quality and depth of religious awareness and commitment. Rather, it can be practiced in order to exhibit the sociological significance of its basic tenets. Thus, an attempt has been made below to present a resume of Islam tenets.

Basic tenets of Islam

Islam according to Ulfat (1976:193) is "the derivative of the Arabic root words S/L/M, which literally means peace and /or absolute submission to the will of Allah". The religion derives its name from the *Qur'an* as follows: "This day have I perfected your religion for you and completed my favour upon you and have chosen for you Islam as a Religion" (Qur'an 5:4).

The basic concept in Islam is *at tawhid*, an axis around which all the teachings of Islam rotate. Allah, which is the name of God in Islam most emphatically, stresses the monotheistic nature of God, the Creator of the universe, the Lord of all Lords, and the King of all Kings. This is the resume of the first part of the *kalimatu- sh-shahadah* i.e., Declaration of the testimony. The second part of the Declaration recognizes the unique prophet-hood of Muhammad. Islam is a complete code of life. It strikes a harmonious balance between the world of faith and the world of action. In other words, Islam is better understood as a system of social obligations than as a system of belief. The obligations of orthodox Islam are enshrined in the *shari'ah*, a word usually translated as "Islamic law" but actually meaning a whole way of life. Muslims believe that the *Holy Qur'an* epitomizes this way of life, acting as its primary source and regulator. Those who submit themselves to the will of Allah are the adherents of Islam and they are called Muslims.

Secondly, Islam is discussed as a religious culture rooted in Arabism. However, the Arab ness of the *Holy Qur'an* or the prophet, Muhammad, is not an essential conflict in its universalism. This is obvious in the fact that in the span of fourteen centuries, after the death of the Holy prophet, Islam has continued to absorb as much of the non-Arab customs and usage as it came in contact with. Owing to this cross-fertilization of cultures, as pointed by Raji, "there is always an increasing divergence between the ideal Islam as contained in the classical jurisprudence and Islam as it is practised from time to time in different cultural units" (xi.).

Sources of Islam

The whole of Islamic historiography and tenets are sourced from four categorical sources. The four are paired viz.; the *Holy Qur'an* and the *Hadith*, which are classified as *al-adillat al-qat'iyyah*, i.e absolutely sure argument, the *Ijma'* (consensus of opinion of Muslim jurists) and the *Qiyas* (Analogical reasoning). These are classified as *al-adillat al-ijtihadiyyah* i.e arguments obtained by exertion.

Of these four sources, the parent source is *Al-Qur-an* which is a derivation of the Arabic root words *Qara'a* i.e., that which is to be read. It is known as *Umm al-kitab* i.e., mother of all books. This status derives from the fact that previous revelations were limited in their scope in that each was designed to meet the needs of the people to whom it was sent. Admittedly, some elements of these revelations contained fundamental truths, which are valid through the ages in respect of mankind. Basically, such revelations contained guidance, directions, commandments and prohibitions, which were of a local and temporal character.

Moreover, in the course of time, portions of these revelations were lost, forgotten or distorted through the processes of theoretical fabrications and interpretations. The various references that are contained in the *Holy Qur'an* about past prophets and peoples of God, their life styles, tribulations, heroic acts or the references to the tyranny and villainy of certain monarchs and tribes are all calculated to enhance man's broad perspective of life and to breed moral and spiritual development among mankind.

With the *Hijrah* of Muhammad in 622 C E, revelations assumed a new dimension. The *Makkan surahs* comprise spiritual messages and injunctions while the *Madinat surahs* contained provisions on administrative injunctions and reforms. The revelations covered a period of twenty-three years during which the Holy Prophet and some of his companions memorized all the revealed verses. A person who memorizes the *Holy Qur'an* is called *al-Hafiz*. The preserved manuscript was later to be standardized in its present form under the caliphate of Uthman b. Affan- (7644-656 CE). There are one hundred and fourteen chapters in the *Holy Qur'an* with *Al-Fatiha* as the first and *an-Nas* as the last.

The other source of Islam, which is categorized as secondary is the *Sunna/Hadith*. *Sunna* literally means way or rules or manner of acting or mode of life, while Hadith is a saying conveyed to man either through hearing or through revelation. Basically, *Sunna* indicates the practices, while *Hadith* is the sayings of the Holy Prophet. Both cover the same ground and are applicable to his actions, practices and sayings. Succinctly, *Hadith* is the narration and record of the *Sunna*.

While the *Holy Qur'an* gives the Muslims a primary rule of life, there are many matters where guidance for practical living is necessary. In such cases, the prophetic examples and precepts became the tradition for the *Umma* (Muslim community). This is the subject matter of the Quranic verse. "Verily, you have in the prophet of Allah an excellent model for him who fears Allah and the last Day and who remembers Allah much" (*Qur'an* :33:22). The science of *Hadith* brought about the categorization of *Hadith* works according to their degree of reliability. This owned largely to the schism of the post- Muhammadan era when various individuals and parties resorted to philosophical and theological fabrications of the *Hadith* in order to support their extreme positions. These categories are the *sahih* - which are sound traditions, chains of transmissions, and subject matters that are unbroken and rational. There are also the collections that are classified as *Hassan*, i.e. fairly genuine traditions and *Da'if* - weak traditions. Islam derives the interpretation or subject classifications from the *Sahih* under which there are six authors viz *al-Bukhari*, Muslim, at - *Tirmidhi*, *Abu Dawud*, *Ibn maja*,' and *an-Nasai*. In the latter stages of Islam historiography, the advancement of knowledge and the cross fertilization of ideas brought about *Ijma*,' (consensus of opinions of Muslim Jurists) and *Qiyas*, that is analogical reasoning. These modes were employed to the extent of exercising *ijtihad*, i.e. self-exertion.

The theology of Islam

The edifice of Islam rests on five pillars. These are *Iman, as-salat, az-Zakat, as-Sawn* and *al-Haji*.

(i) *Iman*, literally means faith. It embodies *Kalimatu sh-shahadah*, which is the Declaration of the Testimony. It is a simple but firm declaration that 'I bear witness that none deserves to be worshipped except Allah. He is one, without any partner. I also bear witness that Muhammad (SAW) Is His prophet and Messenger. The basic concept of monotheism in Islam is *at-tawhid*, i.e. unity of God. The second part of the *kalimah* is to discourage other kinds of associations. Hence, it emphatically identifies Muhammad as the prophet and Messenger of Allah.

As a corollary, Islam places certain responsibilities on mankind. These are contained in the six articles of faith. They are:
1. Belief in God. See *Qur'an*, chapt. 2v.256 for more explanation.
2. Belief in Angels. See *Qur'an*, chapt. 35 v. 2 for more explanation.
3. Belief in the Revealed Scriptures. See *Qu'an*, chapt. 2 v 5-6.
4. Belief in all the Prophets from Adam to Muhammad. See Qur'an chapt. 2 v 286.
5. Belief in Life after Death. See *Qur'an*, chapt. 75.v. 7-26.
6. Belief in *Taqdir*-predestination. See *Qur'an*, chapt. 87 v.2 –4.

ii. **As-Salat:** This means prayer which is the canonical worship in Islam. The Islamic Prayer like any prayers has certain forms, which comprise series of actions, genuflections and recitations. Ablution, *Al-wudu*, is the basic prerequisite for prayer in Islam. (See also the Holy Bible Exodus 30: 17-22, John 13: 2-9, Nehemiah 8ff, for references to the Islamic form of worship). The obligatory prayers include *al-fajr*-Morning Prayer, *zuhr*-prayer, *al-Asr*-afternoon prayer, *al-Maghrib*-sunset prayer and *al-Ishai*-night prayer. There are other prayers, which are supererogatory, occasional, ceremonial or voluntary in nature. *As-salat* in Islam is better offered in congregations by the *Ummah*. This has been responsible for the strong bond of Islamic brotherhood.

iii.**Az-Zakat:** Technically, *Zakat* refers to obligatory charity. It is an economic leveller in Islamic sociology. *Az-Zakat* is a Qu'ranic injunction as we read that: "Those who observe prayer and those who pay the *Zakat* and those who believe in Allah and the last Day to these will we surely give a great reward" (chap. 4:163). *Zakat* is paid by Muslim in an Islamic state where the Shari'ah is operative while the non-Muslims living therein pay *Jizyah* – capitation tax. In the sphere of economy, people who are eligible to pay *az-Zakat* are those whose incomes are above *an-nisab* i.e maximum exempted income. In other words, this limit is known as the poverty line. *Zakat* is mandatory on treasure, merchandise, animals, minerals and crops.

Unlike taxes, *zakat* as recorded in the *Holy Qur'an* (5;7) "is collected from the rich and distributed among the poor". Other categories of *zakat* in Islam are the *zakat al fitr* a special form of *zakat* payable during the month of Ramadan fasting and *sadaqah* voluntary charity which has no fixed amount or time of payment. Rather than encourage beggary, these two are economic levellers in the society.

iv. **.As-Saum** is also called *Siyam* i. e. Fasting. It means abstention from food, drinks and other sensual engagements from dawn till sunset. This spiritual activity occurs in the 9th month of the lunar calendar, which is called Ramadan. This is why the activity is fondly called Ramadan fasting. This pillar in Islam is formally presented in the *Holy Qur'an* thus "O ye who believe, fasting is prescribed for you as it was prescribed for those before you, so that you may become righteous" (2:183). The rules guiding the obligatory activity of fasting are outlined in the subsequent verses, (see *Qur'an* 96: 1-6). This night is called *Lailatul. Qadir,* i.e. night power. In the Islamic tradition, the Ramadan fasting terminates with a feast called *Eid ul fitr.* This and *Eid I Adha* – festival of sacrifice held in the 12th month *(Dhul Hijjah)* of the lunar calendar are the biggest annual festivals among the world Muslim *Ummah.*

Moreover, fasting is an exercise in atonement and self-control. It is designed to cultivate self-discipline, awareness of the diverse human environment in terms of empathy and sympathy. It also promotes healthy nutritional habits and sanitizes the anatomy and physiology of man. In Islam, there are other types of fasting. These include voluntary fasting, fasting for atonement, vows and propitiation.

v. **Al-Haji:** This means pilgrimage to the Holy lands of *al-makkah al-mukarramah* and *al-madinah al-munawwarah* in Saudi Arabia. Al-hajj occupies this fifth position because a Muslim must fulfil all the prerequisite tenets of Islam before he or she can be adjudged as qualified for the Holy pilgrimage. Even then, a Muslim must possess the means, good health and stable home before he embarks on such a religious journey.

The sacredness of this institution and its connection with the names of prophets Ibrahim (AS) and Ismail (AS) finds clear mention in the *Qur'an.* (chap. 9:60). Hajj is performed as from the second week of *Dhul Hajjah* on the *Hijrah* calendar. The chief features of *Hajj* centred on the *ka'abah* which is called the first house of Divine worship for mankind. (chap. 2:183-284). After the bloodless conquest of Makkah in 630, AH Muhammad and the Muslims purged the *kaabah* of its idols. The institution of Hajj is a sociological leveller as it is the greatest single assembly for mankind in the whole world.

As a religious culture, Islam aims at a total cultural assimilation of its adherents. The tenets outlined above go beyond the theological sphere. It covers a wider social, political and economic system, a political philosophy and a way of life, which regulates and provides guidance to an individual, right from his cradle to the grave for the discharge of his responsibilities to his family, his neighbours, his society and his country.

The Islamic concept of religion

The Islamic concept of religion is unique in the broadest sense of the word as it maintains that religion is not only a spiritual and intellectual necessity but also a social and universal need. In an interpretative analysis, religion is not to bewilder man but to guide him. It is not to oppress his qualities but to open for him inexhaustible treasures of logical reasoning and right action. A purposeful religion unites the psychological knots and complexes of man, sublimates his instincts and aspirations, and disciplines his desires and the whole course of life. It improves his knowledge of God (the Highest Truth in the universe) and his own self. It teaches him about basic concepts that characterize man's existence such as good and evil, right and wrong. It purifies the soul from evil, clears the mind from doubts, strengthens the character and corrects the thinking and convictions of man. All these can be realistic when the spiritual duties and physical regulations introduced by Islam are faithfully observed.

Islam conceives of religion as one, which inculcates in man hope and patience, truthfulness and honesty, courage and evidence, one which insures man against tears and spiritual losses and assures him of God's aid and unbreakable alliance. The resume of it all is that it provides man with peace and security and makes life meaningful. According to Hammudah Abdalati, "any religion which fails to bear these fruits is not Islam, or rather, is not religion at all, and any man who fails to draw these benefits from religion is not righteous or God-minded" (H-Abdal Ati n.d.,34). Islam as a religion has based itself on personal thinking and intentional logic. The relation between religion and its propositions on the one hand, and civilization and its foundation on the other, is binding and firm, Islam links metaphysical thought and personal feelings with the rules of logic and the precepts of science with an imperative injunction that all Muslim must discover and grasp, if they are to remain Muslims.

From this perspective, the interpretation of religion by Islam is radically different from that of western interpretation. The two are different in their description of life as well as the foundation on which they base such description. The difference is due to a number of historical causes. In Christendom, the unending struggle between the religion and secular powers or between church and state led to their separation and to the establishment of the state upon the denial of the power of the church. This had many effects. The first of these effects was the separation of human feeling and reasoning from the logic of observation and evidence.

Islam made reason the judge in everything, whether in religion or in conviction and faith itself. Thus the *Qur'an states*, "And the case of those who disbelieve is like the case of one who shouts to that which bears nothing but a call and a cry. They are deaf, dumb and blind so they do not understand (3:97). Commenting on this verse, Muhammad Abduh wrote:

> *taqlid* (i.e. conservation) without reason or guidance is the prerogative of disbeliever, that man is not a convinced Muslim unless he has reasoned out his religion; known it in person and become personally convinced of its truth and validity... religious conviction does not have for its purpose the subjugation of man to the good as if he was an animal. Rather, its purpose is that man, by the use of reason and the pursuit of knowledge rise to the level where he will do

the good because he fully knows that it is in itself good and acceptable to God and avoid the evil because he fully knows its undesirable consequence and harm. (507-544)

As a corollary to this fact, Sayyid Mujtaba Lari says:

> Illogical beliefs do not pertain only to religious question. Before they were properly defined, many of the sciences were commingled with superstitions. Men found their way from incantation and magic to true and beneficial medicine and from unrealistic alchemy to realistic chemistry. No one can claim that if men once committed an error in searching for something, he is bound always to remain in error and will never find the way of reaching the truth... (88).

The study of different stages in the life of primitive man, and the discovery of evidence that fear pervaded his thoughts, do not prove that fear and ignorance were the fundamental factor in man's inclination to religion. Such an assertion would be the product of one-sided assessment. General conclusions can be drawn from historical researches and studies only when the entire history, with all the different periods in the life of man is investigated and researched. A series of special modes of perception are inherent in man. Among these perceptions are the sense of commitment to trust, justice, veracity and honesty. Before he enters the realm of science and knowledge, with all its concerns, man is able to perceive certain truths by means of these innate perceptions.

However, having entered the sphere of science and philosophy; and filling his brain with various proofs and deductions, he may forget his natural or inborn tendencies or begin to doubt them. It is reason that when man moves beyond his innate to delineate a belief, differences begin to appear. It is in cognizance of this that the *Qur'an* says:

> Surely, the true religion with Allah is Islam, (complete submission). And those who were given the book did not disagree after knowledge had come to them, out of mutual envy. And whose denies the signs of Allah, then surely, Allah is quick at reckoning (chapter 2:172).

Scholars have agreed that religious beliefs have always been intertwined with human life. Their opinions differ concerning the fundamental root of religion and the factors that have played a primary role in its establishment and development. Their judgments in this respect are generally based on studies of superstitious religion and primitive beliefs, with the result that their conclusions are, in the final analysis, defective and illogical religious thought. Hence, Sayyid Mujtaba remarked that despite the primacy, autonomy and effectiveness of the sense of curiosity, virtue and beauty and the role they played in the emergence of science, morally and art, it was the religious sense that prepared the ground for the activity of these senses, helping them to advance on their path and to discover the secrets of the created world.

Religious thought has also been a factor throughout history in cultivating the aesthetic sense. Primitive men produced their most creative works of art in order to glorify their gods. The remarkable temples of China, the great pyramids of Egypt, the distinctive statutes of Mexico, the refined and astounding architecture of the Islamic east, all draw on religious sense. However, certain factors such as contrary propaganda can decrease the growth and development of inward feeling and correct thought. If such hindrances are removed, sound instincts resume their activity and display themselves by means of their inward creative effort. In recognition of this inborn self controlled mechanism, the *Qur'an* says, "Call unto the way of the Lord with wisdom and goodly exhortation, and argue with them in a way that is best. Surely, thy Lord knows best who has strays from His way and He knows those who rightly guided." (Q. 16; 126).

Also still in recognition of the inviolate delicacy of man's nature, Cantwell Smith and Idowu (1976:16) also warn, "Particularly, in a study of a major civilization other than one's own, and most of all, all of the religions of that civilization, one must learn rather slowly, perceptively, painfully, creatively, to ask new question, to discern new categories, to sense new visions..." In essence, no worthy scholar should create the impression that his own is the last words on the subject of religious studies and no evangelist should emphasize particularly to the detriment of caution. As fresh visions are vouchsafed to man, new material is added to existing knowledge to modify, enrich or correct our views with regard to past acquisitions and intellectual position. It is necessary to be cautious with regard to statement and concepts, which have to do with deity in relation to man. But alas! The contrary has been the case with the result that religion has come to be bastardized in contemporary times.

In this connection, religion has been blamed for sowing discord in the world. Recognizing therefore the hypothesis of Walker Capps that, "Men sometimes view religion from the outside looking in, sometimes from inside looking out and sometimes from inside looking around. Where they stand has a bearing on what they do. What they do influence what they discover and how they stand." (1).

Islam seriously disagrees with the dysfunctionalist approach which, *inter alia*, considers God to be a product of human feeling, and reject religion on the ground that it seduces humanity away from its true task and challenges. In view of this intellectual fraud, it is considered appropriate to examine the role of religion in national development

Religion as a factor in national development: the Islamic perspective

Religion has produced both good and bad results. On the one hand, it has contributed greatly towards peace and progress. The good aspects according to

Onwu include, "building hospital and charitable institutions and promoting art and literature. The bad on the other hand, is that in the name of God, men have engaged in war, persecuted fellow human beings, and destroyed monuments of human culture. And this is going on even today." (159).

The above statement significantly portrays the dual role in which religion has been made to function in medieval and contemporary times. In the critique of any concept, the philosophical basic is often necessary. The fundamental human needs that religion seeks to fulfil, whether be it the needs for social stability or for personal integrity, have been explored and weighed perceptively by numerous theorists. Dysfunctionalists like Karl Marx and Sigmund Freud discredited religion as a smoke screen and subterfuges that allow people to avoid dealing constructively with suffering and injustice.

In the case of Islam, religion is espoused as a determinant factor in National Development. The philosophy of National Development, to wit, the Islamic perspective is explicitly stated in the *Holy Qur'an*. *Ab initio,* the *Qur'an* is a book essentially religious, not philosophical, but it deals with all those problems, which religion and philosophy have in common. Both have to say something about problems related to God, the world, the individual soul, the inter relations of these, good and evil, free will, life after death and also throws light on such conceptions as appearance and reality, existence and attributes, human origin and destiny, truth and error space and time, permanence and change, eternity and immortality.

Conversely, the world is not without a goal or purpose. It is throughout teleological and to this universal teleology, human beings and nation building are no exceptions. To every one of them, there is a goal and that goal is God Himself. Emile Durkheim (1917) was one of the first to attempt an in depth analysis of the functional value of religion for the social order. Religion for him, as quoted by Walter (1) "consists primarily in a system of 'collective representations' such as concepts of God, notions about sin and evil etc. that the patterned essentially after the structure of community life."

In an interpretative analysis, Peter Berger (1969) opined that religion carries through the dialectic of self and society by creating a system of symbolic order that resolves all potential conflicts of the individual with the norms and intentions of those to whom he must remain loyal and trustworthy. Religion performs the dual role of both "world building" and "world maintenance" viz it expresses that members of a society take to the binding rules of experience and behaviours as a set of objective facts about things in general and in fact to concretize these facts as holy and inviolable. However, the developmental function which religion can perform in any society depends on the perspective to be adopted. This perhaps informed Walter Capps' declaration earlier and also prompted Alfred Whitehead to appraise religion as:

> The inspiration of something which stands beyond, behind, within the past influx of immediate things. Something which is real and yet waiting to be realized, something which is a remote probability and

yet the greatest of present facts, something that gives meaning to all that passes and yet eludes apprehension. Something whose possession is the final good and yet beyond all reach, something which is happiness and quest (1).

In the Islamic context, the theology, or for that matter, the philosophy of national development rests squarely on the theory that God, the most High is the Creator and Sovereign of the Universe. Essentially, religion defined the political and socio-economic structure of any given society whether homogenous or heterogeneous. That religion plays a role in national development is an indisputable truism more so, when Oniayekan contends that:

...history has shown that even countries which tried to eliminate religion have not enjoyed peace as a result...Any religion worthy of the name must have an impact on society at large. Besides, the individual and social dimensions on of man are in the same human person, so that whatever affects him as an individual eventually touches him as members of the larger society. Both areas are interrelated (123-124).

Thus, Islam is opposed to the contagious disease of prevalence of sophistry and obsession in a society with a major danger: the danger of being without an ideology. In such a society, there can hardly be traced a few co-thinking individuals. No sooner a few persons come together that fallacy, obsession and unfounded doubts influence them beyond sanity. There neither exists any unity in such a society nor can there be stability and ideology. In the study of World religions, Islam occupies a unique place as an ideology rather than a system of beliefs. Islam distinguished itself by its own unique philosophy of welfare, which is comprehensive and consistent with its concept of human nature. Hence the philosophy of national development in Islam cannot be exclusively "other-worldly" or purely "this-worldly". Islam takes note of the diversity that exists among nations and peoples, and as Manna points out that...in as much as God's sovereignty extends over the whole universe, the ultimate ideal of a state in Islam is a universal federation, or confederation, of autonomous states, associated together for upholding freedom of conscience and for the maintenance of peace and cooperation in promoting human welfare throughout the world" (70).

In contemporary times, arguments have been advanced in support of political and religions secularism. Political secularism, which people argue for is atheistic in its genesis, inspiration and aspiration because, it socially and politically seeks to divert the state from the cosmic order. In this connection, Uka correctly observes that, "it (secularism) falsely assumes that religion and spiritual interest are of no consequence in the temporal order. Secularism advocates absolute separation of religion and politics. Here is a political extremism and a false interpretation of the secular nature of the state" (20).

As a matter of fact, political secularism is a distortion of the political compass and evolution of human history. In an apparent reference to the shallowness of the secularist argument, Ahmad Lemu correctly observes that "any ideological goal...which is opposed to God the Supreme Being is culturally alien, socially unrealistic and doomed to be frustrated by all forces. The right ideological goal for the nation, must be integrated with their belief in God, the Supreme Being, who created man and placed him on earth with a purpose... such an integrated ideology is called submission to the will of God" (7).

In the opinion of Leo Pfeffer,

> "the difference between the Religion and the secular is itself a comparatively modern development in the evolution of human society. To the primitive, all of life may be said to have been religions. Tribal society was kept together and survived because religion sanctions and effectively enforced adherence to social customs; one who broke a custom violated a taboo which could bring upon him, the wrathful vengeance of a super-human mysterious power..."

In the Islamic context of religion, secularism is unrealistic. The concern and role of religion in national politics and development is to help in making the people in society morally responsible and to avoid all acts and practices that dehumanize humanity. Islam opposes secularism in all its facets because Islam is a way of life. In his book, *Al-Islam wa al-Nasraniyyah*, Muhammad Abduh wrote,

> Islam, therefore, and its demand for faith in God and His unity depend only on rational proof and common sense human thinking. Islam does not overwhelm the mind with the supernatural, confuse the understanding with the extraordinary, impose acquiescent silence by resorting to heavenly intervention, nor does it impede the movement of thought by any sudden cry of divinity (13).

Religion is not a misnomer, neither is it an anomaly. Religion, as perfected by Islam laid the basis of a unification of humanity or which no other reformer or religion has ever dreamed. Summing up the social ethics of Islam, Haykal has the following to say:

> Islam has the merit of standing for very egalitarian conception of the contribution of each citizen by the title to the resources of the community. It is hostile to unrestricted exchange, to banking capital, to state loans, to indirect taxes or objects of Prime necessity, but it holds to the rights of the father and the husband, to private property and to commercial capital. Here again, it occupies intermediate position between the doctrines of bourgeois capitalism and Bolshevist communism (522-523).

This is the essence of Islam. It is by solving these and a hundred other problems that religion, when approached from the Islamic perspective, can bring true happiness to the human race. Islam of today manifests its universality in the ability of knowledgeable adherents to reasonably and discouraging misdirection of zeal and misappropriation of responsibilities – a factor which has been a cankerworm in the fabric of the understanding of the religions question.

Conclusion

An attempt has been made in this chapter to facilitate the understanding of the concept of religion from the Islamic perspective. It has been established that the perception of great truths is impossible without logical examination, deduction and comprehensive study. If superstitions and religious myths are to be found among ancient peoples, constantly being infused into new moulds because of deficiency and weakness in thought and restriction in knowledge, this does not mean, then, that religion with its doctrinal content is false.

Rather, it demonstrates the primacy and autonomy of religious aspiration in the very depths of the human soul and heart. Since human conduct and activity are always accompanied by these two clear characteristics i.e. primacy and autonomy on the one hand and comprehensiveness and universality on the other, it appears entirely logical that one should posit some origin for that conduct and activity in the depths of the human spirit. The existence of such a continuous phenomenon in an eternal and universal form, in historic and pre-historic times cannot be regarded as the effects of customs and habits. It is the manifestation of a primordial thirst, an imperative instinct for seeking the truth.

In this perspective, Islam upholds that all religious beliefs, with their different aspects and forms, arise from a single, gushing, abundant source, the primordial nature of man, which is neither eternally imposed nor paternally accidental. The fact that many centuries of argumentation have not produced a coherent and convincing alternative to the concept of religion among sociologists, anthropologist, historians, scientists and philosophers, makes it indisputably altruistic that religion does not deserve such semantic or egotistic bastardization. One cannot but agree with William James' liberal assertion that Religion shall mean for us the feelings, acts and expressions of individual men in their solitudes, so far as they apprehend themselves to stand in relation to whatever they consider the divine.

It is a monstrous misconception to say that hatred and bloodshed have characterized the principle and practice of religion in the world. Rather, love or concord, sympathy, kindness to fellow men, has been the message of every religion. If there had been hatred and bloodshed, in spite of religion, it is because human nature is prone to these things. This is how fundamental and dominant the theme of peace is in Islam. The individual who approaches God through Islam cannot fail to be at peace with God, himself and with his fellow men. Taking all these values together, putting man in his proper place in the cosmos and viewing life in the Islamic perspective, men of good faith and principle cannot fail to make our world a better world, to regain human dignity, to achieve quality to enjoy universal brotherhood, to build a lasting peace. Hence the *Qur'an* says: "There should be no compulsion in religion. Surely, the right has become distinct from wrong" (*Qur'an* 2 v 257). Islam adopts this stance because religion depends upon faith, will and commitment. These would be meaningless if induced by force.

Works cited

Abd 'Al-Ati, H., *Islam in Focus*, Lagos I.P.B., n'd.
Afonja, S., Olu-Pearce, T, (eds.), *Social Change in Nigeria*, London: Longman, 1986.
Ahmad, G., *The Philosophy of The Teachings of Islam*, London: Ahmadiyya Centenary Publications, 1979.
Ahmad, T., "Revelation, Rationality, Knowledge and Truth," *Islam International Publications*, London: Tilford, Survey, 1998.
Ali, M., *The Religion of Islam*, New Delhi: Taj. Co.1986.
Aziz-us Samad U, *The Great Religions of the World*, Darūl Kutūb Lahore, 1976.
Balogun I.A.B., "Utilizing Religion for Peaceful Unity and Progress in Nigeria," Ilorin, Univ.of Lectures, Notes 1981
.Berger, P., *The Sacred Canopy*, New York, Double Day Press, 1969
Bertocci, P.A., *Religion As a Creative Insecurity*, New York, Assoc. Press, 1958.
Capps, W., *Ways of Understanding Religion*, New York, Macmillan, 1972.
Clarke, P.B., *West Africa and Islam*, London, Edward Arnold, 1982.
Doi, A.R., *Islam in Nigeria*, Zaria: Gaskiya Corp. Ltd., 1984.
Engineer, A.A., *The Islamic State*, New Delhi: Ulkaa Publishing House, 1980.
Eniola, S.O., "Religious Crisis in Nigeria: Causes and Effects," Unilorin, 1990.
Eliade, M. (ed) *The Encyclopedia of Religions*, New York, Macmillan, 1984.
Erivwo, S.U & Adogbo, M.P. (eds.), *Contemporary Essays in The Study of Religion*, Fairs and Exhibitions Nig. Ltd., Lagos, 2000
Farid, G., (ed*.). The Holy Qur'an*, Eng. Transl. And Commentary, Rhwah The Oriental and Religious Publishing Corporation Ltd., 1969.
Guillame, A., *Traditions of Islam* Oxford: Clarendon Press, 1924.
Haykal, M., *The Life of Muhammad*, Transl. I.R.A. al. Faruqi, North American Trust Publications, 1976.
Idowu, E.B., *African Traditional Religion, A. Definition*, London: SCM. Press, 1976.
Jung, *et al* (eds.); *Relations Among Religions Today*, London, 1963.
Lemu, A., "The Quranic Basis of Ethical Revolution". Conference Papers on Religion and Ethical Revolution in Nigeria; Dept. of Religious Studies, University of Ibadan, April 1983.
Mala, B. & Oseni, Z.I., (eds.), *Religion, Peace and Unity in Nigeria,* Ibadan: NASR, 1984.
Mannan, M.A., *Islamic Economics, Theory and Practice*, Sh. Muhammad Ashraf, Lahore, Pakistan, 1970.
Montgomery, W. *What is Islam?* London, Longman, 1979.
Parrinder, G. *The World's Living Religions*, London, Pan Bks., 1974.
Pfeffer, L., *Church and State and Freedom*, Beacon Press, Boston, 1967.

Raji, M.G.A., *Background to Islamic Culture*, A.B.U. Press, Zaria, 1991.
Siddiqi, M.I., *Asharah Mubash-Sharah*, Lahore, (n.p.), 1989.
Smith, D.E. (ed), *Religion, Politics and Social Change in the Third World*. New York, Free Press, 1971.
Wessels, A. *A Modern Arabic to Biography, of Muhammad, A Critical Study of M.H. Haykal's Yayat Muhammad*, Lei den, E.J. Brill, 1972.

Chapter 8

The spread of Islam in Nigeria: the case of Ijebuland

- T.A. Oladimeji

Introduction

Shortly after the death of Prophet Muhammad in A.D. 632 (8 June), Islamic conquest spread to Africa. One route was the Nile valley southwards to the Sudan while the second was along the coast of North Africa. Islam in Sudan at this early period was initially for the trading class and the rulers with strong Muslim empires emerging. Scholars could not agree on the date of the Islamic spread to West Africa. While Awolalu (c: 52) as well as Fajana and Biggs (161) suggest the eleventh century as its probable date of inception, Watt (IV) submits the seventh century date. Bourgeosis specifically traces the history of the Great Mosques of Djenne to between the thirteenth to the nineteenth century.

The motives which brought the peoples of North Africa into touch with Negroland, according to Fage (9), were primarily economic in origin. The trans-Saharan trade provided opportunity for the export of gold, Negro slaves, kola-nuts among others, to North Africa while in return, West Africa received salt, copper, cowry shells, cloth, figs and dates, horses, cattle, beads and other ornaments. The influence of the peoples from North Africa on the Sudan and the Negro peoples in particular may be said to have developed in the following general terms. First the North Africans traded with the Negroes and raided them for slaves. Then they began to settle in the northern districts of Sudan, first establishing political domination over the Negroes and then increasingly merging with them. From this point they began to extend their commercial activities farther south to the edge of the forest. In the process the people were converted to Islam. Everywhere in the north of West Africa, the character and composition of the black race became modified by contact and intermarriage with the Arabs. From the fourth century onward, as Conton (26) observes, the camel was increasingly used by the Berbers of North Africa as a means of transport in the trade across the Sahara. By the use of the camel, the Muslims spread in increasing numbers in the late seventh century and many of the pagans were converted to Islam.

The forceful conversions of West Africans by the trained fanatical sects (*Murabits*) led by Abdullah Ibn Yasin in Morocco, and the natural spread through Muslim merchants from North Africa were the major factors responsible for the establishment of Islam in West Africa. The conversion of the ruling elites in Ghana, Mali and Songhai and their eventual influence among their people as well as the dissemination by individual scholars (*marabouts*) were the major factors that accelerated the spread of Islam in West Africa (Watt: 43– 1 & Bravmann: 13). It is against this background that the remainder of this chapter focuses on the spread of Islam in Nigeria, especially among the people of Ijebuland.

Studies on Ijebu people done by a good number of scholars gave a lot of information on the people and their cultural traditions. The studies of Law (245–260), Odumuyiwa, Adebonojo, Ayandele (264–299), Aronson, Ogunkoya and Seriki (387–400) discuss extensively the traditions of origin, later developments after European contacts as well as their cult and religious practices. Only Seriki (387–400) and Ayandele touched on the history of Islam in their accounts of the origin and settlement of the Ijebu as a people. Other notable aspects of Ijebu culture written on by most of them focus on their cultural organizations such as *Agemo*, *Obinrin-Ojowu* in their religious system and the *Osugbo, Erinkiran, Eluku* and *Akalamasa* for political and judicial roles under the spiritual overlordship of the *Awujale* - their paramount traditional ruler. All the studies gave some insights on the spread of Islam in Ijebuland, their works are not focused on the Ijebu field, making this study essentially unique.

In the bid to trace the routes of Islam into Ijebu land, this paper combed the relevant literature, the archive and equally interviewed the Imams and other relevant personalities in about twenty-five (25) settlements of Ijebu land. These include even some highly placed traditional rulers. It equally examined the advent of Islam into Nigeria, the Ijebu people and their religion before the arrival of Islam so as to be able to understand how and when Islam got to them. It examined the dates and the nature of the spread of Islam into Nigeria and Yoruba lands in particular and concludes that Islam in the new land of Nigeria, as erroneously believed was not necessarily and totally forceful.

Islam in Nigeria

The spread of Islam in Nigeria was greatly influenced by the earlier Islamization of some West African empires, such as Ghana, Mali and Songhai. The Chad, Bornu and some parts of Hausa land accepted Islam willingly first because it was a teaching from better educated people. The nature of the spread in Nigeria was generally simple and peaceful through the activities of Muslim traders and teachers. During this period, between the fourteenth and eighteenth centuries, the Islamic teachers were still allowing those who had accepted it to practice their traditional religion. Not too long the ardent adherence of the Islamic religion, especially the Gogobir-born Fulani - Uthman-dan Fodio – started to accuse the Habe kings of mixing traditional practices with the faith and also of imposing illegal taxation on the population of the states. There were obvious cases of bribery and corruption and Muslims were forcefully conscripted into military services. It became legitimate to rebel against these anomalies and to establish a purer form of Islamic administration.

In 1804, under the leadership of Uthman dan Fodio, the holy war, commonly called Fulani Jihad, started. The death of Yunfa, king of Gobir in 1808 and the subsequent conquest of all important Hausa states marked the end of the Habe rulers and the beginning of the great Fulani Empire which later became known as Sokoto Caliphate. The Nupe people in the North of Yoruba land had been credited for the spread of Islam into Yoruba land along the trade routes, but the exact date for this can still not be ascertained. Balogun (218) has suggested a seventeenth century date while Gbadamosi (87) suggested the sixteenth century. The latter used the non-incorporation of Christianity into *Ifa* literary corpus - *Odu* after its 150 years of inception in Yoruba land to project that Islam must have been about 200 years before its references in *Ifa* literary corpus towards the end of the eighteenth century. This is corroborated by the oral tradition gathered among the people: *'Aiye la ba'fa, Aiyela ba'mole, osan gangan n'Igbagbo wole.* Thus expressing the fact that *ifa* worship and Islam were in existence before Christianity came at 'the afternoon of time'. Balogun (218) based his eighteenth century suggestion on the presence of a Muslim community in Old Oyo, and using the accounts of 'the Lander brothers' he identified the spread of Islam in Yoruba land along the trade routes in Oyo, Igboho, Kissi, Saki, Iseyin, Ikoyi, Ogbomoso, Ijanna, Owu, Ketu and Badagry. It seemed not to have spread to Ijebu land then. Scholars have inadvertently not provided specific information on the spread in Ijebu land. In actual fact, Ijebu-land was the last of the Yoruba sub-groups to be reached by Islam.

The nature of the spread of Islam in Yoruba land changed into a forceful one with the forceful intrusion and activities of Uthman Dan Fodio and Mallam Alimi in the nineteenth century changed. Ilorin, a former Oyo provincial town then became a Fulani emirate and part of Northern Nigeria. Ilorin later influenced most of its neighbours. According to Eades (7), Large Muslim communities invariably grew up in Oyo Ile, Ikoyi and Igboho. Islam also spread eastwards into Osun and Igbomina-Ekiti divisions; Offa and the Kabba-Yoruba (Yagba, Ikiri, Abinu, Igbede and Ijumu) came under the influence of the Islam of the Fulanis.

The return of the liberated slaves from Sierra Leone and Brazil in the nineteenth century accelerated the expansion of Islam, even after the Ibadan warriors led by Balogun Oderinlo forestalled the Fulani's further incursion into southern Yoruba land in Osogbo. The returnees eventually introduced Islam into some parts of Lagos, Ijebu and Abeokuta in the coastal Yoruba area and other parts of Yoruba land. Eades (129-130) however, noted the strongest resistance in Ekiti area while the most rapid progress was recorded in Ijebu with the conversion of the wealthy Ijebu military Chief - Balogun Kuku.

Ezzati has listed some factors responsible for the peaceful acceptance of Islam worldwide. These are the mental freedom in Islam, moral factor, free integration of culture, humanitarian factor, and inclusiveness of Islam and Islam's non-connection with colonialism. Others are the emigration and immigration of Muslims, educational activities and its types and finally Islamic dualism and resilience as in the continuous spread in Islam. Besides, the freedom of dual religion among the Yoruba people, certain other factors aided Islam's acceptance in Yoruba land than Christianity. Awolalu (c: 58-59) has observed these similarities between Islam and their traditional religions. They include the art of divination used to ascertain the future, and the wearing of girdles, amulets, rings etc to ward off evil forces. Also both religions allow polygamy while other social ceremonies connected with birth, naming ceremony; marriage and burial are not too different in the two religions. The act of worship – *ibadat* in Islam is similar to the ceremonial act of devotion in the traditional religion. The headgears of the Orisa-nla worshippers resemble the turbans of the Muslims. All these attracted the adherents of the traditional religion of the Yoeuba to Islam.

The Ijebu people

Ijebu land is in the coastal area of the South-Western Nigeria and covers a territorial land space of about 2,000 to 3,000 square miles. It constitutes a large area of the present Lagos and Ogun States of Nigeria (Smith: 895) and is bounded in the South by the Lagoon in Lagos State, in the East by Ondo State, in the North by Oyo State and in the West by the Egba area of Ogun State. Ijebu land is inhabited by the Ijebu proper (*Akile-Ijebu*) and the Remo subgroups. Traditionally, its people are dominantly farmers, fishermen and traders who served as middlemen between the Europeans in the coast and the other Yoruba subgroups in the hinterland from the fifteenth century to the end of the nineteenth century.

By the fifteenth century, they had already formed a large kingdom that had become a distinct cultural entity with institutional bonds and a dialectal peculiarity (Ayandele, 2). They are very enterprising and highly feared by their neighbours. Hence, they were the least suffered of the major Yoruba subgroups from the nineteenth century wars in Yoruba land. A less urbanized pattern of settlement in Yoruba land was found among them whereby the principal city was surrounded by substantial and permanently organized dependent villages. Lloyd (220) has suggested this as a preserve of a pattern of settlement formerly more widespread in Yoruba land.

The traditions of origin among the Ijebu people is linked with their descent from Oduduwa – the progenitor of the Yoruba race that migrated from Nubia (Upper Egypt) or Wadai through Arabia (Mecca) and Nupe land to establish Ile-

Ife, the revered cradle of Yoruba civilization. The semblance of various traditions found in the two areas and among the Yorubas support this particular tradition. The account is also supported by Sultan Bello of Sokoto as reported by Captain Clapperton in his travel memoir, which suggests some kinship with the Gogobir (Gobirawa) people of Northern Nigeria in the mist of whom they allegedly had a brief stop – over during their migration (Akinjogbin & Ayandele: 122, Ogunkoya: 48). These Yoruba emigrants eventually settled into several subgroups in different parts of the present Yoruba land.

The first group to settle in Ijebu land was led by Olu-Iwa to establish Ijebu-Ode and other smaller settlements such as Ibefun, Ososa, Ala, Idowa, Isonyin, and Atan. Others are Odo-Oniwa, Idomowo, Erinje, Odele and Etisa. The second group was under the leadership of Arisu, who settled at Ijasi – a quarter in Ijebu Ode. This group stretched Ijebu land from Idomowo through Iwaya to Iwopin and other coastal towns. The emigration of Obanta, then known as Ogborogannida or Ogborogan through Imesi to Ijebu land was the third group. He is claimed to have been the son of the daughter of Olu-Iwa; given to Oduduwa as wife during a brief stay in Ile-Ife. Obanta – the grandson of Olu – Iwa became the first Awujale – the traditional ruler of Ijebu land. These emigrants have been traced to Ala, Ogere, Ilaporu, Ilisan, Odo-Obanta (part of Ayepe), Ilada and Odo (part of Odogbolu) (Seriki: 15-16).

The settlement of Ajebu, Olode and Olorise who had earlier settled in Orile Oko, a village between Abeokuta and Sagamu was the next. This group later founded Ijebu-Imushin. The fifth emigrant group was led by Ajalorun and Balufe. They extended Ijebu territory to Ijebu-Ife and Abigi. Their emigration is said to have been in the fifteenth century when Koko who founded Abigi settled at the present site with his brothers – Kelu, Lumuken and Ebiwo (Obanta Newsday: 26). The sixth group led by Ebumawe and Osimawe settled at Ago-Iwoye while the seventh which is the last group came under Kayolu and the first Elepe from Ile-Ife to search for Obanta's group. Their descendants now occupy Offin, Epe, Pakodo and Igbogbo.

All these settlements today refer to themselves as either 'Ijebu proper' – *Akile* Ijebu or the Remo subgroups. The phrase 'Ijebu proper' does not suggest that others are actually inferior or bastards. No. It is just a name used to denote the group outside Remo. However, a counter tradition claims that the Remo people migrated from Iremo quarters of Ile-Ife and not part of 'Ijebu proper' and are believed to be a separate immigrant group from North Africa. While some of them such as Illisan, Ikorodu, Ilara, Irolu, Ikenne, Akaka and Ipara claim a direct migration from Ile-Ife after their arrival in Yoruba land. Iperu, Isara, Ogere, Ode and the Makun division of Sagamu claim the same ancestry with Ijebu-Ode.

There are some conflicting dates for the first Ijebu settlement. The work of Odumuyiwa, (12.) citing Talbot, claims that the settlement of Olu-Iwa must have been preceded by an earlier group, which is put at about 1000 A. D. Ogunkoya (53) who gives a 20-year average for each of the thirty-eight (38) reigns of the *Awujales* before the first Gbelegbuwa ascended the throne in 1760 A. D. agrees with Talbot's date of 1000 A. D. for the reign of the first Awujale.

However, the two do not agree with the position of Adebonojo (9-20) who listing out the past rulers of Ijebu-Ode from Olu-Iwa's time to 1400 A. D. Out of the fifty-three (53) reigns listed, only eight (8) rulers including Olu-Iwa and the present *Awujale – Ogbagba II* ever reigned for twenty years or more. It is a fact of history that four (4) of kings even reigned for only one or less than a year. This contradicts Ogunkoya's twenty-year average for each of the rulers' reigns. A reconciliation of Adebonojo's list and Ogunkoya's seems to make an average of eleven (11) years per reign more realistic and makes up 1352 A. D. for the settlement of Olu-Iwa, which seems to tally with Adebonojo's date of 1400 A. D.

Immediately after the settlement of the Ijebu people into large communities, there were some early contacts between them and the Europeans, which developed into mutual interests for centuries that followed (Law: 245–260). Dated to around 1352 A.D, Ijebu land had been appearing in early European maps of Africa since the fifteenth century with its trade contacts with early Portuguese travellers (1505), Dutch (circa 1630-1668) and Spain (circa 1627). Several records of early European explorers and traders described Ijebu-Ode – the capital city of Ijebu land as a 'large city' as early as 1505, and mentions of *Awujale* were made as the titled king of the land. There was even the belief in Ijebu-Ode that Portuguese's traders once lived there.

Other things recorded by the Portuguese traders were the importation of slaves, cloths and ivory from Ijebu land. Extensive accounts of the Ijebu's contact with the Dutch people around 1668 also attest to the existence of cotton cloth, beads – *akori* and slave trades with the Ijebu. The Dutch drove away the Portuguese in the 1630s as European attentions became increasingly focused on Ijebu and around the seventeenth and eighteenth centuries A.D., Ijebu cloth had become known in the entire West African coast and Europe.

The Spanish writers' accounts published as early as 1627 explicitly indicate the presence of Ijebu slaves in the Atlantic slave trade. However, as Lagos and Benin were becoming more popular in the European world, less attention seems to have been paid to Ijebu, especially between 1660 to the early eigntenth century. It returned to European consciousness only in the 1770s, as a map published in 1789 located Ijebu ports as Ikorodu - cradoo and Ikosi - Quassee). 'Ijebu' in the early European records was also mis-spelt as Jabu, Geebu (Duarte Pacheco) Iabum, Jabu, Jabon, Jaboe and Gboe. (Law: 254). With the arrival of these early European travellers, Ijebu people started to trade in farm products, which they exchanged with Europeans for tobacco, salt, alcoholic drinks, guns and gunpowder, as well as bales of velvet cloths. They became middlemen between the European traders and other Yoruba sub-groups in the hinterland. With the European interest in West African slaves, the Ijebu people later exchanged slaves bought or captured from the hinterland for imported articles. Slave trade soon became the main source of their buoyant economy.

Ijebu people were a powerful and homogeneous group that refused to be included in the Yoruba state, such as Oyo, Ilorin, Abeokuta and Ondo and their kingdom was at its peak between 1700 and 1870. Ijebu then was an exclusive state that sealed off other Yoruba sub-groups from its North on the one hand

and the European agents, traders, missionaries and later the educated Africans on the other. They also opposed and prevented European direct trade route and the spread of the Christian gospel by British missionaries in the 19th century into their state and Yoruba hinterland. A war declared on them in May, 1892 quashed their monopolies and the corollary was an imposition of British rule on Ijebu people This development influenced their culture, formal education, health care delivery system, good roads and other physical developments. The abolition of slave trade and the introduction of foreign religions also influenced their economic activities and traditional religion respectively.

During the reign of the twenty-fifth *Awujale* – Oba Jadiara (*Olowojoye meji*) guards were still ordered to keep vigil on city gates and to collect taxes (Adebonojo: 10). Its capital - Ijebu Ode was *personal-non-grata* to strangers. The town was dreaded and hated too by their neighbours, as death would befall any intruder. An Ijebu tradition in Ijebu land confirms this thus: *'Ijebu-Ode: ajeji ko wo; bi ajeji ba wo laaro, won a fi s'ebo l'ale'* – meaning, Ijebu-Ode – was never entered by strangers, any stranger who entered it in the morning, will be sacrificed in the evening (Ogunkoya: 58, Odumuyiwa: 16 & Ayandele: 2).

Traditional religion in Ijebuland

Before the advent of Islam, religion among the Ijebu people is a thoroughly social phenomenon. Religious practices were closely tied to societal values, experiences and expressions. Unlike their controversial sources of origin, the Ijebu people are bound together by their religious beliefs and practices. They believe in the concept of the Supreme Being, *'Olorun'* – Lord of the Heaven, or *'Olodumare'* – Almighty (Idowu: 5). His position among this people generally as the impersonal order of the universe and one that created the universe is unequivocal.

The mode of worship of God with several gods as intermediaries is common to most African societies. The religion has no founder and no written literature yet its essence is the 'heritage from the past and that, which connects the past with the present and the present with eternity'. It is never a religion of the dead but of the living. It has different layers of spiritual beings; - the Supreme Being, who is too exalted to concern Himself directly with men and their affairs, a number of divinities or spirits including the ancestral ones and mysterious powers (Awolalu, c: 49-64). The divinities are regarded as semi autonomous agents and functionaries of God in the universe. The common divinities among the Yoruba people including the Ijebus are *Obatala* – the creator divinity, *Ifa* or *Orunmila* – the oracle divinity, *Ogun* – the god of iron and war, *Sango* – the god of thunder and *Egungun* – the spirit of the ancestors.

The worships of these divinities are elaborate in some communities and sometimes next to being forgotten in others. Consequently, in Ijebu land some divinities are known with specific communities. Iperu and Ago-Iwoye are known for the worship of *Sango*. *Oya* is known only in Iperu. Ikorodu is known for *Eluku* and *Mapo,* Epe for *Ayelala,* Ilushin for *Ogbodu,* Agbo and Igodo for *Sango,* Ijebu-Ife for *Oduduwa* while Isonyin is for *Oro*. Strictly attached to the belief in *Orisa* is the headship of *Awujale* – the traditional ruler of Ijebu-Ode who like all other Yoruba rulers is referred to as *Alase! Ekeji Orisa* – 'the commander, next to the gods'. The *Awujale* wears a crown, to provide spiritual over-lordship through the *Agemo, Oshi* cults and his chiefs. The *Awujale* was regarded as a fetish whose name must not be mentioned; lest death befalls the person.

Agemo is uniquely the chief ancestral spirit found among the Ijebu people. It is a secret cult and one of the 256 deities of Ile-Ife that the *Awujale* had to keep and settle at the sacred groove – *agbala* near Porogun in Ijebu-Ode. It is a masquerade tradition in which the masquerade members are propitiated during their annual visits to the town. *Onire* – the chief priest heads the *Agemo*. The secrets of *Agemo* lie in their 'loads' – *eru* which are dreaded by women and the uninitiated. Death is the ultimate punishment for any offence after series of warning and *epe* – curses from the *Agemo* cult members. The members, sixteen (16) of them are from Odogbolu, Imoro, Isiwo, Oru, Imosan, Okenugbo, Muku, Igbile, Odo Nopa, Ago-Iwoye (Idebi), Ibowon, Ayepe, Okun-Owa, Imosan (Posa), Ago-Iwoye (Lubamisan) and Imosan (Jagbori) settlements (Adebonojo: 36). Their prominent essence in Ijebu society is the performance of ritual and funeral rites.

The *Osugbo* is another secret cult. It is the cult of elders, male or female. As a version of the *Ogboni* cult present in all other Yoruba sub-groups, it is a strong leadership institution to which the rulers often belong. The cult is a major force with integrated religions, social and political importance in Ijebu land. It is devoted to the worship of the earth and the main symbols of the society are metal images of human figures, *edan*. (Adepegba: 22). The use of *itagbe* – a shoulder cloth is also common among the *Osugbo* members. This is used not just for identity but also as highly personalized symbol of status, and therefore an emblem of authority (Aronson: 56–57). It is an essential outfit during chieftaincy installations and members have their cloths buried with them to affirm their status. Over ninety per cent of Ijebu chiefs belong to *Osugbo* and their activities presently seem confined to funeral rites of members.

Other secret cults in Ijebu land are *Egungun* and *Oro*. These cults are also connected with the *Osugbo* cult members. Evildoers and witches condemned by the *Osugbo* are usually executed in *Oro* groove – *Igbo Oro* by the *Oro* society. *Oro* is purely a male secret cult to boost male prestige in performing essential rituals especially during burial rites. Whenever *Oro* is out, all women keep indoors. It is an essential cult in the installation of a traditional ruler in Isonyin community. The Oro grove in Isonyin was dismantled early in the twentieth century but a new and smaller one had to be built around 1991 when the traditional ruler – the *Oba* of the town was to be installed.

Egungun is the masking tradition amongst most Yoruba sub-groups. They are of different types and functions but are principally associated with the veneration of ancestors. *Egungun* masquerades perform socio-religious, political and military functions in the traditional society. Known as '*ara-orun*'– 'dwellers of Heaven', their spirits are usually invoked when needed (Oladimeji: 109). The *Igunnuko* is a masquerade cult that originated from Nupe land (Parrinder: 132–133). It first migrated to Lagos colony before 1851 through Balogun Oshodi Tapa alias *Landogi*. The banishment of Oba Kosoko to Epe popularized it the more in the town.

Obinrin Ojowu – 'the envious woman' - is another important deity among the Ijebu people. It is a stone image collected by an *Awujale* while passing through Ibu - the home of the cult. The stone was eventually deposited at Odo-Esa in Isale Iwade compound of Ijebu Ode. A young Iroko tree – *militia excelsia* was planted near it. With a dog sacrifice offered it every year, *Obinrin Ojowu* has become a deity in Ijebu-Ode from which barren women pray for children. The *Awujale* till date still performs its rites every year. *Olowa Iberu* is its chief priest (Seriki: 39).

Another religious practice found among the Ijebu people is the worship of *Aiyelala*, which only spread to the land from their coastal neighbours - the Ilaje and Ijaw people at Okitipupa. *Aiyelala* is a female deity said to be a woman-slave who later became revered and popular. She is believed to be the guardian of social morality and an anti-wickedness goddess. She detests stealing, witchcraft, bad medicine and other vicious practices. *Aiyelala* punishes any infringement of social virtue. She is also worshipped for protection. The resident officer of Ijebu Province recorded that the *Elero* of Ijebu (Ilaje Area) in May 1947 claimed to have the protection of *Ayelala*. (Awolalu a: 41–45. Also see archive document – IJE N0 3435/7). Her symbols are five cowries specially consecrated and wrapped in a white cloth inside a white bowl (Awolalu b: 79–89 & a: 41–45. Also see archive document – IJE N0 3435/4 of 21/11/1947). The Ijebu Native Authority in Ijebu Province excluding Remo in 1949 banned *Aiyelala* however, individuals in Ijebu land still keep simple forms of *Aiyelala* altars.

The advent of Islam in Ijebuland

Although the Ijebu kingdom was of considerable antiquity and size when Islam was spreading to other Yoruba kingdom, it did not reach it then. Ijebuland was late to be Islamized. It was closed to 'strangers' including those who were to introduce Islam even after the Northern Yoruba land had been Islamized. This was also the situation in the introduction of Christianity, as already noted by Olayiwola in this book. How and when Islam entered Ijebu settlements are therefore not certain. However, traditional sources seem to suggest that it was through some converted freed slaves, itinerant preachers from the Northern Yoruba area or converted indigenous traders on their home-return towards the end of the nineteenth century (Seriki: 388). However, by around 1879, Islam had been introduced but the early Muslims in Ijebu then were not 'strong' enough to build long-lasting built-up structures as mosques. The early mosques were 'mud and thatch' built.

Even, when it did, it did not simultaneously spread to all Ijebu settlements. Islam was first noticed in Ijebu-Ode, the capital city in 1877 during the time of Oba Fidipote (1850-1886), the forty-third *Awujale* of Ijebu land. However, some Muslims led by Imam Audu who later became the first chief Imam of Epe accompanied Chief Kosoko who was banished from Lagos to Epe in 1851. By the permission of *Awujale*, he settled in Epe – an Ijebu seashore earlier inhabited by the fishing Ijaws. With this incident of 1851, Epe most probably accepted Islam first in Ijebu land. Apart from Avoseh *'s history of Epe*, Alhaji Amidu Usman - the Chief Imam of Epe confirmed this. Seriki has earlier dated the advent of Islam in some Ijebu settlements. In the *Akile-Ijebu* area are: Ijebu-Igbo and Ago-Iwoye - 1880, Ijebu-Imushin - 1882, Ijebu-Ife - 1885, Abigi - 1886, Ogbere - 1888, Ilushin - 1890, Isonyin - 1893, Okun-Owa - 1895 and Ayepe - (1900).

In the Remo area, the inception was around the same time. Sagamu and Iperu received Islam in 1869 and 1875 respectively, some few years before Ijebu Ode. The other Ijebu-Remo settlements where Islam was established are Ilishan and Ikenne – 1880, Isara and Ode–Lemo – 1885 and Ogere – 1889. It should be noted that apart from Ijebu Ode, Epe and few other settlements that has formal records of dates or their dates being linked with a recorded event or tradition, most of the dating are not absolute. Recording an event in African traditional societies was mainly through oral traditions. It is therefore not strange that most informants were not sure of the exact dates. In some cases, as in Ibiade, Ikorodu and Mamu, not dated by Seriki; informants were not sure of the exact dates of the arrival of Islam. For example Alhaji Abdul-Salam Hazzan - the chairman, league of Alfas in Ibiade. (aged 80) just gave 'over 100 years' for the inception of Islam in Ibiade. The nature of the spread of Islam to each Ijebu settlement is slightly different from one another.

There are four main approaches of Islam into the various settlements under study. The advance of Islam into Ijebu land started with its practice by the slave servants of wealthy indigenes of various Ijebu settlements. These include the slaves of Chief Tubogu and chief Role Ikanigbo of Ijebu Ode, Balogun Onihale Onabegun of Ago-Iwoye, Olowolayemo and Oliwo-ile of Okun-Owa. It should be noted that Ijebu land was generally a wealthy kingdom from the proceeds of slave trade and other exchange business with the Europeans at the seashores. They were rich and very proud people. Islam also spread to Ijebu-Igbo, Ijebu-Ife, Sagamu, Ikorodu, Iperu and Isara through the activities of these slaves who were mostly of Ilorin, Nupe and Hausa origins. Islam was then therefore regarded as an exclusive religion of the *Hausas* and popularly referred to as *esin Gambari* then. They allowed their *Hausa* slave-servants and the itinerant *mallams* and preachers from Hausa land, Ilorin and Nupe land to practice the religion unmolested.

However, certain incidences in some of the areas made the indigenes accept Islam eventually. For example, in Ago-Iwoye, the masters of the slave-servants allowed them to perform the five daily prayers in the open spaces outside their houses. Because they normally called the adherents to prayers (*adhan*), other slaves-servants joined them. They also attracted some indigenes of low status while performing the five daily prayers – *salat*. There was even the case of Chief Onihale Onabegun – the Balogun of Ago-Iwoye whose son - Abosede fell seriously sick. He spent a lot of money and made very frantic efforts to cure his son; but all went in vain until the slave-servant begged for the son to perform *salat* with them. The son did and got well. This impressed the highly influential master who was converted and his son was given the name - Abdul Qadri. Consequently, he freed Mohammad, his slave-servant, and embraced Islam with all members of his household (Seriki: 94–96). The return of indigenous traders who had been converted from their traditional idol worship to Islam while on their business trips to Ilorin, Nupe and Hausa lands reinforced the introduction of Islam by slaves in settlements like Ijebu-Ode, Ijebu-Ife and Ogbere. The return of Ali Akayinode of Ijebu Ode and Pa Agufon of Ijebu-Ife, who later became the first Imams of their settlements, increased the number of adherents of Islam. Wealthy and influential indigenes that saw their colleagues in these new religions rushed in to embrace Islam. It was these later groups that usually asked the traditional rulers for a piece of land to build their house of worship – *masjid*. In Yoruba traditional society, it is the ruler that owned all lands, and it was only he who had the right to give it out for use to anyone or group of people. The return of these indigenous traders was responsible for the introduction of Islam to Ilishan. Abdul Salam Okunusi Sofumowo was an indigenous trader dealing in oil and palm-kernel. He returned from a market in Mokoloki – an Egba land to introduce Islam in Ilishan. (Seriki: 11)

The conversion of some influential personalities to Islam in Ijebu land also spread the religion like the case of Chief Balogun Bello Kuku. This late nineteenth and early twentieth century *Seriki* of Ijebu-Ode was a wealthy Muslim trader and a successful war-lord. After his conversion to Islam in 1902, Kuku was given the name Muhammad Bello. For his singular conversion to Islam, Ijebu land was remarked by Ayandele (269) to have had the most rapid spread of Islam in Yorubaland. Being a powerful and highly influential man in the land, he assisted to secure a land for the first central mosque of Ijebu-Ode at Etitale area from the then *Awujale*. The current central Mosque is at Oyingbo area of Ijebu-Ode.

The spread of Islam was also made easy by the interaction of Ijebu traders who had been converted to the Islamic faith with their fellow kinsmen. For example, traders from Ijebu-Ode introduced Islam to Ogbere while Prince Ismaila of Ijebu-Ode royal family established it in Ikenne. Alfa Lawal from Isado quarters of Ijebu-Ode also spread it to Abigi, which is eventually credited for its advent in Ibiade and other sub-urban settlements. A trader and farmer; Abdul Salam introduced Islam through Ijebu-Ife to Isonyin while Islam entered Mamu through Ijebu-Ode. Some of Seriki's (90–117) nature of the spread corroborates most of the statements of the chief Imams of these towns interviewed at various times.

The last tactics of Islam for its spread to Ijebu land was through the activities of itinerant Muslim preachers mostly from Ilorin and Oyo as well as Northern

Nigeria. This is the only approach similar to the general spread in West Africa as observed by most scholars. This was the situation in Ilushin, Ayepe, Ode-Lemo and Ogere only. Epe can be grouped here with the inclusion of Chief Imam Audu in the Kosoko exiled group from Lagos.

Besides these major approaches of Islam in Ijebu land, there were also cases of some people who were pre-destined to be Muslims in Ijebu land. During the consultation of the *Ifa* oracle, which is common for all newly born - e*sentaye* in all Yoruba groups, *Ifa* revealed that some children were predestined to be Muslims. Gbadamosi (89–91) reported the case of Asana of Iperu and that of Kasumu Ojeneiye of Idowa in Ijebu land.

Conclusion

The advent of Islam into Ijebu land was a delayed as well as an organic phenomenon, spreading from one settlement to another in a periodic chronology. The nature and spread of Islam into most Yoruba settlement was a forceful historical event. This is unlike the circumstantial incident and peaceful means of its spread into Ijebu land. Despite Ijebu-Ode's considerable antiquity and size, Islam got there only around 1879 when other Yoruba sub-groups were receiving it between the seventeenth and eighteenth centuries. The incursions of Uthman Dan Fodio, which forcefully converted the rest of Yoruba land did not get to Ijebu land as Ibadan people led by Balogun Oderinlo stopped it at Osogbo.

With this unique incident, Islam in Ijebu land remained unpurified as Uthman did in other Yoruba land. This was therefore, supposed to affect the cultural framework of Ijebu people. Despite these, it was discovered that the most rapid spread of Islam in Yoruba land was recorded in Ijebu land with the conversion of Balogun Kuku and other high chiefs of the period. Moreover, and despite their early contacts with Europeans, Islam still became more powerful and better received than Christianity. Early Europeans were more interested in their economy rather than the spread of Christianity.

In actual fact, the nature of Islam in Ijebu land generally allowed the converts to practice their traditional religion simultaneously. It was claimed that 'Islam does not prevent us from practicing our traditional rites - '*Imale o pe ka ma s'oro ile wa'*. However, the situation now is different. Muslims now will not want to associate in any way with traditional religious practices, especially not in the open anyway. The chief Imams of the settlements under study confirmed that Islam does not allow the worship of the traditional divinities.

Works cited

Adebonojo, B.O. *Itan Ido Ijebu*, Ikeja, John West Publications Ltd., 1990.
Adepegba, C.O. *Yoruba Metal Sculpture,* Ibadan, Ibadan University Press 1991.
Akinjogbin I. A. & Ayandele, E. A. "Yoruba-land up to 1800" in Obaro Ikime (ed.).

Groundwork of Nigeria History, Ibadan, Heinemann & Historical Society of Nigeria, 1980.
Awolalu O. J "Ayelala – A Guardian of Social Morality," *Orita – Ibadan Journal of Religious Studies* (11) 2, Dec. 1968.
-------------- *Yoruba Beliefs and Sacrificial Rites,* London, Longman, 1979.
--------------"The Interaction of Religions in Nigeria" *Orita – Ibadan Journal of Religious Studies, (XV)* 1, 1983.
Aronson, L. "Ijebu Yoruba Aso Olona – A contextual and Historical Overview" *African Arts* (XXV) 3, July 1992.
Avoseh, T.O. *A short History of Epe,* Parochial Committee, St Micheal's Anglican Church, 1960.
Ayandele, E. A. *The Ijebu of Yorubaland: 1850-1950: Politics, Economy and Society,* Ibadan, Heinemann, 1992.
Bourgeois, Jean-Louis "The History of Great Mosques of Djenne" *African Arts* (XX) 3. 1987
Balogun, S. A. "History of Islam up to 1800" O. Ikime (ed), *Groundwork of Nigerian History,* Ibadan, Heineman for theHistorical Society of Nigeria, 1980.
Bravmann, R. A. *Islam and Tribal Art in West Africa,* London, Cambridge University Press, 1974.
Conton, W.F., *West Africa in History, Vol. 1, before 1800,* London: George Allen & Unwin Ltd., 1965.
Eades J. S. *The Yoruba Today,* Cambridge, Cambridge University Press, 1980.
Ezzati A. *An introduction to the History of the Spread of Islam,* Lagos, Islamic Publication Bureau, 1979.
Fage, J.D., *Introduction to the History of West Africa,* Cambridge: University Press, 1961.
Fajana A. and Biggs, B. J, *Nigeria in History,* Ibadan, Longman, 1964.
Gbadamosi, G. "Odu Imale: Islam in *Ifa* Divination and the case of Predestined Muslims," *Journal of the Historical Society of Nigeria,* (8) 4, June 1977.
Idowu, E. B. *Oludumare –God in Yoruba belief,* London, Longman, 1962.
Lloyd, P. C. "Osifekunde of Ijebu" in Philip D. Curtin's *Africa Remembered - Narratives by West Africans from the Era of the Slave Trade,* Madison, The University of Wisconsin Press, 1967.
Law, R. "Early European Sources Relating To The Kingdom of Ijebu (1500 – 1700): A Critical Survey," *History in Africa,* 13, 1986.
Obanta Newsday (4) 1, Jan-March, 1999.
Odunmuyiwa, E. A. A History of the Anglican Church in Ijebuland: 1892-1984 – A Sociological Analysis', Ph.D. Thesis, 1987.
Ogunkoya, T.O. "The Early History of Ijebu," *Journal of Historical Society of Nigeria* (1) 1, Dec 1956.
Oladimeji, T. A. G. "The Essence of Dwellers of Heaven: A search for new functions and Forms for Ibadan Masquerades" in *JONART – A Journal of Humanities* (St. Andrews College of Education, Oyo) (1) 2, June 1995.
Parrinder, Geoffrey, *West African Religion,* London, Epworth Press, 1969.
Smith, R. S. *Kingdoms of The Yorubas,* London, Metheun and Co Ltd., 1976
Seriki, I. A. A. Islam Among the Egba and Ijebu Peoples (1841-1982) Ph.D. Thesis, University of Ibadan, Ibadan, 1986.
Watt, W. M. "Some Problems Before West African Islam" in *The Islamic Quarterly – A Review of Islamic Culture* (IV) 1, April 1958.

Informants

1. Abdul-Salam, Hazzan (Alhaji) Male, Aged 80 is the Chairman, League of *alfas* in Ibiade and the *Noibi* of the central mosque of Ibiade. He was interviewed on 03/12/1999.
2. Audu, Abdul Gafar Adesanya (Alhaji) Male, Aged 86 is the current Chief *Imam* of Ikorodu. He was interviewed on 08/12/1999.
3. Awonaike, Tahiru Olagun (Alhaji) Male, Aged 78 is the *Noibi* of the central mosque of Isonyin. He was interviewed on 27/11/1997.
4. Ejalonibu, Rabiu Ahmad (Alhaji) Male, Aged 75 is the Chief *Imam* of Mamu. He was interviewed on 04/12/1999.
5. Oguntayo, Adesesan Afolorunso Mohammed Anafi *(Kabiyesi)* Male, Aged 62 (now a Christian) is the paramount traditional ruler *(Oba)* – The *Ajalorun* of Ijebu-Ife. He was interviewed in the central mosque of Ijebu-Ife on 27/11/1999.
6. Olufowobi, A (Pa Alhaji), Male, Aged 82 is an Arabic teacher and elder-member of the central mosque of Ago-Iwoye. He was interviewed in his residence on 24/11/1999.
7. Sode, Fasaasi (Alhaji) Male, Aged 72 is the Chief *Imam* of Iperu. He was interviewed on 09/12/ 1997.
8. Toyobo, Ifasola (Alase) Male, Aged 70 is the *Alase-Agemo* of Ijebu-Ode and the head of all *Agemo* of Ijebu-land. He was interviewed on 12/05/2000.
9. Usman, Amidu (Alhaji) Male, Aged 80 is the current Chief *Imam* of Epe. He was interviewed on 25/11/1999.
10. Wadau, S. A. (Mr), Male, Aged 65 is the Storekeeper of Eko-Epe central mosque. He was interviewed on 25/11/1999.

Part V

African Traditional Religion

Chapter 9

Cosmology and symbolization in Urhoboland

- J. T. Agberia

Introduction

Urhobo religious art is sacred and iconic. As art product, its relationship as a set of cognitive symbols relates appropriately to the worldview of its people. And as a well-articulated concept of idea and experiences by the Urhobo people, their distinctive identities are clearly and sufficiently marked out amongst the various polities that acknowledge the existence of such divinities or deity. As a result of the plural nature of the Urhobo people, their civilisation and culture are replete with various religious festivals from where these symbols are clearly identifiable. Hence, for a proper understanding of Urhobo art and its worldview, we shall examine Urhobo systems from the perspectives of its cosmology and its representation in icons as highlighted in some festivals that the Urhobo people celebrate from time to time.

In addition, it is to be observed that worship in Urhobo religious systems connote a relationship between the human society, which can be personified as man, and the esoteric world, in this instance as represented by supernatural beings. Some of these have become transformational to be revered and regarded as symbols, or icons or images. In this regard, Urhobo art can be placed on two pronged parameters of idealism:
 (1) that of being an icon as inspired from religious worship. The attribute of this connotes regularity of the *numinous* and supernatural entity.
 (2) that which represents imagery of form, and as an image, it denotes a visual cult object of material referent to the numinous. The objects at this level of understanding can be given symbolic interpretation and analysis of stylistic

constructs.

Hence, objects of art in Urhobo cosmology represent such structures of Urhobo worldview as the real, that is the powerful, the meaningful, that is the living and the sacred which are identifiable with such characteristics of multivocality, condensation of meaning and polarity. We shall select and illustrate these with well-known iconic art as the discussion progresses.

Urhobo cosmology

We do not, however, intend to go into the old and speculative arguments and theories of worldviews as already noted by Smart (37). Here worldview seen in the same sense as cosmology implies a complex of whole beliefs, habits, the laws, customs and traditions recognised to hold the Urhobo people together over time. It involves an understanding of the overall picture they conceive about reality, the universe, life and existence, their attitude to life and things in general. It also includes what they do and how they perceive of life, what things are worth striving to attain, what man's place is in the entire scheme of things, and whether or not man has an immortal soul and whether or not life has meaning and purpose.

A close study of the Urhobo society, as well as current enquiries into the vestigial remains of traditional past life and religious practices reveal an identical understanding of the entire world with such other peoples as the Edo, the Igbo, the Yoruba, Igala, Idoma or the Ashanti who are constantly involved in religious practices as their well-being depends largely on the goodwill of the transcendental. Quoting from Ikenga-Metuh, Uchendu made the following penetrating observation: "to know how a people views the world around them is to understand how they evaluate life, both temporal and non-temporal provides them with a charter for action, a guide to behaviour" (Ikenga-Metuh: 50).

Thus to maintain such constant good relationship with the transcendental the Urhobo man in many and various ways tries to observe the prescribed behavioural principles. As a result, Urhobo cosmology consists of recognisable elements in their religion. The hierarchical structure of the cosmology of the Urhobo people can only but be determined from the order and reverence accorded the various supernatural beings recognised among the people in all the twenty-two polities. These attitudes are guided by their behaviour towards the spirit beings. Although these spirit beings are known by different names and appellations in the various parts of Urhoboland, they perform identical functions. It is perhaps their names and theogonies (stories connected with their origins) that may differentiate them. In a simple form, Urhobo cosmology could be briefly discussed under the following subheading: (I) The Supreme Being (*Oghene*) (ii) The Divinities (*Edjo*) (iii) The cult of Ancestors (*Erivwi*) (iv) Personal Guardian Spirits and (v) Lesser Spirits.

The Supreme Being (*Oghene*)

The Urhobo like other African peoples as earlier indicated, have the belief and concept of an Almighty creator of the universe whom they refer to as Oghene. So strong is this belief that Nabofa remarks that the elements that constitute the structure of the Urhobo cosmology interrelate in one way or the other. These elements, according to him, draw their reality and power from one source, Oghene (God), whom they believe to be the *Orovwakpo* (the Owner and controller of the entire universe). To affirm this, Nabofa states thus: "He is Oghene the Supreme Deity, while *Edjo, Erhan* (divinities), ancestors and other spiritual forces derive their existence and power from Him only. [In this regard, all the divinities] are united under Oghene." (220).

From the above observation, it is clear that the Urhobo not only have knowledge of the Supreme Being but also venerate and adore him in clearly defined manner. This is contrary to the views of some early writers on the subject as a being foreign to the people. The idea of God as the Creator of the world and man, and the controller of all matters is firmly entrenched in the religious beliefs of the Urhobo people. For instance Bradbury in his reference to the Urhobo articulation of the Almighty One implied a worship of a high god, Oghene, who he claims is the Creator of the World and of life and death...though indescribable, is believed to be some way connected with the sky. It is not uncommon to find Western scholars associate African gods with the sky, which distinctively portray their ignorance as inability to appreciate the various modes by which the African perceives of the Almighty. Awolalu and Idowu drew attention to this weakness when they state thus: "...all races and people in the world are capable of experiencing God's self-revelation but the difference is that the response to this self-disclosure varies from locality to locality in accordance with the intellectual and spiritual abilities of the people" (140).

In Africa, there are no high gods, the only Ultimate Reality is the One God of the whole universe who manifests itself to the different peoples and races of the world. Although the Urhobo relate Oghene with the sky, they believe that He is Almighty, all-powerful, all knowing, all present and all seeing. For instance, the concept of God in Urhoboland as Almighty and Majestic can be related to when God is referred to in other ways apart from Oghene as *Uku* (meaning The Great One*)*, *Osolobruwhe* - (God who blesses, the Father who blesses) *Orovwakpovwe Erivwi* (The Owner of the living and the ancestral world), *Orhovwara,* (the Fearful One*)*. *Omanomohwo,* (The Creator who created or moulded a person) and *Ohwovotota Otunyo*, One Man whom a multitude must hear when He speaks (Erivwo: 4)

God's attributes also manifest in ways in which His magnanimity is felt among the living: In this way, the people have expressions such as *Oberode rotakpo vwo 'rhurhu,* (the plantain leaf large enough to shelter the entire world), *Oghenekohwo (*God it is who gives) or *Ogheneochuko,* (God is helper) and *Oghenebrorhie,* (God is the Supreme Judge). The authority and almightiness of

God is so well felt in every facet of the people's life that His is believed to be the giver of moral code while the lesser divinities or spirits, such as *Edjo, Erhan* and ancestors, are the custodians of these codes.

The worship of *Oghene*

The general worship pattern of Oghene in Urhobo religion is attested to and classified as the trilogy of worship ably represented by Erivwo (16) and Nabofa (220). The three forms are (I) The casual, or perfunctory worship accorded Oghene during an emergency, (ii) worship by purification and sanctification using *Orhen* (white chalk) and (iii) the veneration accorded Oghene through *Ogwan-egodo* (compound shrine).

i] **The Casual Worship:** The casual or perfunctory worship accorded to God is usually in an emergency. It could be for instance a crew of Urhobo voyagers that are confronted with a shipwreck in which spontaneous prayers are offered to Oghene acknowledging his almightiness and soliciting for help. Such a man when rescued from that danger would acknowledge God's goodness and mercy and say *Oghene woruru gangan* (God you have done well) or *Oghene wosivwu vwe nu'ghwu* (God you have saved me from death). This is perfunctory or casual because it is unexpected and in some cases when the 'saved' wishes to acknowledge this he adds *Oghene vwerhe-he* (My God never sleeps).

ii] ***Orhen* Sanctification and Purification:** The second form of worship takes the form of o*rhen* (kaolin or native white chalk) put on the left palm by a petitioner in the early morning, but this time directed and blown heavenwards. The worshipper does this while facing the East during sunrise as the heaven is believed to be the abode of the supernatural. This is done with offering of prayers. The o*rhen* which signifies purity of God and fertility is believed to be the carrier of the petition to Oghene. The symbolism of *orhen* is given wide recognition in almost all African ethnic groups. They believe that white is symbol of purity, peace, prosperity fertility. E. G. Parrinder (17) notes this form of worship as partial worship among Africans.

iii] **Worship of God through *Oghene egodo***
The third category takes place in the family lineage hall often called *Oghene-egodo*, <u>*Oto-egodo*</u> or *Ogwan-Oto-orere* (town hall) all literally explaining the ground of the compound or centre point of the compound or hall. If the earlier category of worship would be classified as partial, this may not as it involves an elaborate ritual form than the other. An elongated pole towering into the sky, which is twelve feet or more, is erected in the centre of the compound. *Oghene egodo* also called *orise* is profoundly recognised as *Osonobruwhe* or Oghene in Urhobo. *Orise* is also commonly used by the Itsekiri, who are Urhobo neighbours, to designate

the presence of God. It is not unlikely that interactions over the years may have resulted in the intermingling of language influences. At the tip of the *orise* is fastened along strip of white calico cloth, which drops downward along the pole. At the foot is half-burned a fibrous coconut fruit, one end of which is sliced off. An iron bar or preferably a cutlass without handle called *ekperhi* of about two and a half feet is also pinned near the coconut which is slanted toward the pole at an angle or about 600. In some cases, at the tip of the pole is attached a conical basket called *agbedada* also believed to trap and transmit to the family information from Oghene and materials of prosperity to man.

Erected beside the pole is an *agbada* (raised platform) which represents the altar. This is constructed with bamboo around the pole. On the altar are placed offerings to *Osolobruwhe* (God); these include coconuts, eggs, kolanuts, sweet drinks of palm wine or sweet mineral drinks. Other ritual elements used for the worship of Oghene are any edible such as plantain, banana and yam. After the sacrifice, the remaining food item is shared and taken in "communion" by the devotees. A white fowl (without blemish) is also offered to *Osonobruwhe*. Usually, it has its two legs tied and hung on to the top pole, where it dangles by the *agbedada*. Inside the *agbedada* are also some yams and plantain, both of which are painted with white kaolin and pricked with sharp pins (*edada*). The day the *orise* is erected, there is feasting and rejoicing amongst all the members involved. This festival is re-enacted annually. Thereafter the worship of Oghene takes place when occasion demands but not on E*dewo* (traditional day of rest).

The Divinities *(Edjo and Erhan)*

Within the traditional Urhobo society, *Edjo* and *Erhan* are highly revered and recognised as nature divinities who mediate between man and Oghene. The divinities (and ancestors which we shall discuss later) are recognised as immediate messengers of Oghene. Their role is significant because they make the transcendent Oghene immanent in the Urhobo cosmology in the performance of several functions. This is why Nabofa clearly enthused that: "the Urhobo believe Oghene to be the Orovwa'akpo the owner and supreme controller of the whole universe. *He is the Supreme Deity, while Edjo, Erha and ancestors derive their existence from him*" (220) (Emphasis mine).

As I said earlier, each of the socio-political units recognises one form of *Edjo* or *Erhan*, the origin of which is realizable in mythical narratives. However, there are allusions as to how some of these divinities came into existence in relation to their dwelling places and functions. Erivwo (21-46) categorised them into two aspects; the *Edjo' rame* and *Edjoraghwa*. Basically, while *Edjorame* implied divinity that dwells in water or a water spirit, *Edjoraghwa* represents a divinity that inhabits the bush or forest or in the farmlands.

Generally, an *Edjo* is believed to disclose itself to a chosen one usually by possessing that person at times in a trance, or in a state of kidnap to the infernal world while on a fishing, farming or on any business away from his home particularly in the bush. Once such a person is overtaken by *Edjo*, he becomes an *Orheren or Edjo* priest. *Edjo* functions as a guardian and protector when petitions of assistance and help are made to it and in return *Edjo* expects its priest and adherents to reciprocate by offering regular worship and veneration to it. Hence, *Edjo* regulates the attitudes and behaviours of its adherents regarding taboo observances. Although the advent of Christianity in Urhoboland has affected the people's commitment to its worship, evidence abound that a lot of Christian converts in Urhoboland at one time or the other get involved in *Edjo* worship.

Apart from the recognition accorded *Edjo* within the villages or small communities, tutelary divinities are recognised in different communities particularly *Ogbaurhie* in Ughienvwen, *Urhienu* among the Eghwu, *Ekene* in Agbarha-Otor, *Ohworhu* among Ogor, Evwreni and Ephrontor whose fame and authority transcend their immediate lineages to other polities (Erivwo: 220). As a result periodic festivals are organised to honour and worship these divinities. While ancestor worship appears to be an annual event, the tutelary festivals come up in decennial or vicinal. The functions of all these divinities can be categorised into four groups for convenience. These are the War or Guardian divinities, the Prosperity divinities, the Moral or Ethical divinities and the Earth cult divinities.

a]   **The War or Guardian Divinities:** These divinities are recognised in their various polities as having assisted the people to avert an impending danger, internecine war or have practically protected them against the onslaught of enemies at battlefields. This is probably the reason why some of the divinities are sited at spots where the devotees waged successful battles and in cases, the locations become the domain of the devotees. War divinities are honoured with annual festivals. For instance Ughwerun honour *Onidjo, Ophio* and *Ugherighe* with *Ade,* and *Ore,* while Arhavwarien honour *Igbodu*. *Ifie* is honoured with *efabere* and *Ovwuvwe* with *Ore. Iphri-Oroakpo,* a community enterprise, is also honoured with *efa*; (*Ade, ifie and ore are religious festivals in Urhoboland*). The war divinities are believed to render the guns, cutlasses and other weapons of war potent for the devotees and ineffective with the enemies. They are also believed to have the capacity to cause dislocation, confusion and panic in an enemy's camp. The *edjo* are also known to have provided the most effective war tactics for the defeat of the enemy. For instance, Ubrurhe (19) reported that the Ovwuvwe made Avwaeke flee from imminent death by sending a squirrel to warn Avwaeke of an impending attack. In another instance, *Orosi* of the Orogun is very well known and honoured divinity for the protection it gave to their progenitors. The divinity is said to have transported them to safety across the Orogun river during a flight from an enemy. In an interview with late Chief Odiri on 12th June, 1996, he narrated how *Orosi* transmute into an eguana. It was on the back of the

iguana that the Orogun people swam to safety in their present location.
The people of Esaba in Ughienvwen worship *Egba* whose *efa* is celebrated vicennially. It is believed that the Esaba people were made invisible by *Egba* when their enemies launched an attack on them. The headquarters of this *orhan* is centrally located at Ovwawha. As a result of this protection which many of these communities received from their *Edjo*, it behoves of them to observe prescribed taboos which range from avoidance of dog meat, snails, antelope, etc. to sexual intercourse before going into a battle field.

b] **The Prosperity Divinities:** Among the Urhobo people, the occupation of a man or woman makes the spiritual attachment to recognised *Edjo* possible. And because occupation of the people varies from farming, fishing to hunting, different divinities make it possible for their aspirations to become a reality. Hence among the crop farmers in Urhoboland, the palm oil collectors worship *Edjokpa* or *Edjo-edi*. Often before the beginning of the harvest season of the palms, sacrifices are made to it, to ensure ripening and healthy protection of life of the collector during the harvesting and processing of the *edi* (palms). This is so because, it is a taboo for a collector who he climbs a tree to fall from it during harvesting.

In fishing, *Umanoku* is worshipped particularly among the Ughelli people. The Ughelli festival is renowned for *iyerin ehworhe* (horn washing), which is celebrated in honour of the divinity. Similarly, other riverine communities have their appellations; the Ughienvwen recognises *Ogbaurhie*. Also a hunter worships *Edjoraghwa* for protection and guidance during his hunting expedition for game. The guidance from this *Edjo* is to enable him to be sharp at shooting animals. Sacrifices and special worship are undertaken regularly to appease *Edjo* and in the process enlist its sympathy. By this practice, abundance is assured in the community.

Again, with the introduction of trade, shop keeping and businesses for the sale of goods and services all over Urhoboland, prosperity in such occupations are also being associated with divinities. The most popularly one is *Orhenki* or *Oneki;* meaning trader. This is a market divinity for success (Otite: 31). Its function is to assist the trader sell his wares unhindered or transact his business profitably and win customers to himself on regular bases. Its iconic symbol takes the form of a carved male/female standing figure carrying a platter on his head into which the devotee deposits coins and offers regular sacrifices including spraying *Orhen*, kaolin. To install one, an *oboepha* (diviner) determines the causes of the person's misfortunes, especially, why his business is facing hardship. The *oboepha* then prescribes a possible solution.

c] **Ethical/Moral Divinities:** In Urhobo traditional religious system, retrogressive acts are abhorred and are viewed with the seriousness they deserve. Such acts as perjury, stealing, cheating and other related vices that are committed by persons are often referred to the ethical or moral divinities. In most cases oaths are very often taken on their behalf and offenders are punished accordingly. The very serious ones of *ozighe* (homicide and murder) are frowned at. For instance, in the late 1960, *Abasiumo* (divinity Calabar area) and *Onerho* were introduced into Urhoboland. They are said to be effectively charged to take the life of offenders who commit such vices. The significant aspect of these two divinities is that they kill and all property and belongings of such victims are deposited in front of the shrine to rot away as such items are regarded to be smeared with evil. The shrines of *Abasiumo* are located at Agbarho and Orerokpe. Those of *Onerho* are sited at Agbarho, Eku, Abraka, Ughelli, Eruemukohwarien etc. It is also recognised that these divinities in conjunction with the ancestors help in the preservation of the moral codes and well being of the communities. Other divinities of note are *Ughele-Urhie*, *Edjoreya* and *Unurhie* of Okpe, *Ohworode* of Agbon-Olomu and *Urhienu* of Eghwu.

d] **Earth Cult (*Oto*) divinity:** It has been the tradition of every Urhobo man that whenever a new settlement is to be built or established (whether at home or in the fishing port, or a settlement by a lineage) the founder plants a sacred tree called *Oghriki* (newbouldia) at the site. The symbolic identity of this is rightful ownership or first arrival at that spot and it is at this point the Earth divinity is worshipped regularly. As time pass on, the priesthood of this earth cult passes from the father to the eldest son in the patrilineage.

Amongst the Agbon people, as noted by Ubrurhe (19), Okpara who is the senior son to all other children of Agbon, performs this rites. Also with the Ughienvwen lineage, Oroghwe is accorded this authority being the most elderly son to Ovwahwa, Ukpedi and Uhurie. The same is true of other towns that constitute the thirty-two villages of Ughienvwen polity. The worship of *Oto* and *Egba*, a war divinity situated at Ovwahwa among the Ughienvwen, serves as a unifying factor for the people. The ritual process, as similarly observed by Durkheim, "brings about a state of effervescence which changes the conditions of psychic activity. Vital energies are over excited, passions more active, and sensations stronger" (as quoted in Adogbo & Ojo: 5).

The worship of *Oto* is also synonymous with the worship of *Oghene-egodo* in which food such as yam, plantain, banana, kolanut, orhen, soft drinks of Fanta, etc. are presented in anticipation of soil fertility and assurance of success in fishing and hunting expeditions.

The cult of Ancestors (*Esemo re Erivwi*)

The ancestors in Urhobo traditional religion are basically of two types, the *esemo* (pl. fathers of children) and *iniemo* (pl. mothers of children). As Erivwo (33) observed correctly, the ancestors among the Urhobo people are more potent and prominent than they are revered among the Yoruba, as more emphasis appears to be given to divinities by the Yoruba. The average Urhobo person believes that at death, the departed soul is transformed into the spiritual realm to their place of rest known as *erivwi*. At *erivwi* their character and attitudes are clearly dictated by the way and manner they lived their lives on earth and how they eventually died. Hence, they are believed to play very significant role in human affairs on earth. In relative terms, they are considered next in hierarchy to Oghene who is believed to be the final authority in every matter of importance.

They are highly revered once their character and attitudes during their lifetime show positive fulfilment. In fact, Opoku captures the mind of the average Urhobo believer in the ancestors on earth when he clearly distinguished between accidental deaths through heroic efforts and deeds in battle fields, on the one hand, and deaths that result from cowardice in the same battle, on the other. For a person to become an ancestor of reverence, he must have died a good death resulting from a venerated old age. By this, he would have attained a spiritual state of existence after death as he has planted his feet in both the world of the living and the world of the spirits. However, deaths resulting from suicide, violence, unclean diseases as lunacy, dropsy, leprosy and epilepsy are abhorred, (Erivwo: 33). Because of the fundamental role the ancestors played in the integration of society, the Urhobo hold a very strong belief in the continuity of life after death, so much so that the dead continue to exist and remain as members of their lineage, family, clans and community. As a result, the relationship between men on earth and beyond cannot be broken even at death.

Another Urhobo belief in connection with the ancestors is unending obligation at death. The dead are expected to be part of the living and even at death must be protective of the living and show generosity to men on earth. Hence the living-dead bless those on earth with *emo* (children), *efe* (wealth) (prosperity) and *Otovwe* (good health and longevity). These are three wishes often generated during prayers among the Urhobo people. In the same way those who deviate from family or communal moral codes (which involve vices such as stealing, witchcraft, sorcery and vices that are antisocial to harmonious coexistence) are punished.

Among the Urhobo, the worship of the ancestors is in two dimensions: *esemo* (fathers of children) and *iniemo* (mothers of children). The worship of *esemo* and *iniemo* takes place in designated shrines inside an *Ogwan* (family compound hall) where the family head offers sacrifices and prayers every morning and during special ceremonies concerning the *Iphri* or *Edjo* worship. Sacrifices are made in form of pouring libation, offers of kolanut and foods of *emarhen* (pounded yam, plantain, and cocoyam) and assorted food items of *eba* (garri), starch, tapioca, fish, meat etc. This is to maintain the existing cordial relationship between the living and the "living-dead." This reaffirms Mbiti's reference to ancestral worship in African society that libation and food in sacrifices are signs of communion, remembrance, hospitality and good relation between the two (9). Again, apart from the daily and occasional worship which are held for *esemo* and *iniemo,* festival occasions are also avenues for remembering the ancestors.

One final word in this section is perhaps to say that as we have seen, ancestors play such a fundamental role in the worldview of the Urhobo that they are clearly distinguished in their moral life. Therefore, they are accorded tremendous respect and held as role model for the living to emulate. But of great concern and interest is the distinction between the way ancestors and God are worshipped. The ancestors are never seen as the final authority in all matters nor do they have the same attributes as God. By virtue of their attributes and close relationship to Oghene and the *Edjo* the *esemo* are held as the messengers to Oghene. In tis capacity, they mediate between Oghene and the living.

The personal guardian spirits

In Urhobo religious system, numerous guardian spirits abound. For the purpose of this study, I shall discuss five which I consider relevant to the body of this work.

Iphri (symbol of aggression)

Its focal point is that it represents an icon of the spirit of aggression, which often represents the forceful male personality. These attributes are redirected towards a beneficial end. Although owned or acquired as an individual property, *Iphri*, in certain communities over the years, has been known to be on transferral; meaning that they could acquire the status of community property, in which case their worship is at the level of collective ownership by such community. For instance *Iphri Oroakpo* of Agbon polity got a transferral status to a community *Iphri* from a primogeniture whose name is already lost to memory. Also in this category was *Esosuo Iphri* of Edjekota currently housed in the *Ogwan* (meeting hall) of the Ogberakan since 1972. Similarly, the Uvwie-Effurun has one whose original owner is located amongst the Abade ward.

Erhi (Man's Spirit Double)

This is the subject of M. Y. Nabofa's PhD thesis (1978). *Erhi* has its symbolism attached to *atarhe*. Before a child is born, it is believed that his *Erhi* has predestined what life he would lead and this has been signed, and perhaps sealed by his *atarhe* and delivered to him at birth. All these processes take place in the presence of his *Erhi* in which Oghene is believed to preside. This spirit is then, therefore, delivered to guide and guard him throughout his lifetime. A significant aspect of this is that it is only when *Erhi* accept the intrusion of evil forces that harm could be done to a man whose *Erhi* is sealed. Hence incidences of involvement in fatal motor accidents or a tree falling on a man and killing him are attributed to *erhi*. In the same vein, successes in battles or in examinations have often been credited to *erhi* which a man had designed or planned for himself. Therefore, an Urhobo man believes that whatever that happens to a man in this world has been predestined and should be accepted as such. It has also been said that often times a man's destiny could be altered by forces of evil such as witches and wizards. Hence an Urhobo man would say "*Erhi roye voye rhovwere*" (His spirit agrees with him). As a result when a child is born, particularly within the first nine days when his *atarhe* would have been properly sealed, the parents keep watchful eyes on him to prevent witches and wizards affecting him.

Erhi is represented iconically. Bradbury described it as a twig of a sacred tree probably from the *Oghriki* (newbouldia) tree. The twig is adorned with a ribbon-like piece of cloth with some cowrie tied to it (160). The object is in most cases kept in one corner of the four-sided room of the house with it leaning against the wall about 45^0, an enamel plate or wooden platter where sacrifices are regularly offered.

Obo (Altar of Creative Hands)

In Urhobo ontology there is the concept of *Ob;*, expressed further refers to a personal name, *obokohwemu* which means the hand is associated with wealth, food, money children, prosperity. The representative object is found among different neighbouring groups. It is known among the Igbo people as *Ikenga*, the Kobowei Ijo people in the Niger-Delta call it *Amabra* while the Isoko, like the Urhobo people, call it *Obo*. The concept expounds further that when a person is wealthy and has many children, it is acknowledged that such wealth or money and prosperity in children should never slip off his hands. It is believed that one who is a spendthrift has a hot hand, while the rich are those who have cool hands. In Urhobo cosmology *Obo* occupies a veritable spiritual realm and, therefore, in reverence it is propitiated and at times given elaborate rituals depending on emotions of joy the owner attaches to it. It symbolizes an overt expression and dramatization of self-glorification and admiration. This is because whatever work a man does and has achieved in life is associated with the physical and spiritual strength of the hand. Whether in business, in farming, fishing, palm production, gin production, hunting, it is the physical hands that are employed and the fitness of the hand creates the success. *Obo* is so important that its symbolism is taken beyond the physical realm. Thus it is strongly believed that everything and conditions that man brought to life is encoded into his two palms. There are good and precious things and these must be guarded jealously to prevent witches and evil doers from changing the good destiny of the person particularly with new born babies who fold their hands in order to conceal their good fortunes. The parents in this respect aid in concealing the child's fortune by hiding their hands or keeping the baby indoors for the first nine days of its life within which time it is believed, the destiny of the child must have been indelibly engraved in the child's body that nobody can interfere with or change its destiny. According to Nabofa, the number, nine, representing the days in Urhobo, symbolizes longevity and also the number of days the child is being thus symbolically wished life eternity (85). The *Obo* symbol takes an artistic form of a single piece of stylistically carved wooden-hand, at times in full realistic representation. It is in the form of a human hand from the wrist upwards showing all the five fingers. Among other ethnic groups, the form is relatively quite complicated and figurative than it is among the Urhobo.

Ayererivwi/Osharerivwi (Spirit Spouses)

The Urhobo believe that a man or a woman has his spirit partner in the metaphysical world which when not controlled or terminated enters into marital relationship with its partner in the physical realm. Susan M. Vogel in alluding to the Baule, articulated how the spirits show benevolence in helping their human partners generally in their lives. This they do by spreading their goodwill to the children of a spouse's partner (246). S. M. Vogel bemoaned her allusions to overemphasis on spirit spouse's sexual relationship and reproductive problems as factors of maintaining good and fruitful marriages. J. O. Ubrurhe's allusions in accordance with my findings, point conclusively to the fact that among the Urhobo this belief is still very strong but with some difference. For as Ubrurhe puts it:

> marital problems such as childlessness, constant miscarriages emanating from love making with the spirit partner in dreams especially during pregnancy, unsustained love for a specific man resulting to unchastity and divorce, masculine impotency, frequent illness during pregnancy and other marital troubles are associated with *Ayererivwi* and *Osharererivwi* (28).

Once it is ascertained that the causes of such problems emanate from *Ayererivwi/Osharererivwi* an image is carved to assuage the spirit to leave the living alone but this either involve the provision of a similar spirit partner which may be buried or drowned in water. Often times as noted by Ubrurhe, sacrifices are offered at specified period as these are aimed at terminating the jealousy of the spirit partner and consequently the matrimonial relationship that existed.

Urhienvwe (Destiny or Fate)

Often related to *Erhi, Urhienvwe* is interchangeable with *Erhi* which means fate or destiny. It is symbolically represented by a carved figure of a man kneeling before the Supreme Being (*Oghene*) who is believed to seal his destiny. Its posture is often of a supplicant full of life and humility.

Lesser spirits

Generally, the Urhobo believe in some unidentified spiritual beings of the departed which were not given second burial known as *irhi ri'debolo/ ikorumuemu* (evil spirits) or *edjoverivwi* (Nabofa: 227). However, these are known to be both benevolent and malevolent but on the whole they express more havoc than good. Spirits of witchcraft and sorcery are also classified in this category as their expressions are more on the negative; they are in all ramifications rejected, thus offerings, sacrifices, and prayers are often given to the benevolent spirits to do away with the evil ones. We shall discuss witchcraft to support our claims.

Witchcraft beliefs in Urhoboland

Basic beliefs in the spiritual realm and its general effects on man relate closely to mystical forces that manifest themselves in form of witchcraft beliefs and practices in Urhoboland. Some of these forces according to J. O. Mume can be tapped and harnessed by men who have the knowledge and the ability to control them (8-22). As a result, manifestations of witchcraft have been attributed, in most cases, to negative impact of sufferings in men such as sicknesses, death, lack of prosperity in business, failures to pass examination at school, inability to gain promotion at work offices, inability to perform medical feats at hospitals during emergencies and even gain promotion in ministerial and religious duties. Failures in crop yield and general misfortunes of evil powers, which certain people in the community are believed to command, are also attributed to witchcraft activities. Since the existence of witches and its belief is not doubtful, its genesis goes back to over three hundred years ago. Generally, nobody has ever doubted or disproved their existence. Dr. J. O. Mume of Agbarho town who worked closely with Jeje Karuwa (who confessed being a wizard for 60 years at Usiefurun and Agbarho) gave a detailed account of the reality of witchcraft: Narrating the confessions of Karuwa, J.O. Mume said, "Wizards and witches don't usually have interest for earthly things. Material things are for those who operate only on physical bodies without astral senses and vision" (8-22).

He went further to state unequivocally what some of his exploits involved:

> Yes. That was long ago when I was newly initiated to the witchcraft club. I had converted five persons, two males and three females. Two of my converts are now dead, while one is already an elder in coven. Recently I taught an American who approached me to teach him the art of witchcraft. His approach was genuine, so I had to teach him (8-22).

Belief in witchcraft and its effect on people, particularly in Urhobo society is, in no doubt, a part of the peoples heritage. Its fears and impact constantly remind everyone of the existence of the unseen force being manipulated by humans who intend to do evil. And like Idowu clearly pointed out, it cuts across all facets of human endeavours - the religious, the non-religious, the political class and all social strata of society such as the Christians, Muslims, the educated and the unlettered, the civil service, student undergraduates, etc. are all embroiled in this strange and frightening phenomenon (3). Although the Bible is not categorical about defining who a witch and their attributes are, readers of the Holy book and adherents of the various religions and non-religious sects believe very strongly in the evil machinations of men which are attributable to witchcraft.

Divination systems among the Urhobo

To many people across the West Coast of Africa and beyond, particularly, in Cuba and Brazil, divination is declared to mean *Ifa,* a Yoruba system which was made popular through writings. William Bascom (1959) and Wande Abimbola (1976) conjecture that divination, a process of being able to see beyond the ordinary, appears to be one of the most complex and complicated systems in spite of its simple methods of using commonly found strings attached to objects in patterns whose meaning could only be deduced when thrown on the ground (Parrinder: 89).

To the Urhobo, life is an uncharted sea where an individual needs to be guided by the unseen hands of the divinities in order to have successes. As his needs vary, he believes that each divinity is assigned a particular function in his life and therefore his recourse to them for help and guidance must be frequent to achieve his daily needs. Emovon puts it more succinctly when he writes; "In choosing a site for his house or farm, in deciding whom to accept as an in-law or in seeking to restore health to a sick member of his family..., *Ominigbon* and its priests whom he calls *Oka* is the medium by which he communicates with the gods (1).

The need to seek knowledge of the unseen world has arisen among the Urhobo because more and more people today, Christians and non-Christians alike, seek the help of divination priests before they decide on any matter of importance. This is done by means of *epha. Epha* in Urhobo means act of or practice of divination that seeks to know hidden information or mysterious action. It has a genetic origin with Yoruba *Ifa* which we have earlier mentioned. To the Edo, it is *Iha*; the Uneme Edo in Akoko-Edo call it *Ivha;* the Isoko call it *Eva* while the Nupe, call it *Eba.*

My research findings have shown that *epha* remains widely prevalent because it serves an important function in the society; that of reducing anxiety whenever there is cause to do so particularly concerning the mysterious forces. To the practitioners, it is directly efficacious as a method for attaining ends envisaged. In Urhobo religious system, the practitioner, who is here regarded as the priest or diviner, is known as *Oboepha*.

The *Oboepha* and why he is consulted

Throughout the length and breadth of Urhoboland, my investigation shows that the Urhobo have no tutelary divinity unlike the Yoruba who have *Orunmila* for divination purposes. Consequently, among the Urhobo people, *Oboepha* (diviner) literally is a doctor of *epha* which means he is a doctor or expert in divination and thus able to communicate through a process with the unseen and super sensible world. He is able to transmit messages from the living-dead, the spirits and divinities to his clients on earth. He is not only able to foretell the future, but is able to unravel the mystery of the past and possibly proffer solution. This he does through some leading questions. This does not always follow as through telepathy, an *Oboepha* could even at the instance of an inquirer place before him the object of his mission. As a result of these roles, an *Oboepha* occupies a very important position in the village or community where he dwells. It is also of importance that although the act of divination is associated with mostly men, in Urhoboland there are instances where women also perform these roles.

Oboepha occupies a central position in Urhobo divination. This is because no typical Urhobo man will embark on any project without reference to the diviner whom he considers the medium through which he could foretell the future about the project he intends to carry out. Hence in seeking to know whether the time is propitious or whether the ancestors are in favour and whether or not the entire project can be insulated from the reach of evildoers who constitute themselves into veritable negative threat to success. The circumstances may involve saving life due to sickness, birth, circumcision, marriage, death in the new planting season, farming hunting, fishing, or expedition to *ukale* (sojourn) or putting up a building project. All these merit consulting an *Oboepha* for spiritual and psychical guidance. The believers in this system are often unable to accomplish anything until their yearnings are satisfied through the revelations that come from the *Oboepha*. Some of these revelations, for example, if they relate to death can only be accepted as natural if the victim is an old person. But on the other hand, an inquest would have to be undertaken to find out if the deceased committed a heinous crime against an ancestor or perhaps unceremoniously died as a result of witchcraft. If the revelation from the *Oboepha* shows that the cause of sickness is related to a crime against the ancestors, the offender is expected to make confessional statements to the entire family elders. On confession, if the elders are satisfied, specific sacrifices are made to recover the offender. Depending on the nature of the cause of illness, or calamity, a multiplicity of sacrifices may be recommended and offered, to such entities as ancestors, the witches, *erivwi* and *edjo*. In view of the central role which an *Oboepha* plays to the Urhobo society, it needs no emphasizing that the *Oboepha* is indispensable.

An Urhobo consult *Oboepha* to ascertain the danger ahead in the belief that once it is known early measures could be taken to avert it through reparatory sacrifices. Erivwo stresses thus: "*Ofovwi re nyo nu owheogba-a* (a strong warrior is never defeated in a battle he had pre-knowledge)" (21).

The methods of *Epha* divination

Epha methods in Urhobo vary from *Oboepha* to *Oboepha*, depending on his calling and technique by which he operates. Basically, his instruments include *awhawha* (bush mango seeds), strung into four lines or rope chains which he throws down with his two hands onto the ground. He interprets them from the message or communication the *epha* presents to him instantaneously. Some of these seeds are in concave shapes while others are convex. From the throw and their falls, the *oboepha* is able to interpret them from the spoken Urhobo. However, some *eboepha* (diviners) use kolanut seeds and the message and interpretation are deduced from the number systems and their symbolism in Urhobo (Nabofa: 59). Of important consideration in this regard, is the ability of *Oboepha* to freely manipulate his reading from the lots cast since he can read them upwards, downwards, sideways and even diagonally to give meaning to the entire process.

Conclusion

The vitality of symbolization throughout the greater part of history is closely bound up with some form of religion. In Urhoboland, like many other African ethnic groups, spiritual reality is represented by physical objects or gestures. This forms the basis on which art is closely linked with religion. In this vein, most artistic works in Urhoboland are associated with religion, which pervades most aspects of the people's cosmology. The religious genres include votive figures which adorn shrines, charm figures, stools used for initiation to the cults, the apparatus of divination, dance-staffs, musical instruments and a variety of other ritual paraphernalia. The representation of these objects in symbols relates to direct expressionism which has close link with religion.

The civilisation and culture of the Urhobo is replete with various artistic objects which symbolically represent their worldview. Here worldview is seen as cosmology that embraces a complex range of beliefs, habits, laws, taboos and whatever they consider as sacred and reality. Here lies the basis for symbolism. The divinities and religious objects become Hierophanies, that is, the external manifestation of the sacred; the physical representation of the invisible by the visible (Adogbo: 117). This explains why symbol, even in its explicit form, would remain unintelligible to the novice. It is against this background that the present work focused on Urhobo traditional cosmology and the unique significance of symbolization.

Works cited

Adogbo, M.P., "The Spirit World of African Peoples" in Erivwo, S.U. & Adogbo, M.P., *Contemporary Essays in the Study of Religions*, Lagos: Fairs & Exhibitions Nig. Ltd., 2000.

Adogbo, M.P. & Ojo, E.C., *Research Methods in the Humanities,* Lagos: Malthouse Press Ltd., 2003.

Abimbola, W., *Ifa An Exposition of Ifa Literary Corpus*, Ibadan: 1976.

Awolalu, J.O. & Dopamu, P.A. *West African Traditional Religion*, Ibadan: Onibonoje Press 1979.

Bascom, W.R., *Ifa Divination, communication between Gods and men in West Africa,* Bloomington: Indiana Univ. Press, 1959.

Bradbury, R.E., *The Benin Kingdom and the Edo-speaking Peoples Peoples of South Western Nigeria,* London: Int. African Institute, 1970.

Erivwo, S.U., "Epha: Divination System among the Urhobo of the Niger Delta" *African Notes* Vol. VII, No. 1, 1979.

.... "Traditional Religion and Christianity among the Urhobo" in Ikenga- Metuh, E., *The Gods in Retreat,*Enugu: Fourth Dimension Pub., 1986.

.... *Traditional Religion and Christianity in Nigeria: The Urhobo People,* Ekpoma: Bendel State University, 1991.

Emovon, O., "Ominigbon Divination" in *Nigeria Magazine* No. 151, 1984.

Idowu, E.B., *African Traditional: A Definition*, London: S. C. M., 1969.

......."The Challenge of Witchcraft" *Orita, Ibadan Journal of Religious Studies,* Vol. IV, No. 1, June, 1970.

Ikenga-Metuh, E., *Comparative Studies on African Traditional Religions*, Onitsha: Imico Press, 1992.

Mbiti, J.S., *African Religions and Philosophy,* London: Heinemann, 1969.

Mume, J.O., *Confession of the Wizard of Igbinse* (Ughelli: Jom Nature Cure Centre, Agbarho): 1972,

Nabofa, M.Y., "Erhi: The Urhobo Concepts of the Human Double and the Paradox of Self-Predestination in Urhobo Religion", Ph.D. Thesis 1978.

.... "A Survey of Urhobo Traditional Religion" *The Urhobo People*, Ibadan, Heinemann 1981.

.... "The Symbolism of Obo: The Urhobo Altar of Hand" *Owu: Port Harcourt Journal of Humanistic Studies,* Vol. 1, No. 1, June,1994.

Opoku, K.A., *West African Traditional Religion,* FEP Int. Private Ltd., 1978.

Parrinder, A.G., *West African Religion*, London: Epworth Press, 1961.

.... *African Mythology*, London: 1967.

Smart, N. "Worldviews: An Inventory" in *Worldviews: Cross Cultural Explorations of Human Beliefs*, New York: Charles Scribner's Sons Publishers, 1983.

Ubrurhe, J.O., "A Functionalist Approach to the study of Taboos: A Case Study of Urhobo Traditional Society", Unpublished Master's Thesis, UNN, 1986.

……. "Urhobo Cosmology: A key to Understanding Urhobo Art" in, Ubrurhe, J. O. (ed.), *African Beliefs and Philosophy* Warri: International Publishers, 1992.

Vogel, S.M., Baule: *African Art Western Eyes.* New Haven, Yale University, 1997,

Chapter 10

Clairvoyance in Urhobo traditional religion

- M.P. Adogbo

Introduction

Clairvoyance in this chapter refers to the power to relay events which happened in the past, and of seeing in the mind what is happening or what will happen in the future. Specialists in this special area of spiritualism are called clairvoyants because of their natural or acquired gifts of emotional and ecstatic insight. Bouquet (216) notes that "in earlier times they have been confused with sub-normal or abnormal states of a pathological character, approximating to hysteria or epilepsy; and some times, the discovery of the effect of certain herbal drugs or alcohol has led to the employment of artificial means to induce abnormality." This is certainly not the case in Urhoboland. The remainder of this work will focus on the prevalence and religious significance of this phenomenon in Urhoboland.

Mediums in Urhobo cosmology

The challenges posed by spiritualism in Urhoboland have resulted in the emergence of persons who act as intermediaries between the physical and spiritual realms of existence. The two important categories are *Oboepha* (diviner) and medium *(omraro)*. Our emphasis here shall be on mediums as divination has been treated in the preceding chapter.

Medium is used among the Urhobo as a broad designation for any one who acts as a channel of communication between the human and supernatural realms. People came to the medium to ask question about the spirits, and the spirits, in turn, speak to the inquirers in a recognizable way through the medium. Mediums perform this role only when possessed by a spirit. The unique feature of this institution is the ability to be possessed or get into communication with the spirit beings. This gives a clear distinction between the medium and the diviners. The diviners depend on the manipulation of magical objects. They may not be possessed.

Mediums may be men or women. It is generally believed among the Urhobo that women are particularly adapted to trance state than men. In a questionnaire widely circulated among randomly selected people of Urhobo origin on why women are more susceptible to spirit possession, the following answers were re turned:

(i). Mrs. T.E. Kwakpovwe of Ughelli writes, "Women are interested in virtually everything and could be easily moved."

(ii). Mrs. M.E. Mariere of Agbon says: "Women are weaker physically and, therefore, could easily be moved by spirits."

(iii). Mr. M.O. Jehwe of Udu claims: "Females are easily moved by any wind of religious faith thus they join in large numbers. Men, on the other hand, are more critical in examining religious issues."

(iv). Mr. M. Oseruvwoja of Agbon records: "As bearers of babies from the spiritual world, women are assumed to be nearer the spirits than men. They are also more attractive than men. By the use of scents and attractive dresses, they draw the attention of the spirits to themselves."

(v). Mr. Emumejakpo of Agbarha writes. "They serve as the earthly mothers of the spirits and, in the same vein, as their wives. Most of the possessed women are not married and must not have sex on *Edewo*, the sacred day when the spirit manifest."

Mediums are found all over Urhoboland. Some of them live in communes or convents called *Igbe* in Urhobo language. Virtually all villages and towns in Urhobo have *Igbe* houses. In Ughelli Township alone, over two hundred and fifty *Igbe* houses were counted. The writer entered into the well established ones and had useful interview with the mediums (*emraro*).

A typical *Igbe* house is an open *ogwan* (hall) with houses at both sides for the devotees, as well as sick people. There is an altar at one end of the *ogwan* (open hall). It is clearly demarcated and decorated with white clothes. Only the head of the medium can enter into the *Igbe* altar. If a woman, she must not enter when she is under menstruation. Indeed, no woman under menstruation may enter into the *Igbe* hall. Menstruation, in belief of the Urhobo, is a period of uncleanliness. It is believed that the impurities discharged with the blood can neutralize the potency of spirit and magical forces.

Before the altar is a mound of *orhe* (kaolin), on which a candle continually burns. This is common practice among *Igbe-orhen* adherents. The walls of the *ogwan* are painted with *orhen* and beautiful buntings of several colours hang from one end of the hall to the other. Small benches or stools are arranged at both sides of the hall, leaving sufficient space in the middle for dancing. No one must enter the *Igbe* house with shoes on; they are dropped at the entrance of the hall. While the idea of a "holy ground" in the manner of the biblical injunction to Moses (Ex.3:5) may apply, what is more pertinent is the belief that spirits manifest more when there is direct contact between the legs and the ground. In the same vein, most potent medium wear only skirts and expose the other parts of the body including their breasts. This is to attract the spirits.

At the middle of the compound or the threshold of the *Igbe* house is an *orise* (the symbol of God's presence). A plat-form of stick or mound of mud covered with *orhe* is made at the foot of the *orise*. Occasionally, a candle is made to burn all the night at the foot of the *orise*. Minerals, biscuit and coconuts may be deposited on the top of the *orise*. This is a common feature during the annual festivals of the *Igbe* devotees.

The origin of medium is not known in Urhobo. In an interview with S.O. Ikogho-Ovu at Ughelli, he explained that mediumship is a common and potent factor in Urhobo traditional religion. He opined that the need to know the problems of man and desire to proffer solutions to them must have necessitated the emergence of mediums in Urhobo traditional religion. The duty of the mediums is to probe into the events of the supernatural realm as they affect man and to provide explanation and solutions to them.

Several *Igbe* mediums who gathered a large number of followership had declined and eventually collapsed. The reason for the collapse is either the death of principal actor or his inability to have effective and factual communication with the spirits. This may also include the lack of effective successor. The following are examples of *Igbe*, houses, which originated in Urhobo, gathered a large number of followership but are no more:

(i) **Ugo:** It originated in Ubogo, a town in Udu polity. It gathered a large followership in virtually all the geo-political groups in Urhoboland and spread to neighboring ethnic groups such as Isoko and Itsekiri before it declined.

(ii) **Igbe re Eghragbomi Idjesa:** This originated in Otovwodo, the headquarters of Ughelli polity. At a time, it became so popular that people were coming from various parts of the country to inquire into the events of the spirit world. After the death of Eghragbomi, his children were unable to keep the tempo. The mediums who practised under him formed movements with several other names. However, some of the relics left behind by Eghragbomi could be found at Otovwodo – Ughelli today.

(iii). **Igbe re Tareri** - This was founded by Tareri at Owhrode in Udu. Like the ones before it, it fulfilled the basic conditions of perdition, explanation and control of events in time and space. It declined when Tareri died.

(iv). **Everhe:** The actual founder in not known. It was as popular as Ugo. Its spread and importance were dramatic that no one ever suspected that it would collapse like the ones before it. The principal centres were Agbon, Ughelli, Orogun, Agbarha, Ewhu, Udu, Ughievwen and Okpe. Late Madam Oghenebrume Esapo founded a branch at Okuama in Ewhu polity from the parent body at Okpara Inland. Many people came from the various Urhobo communities in the riverine area to consult with Oghenebrume. No trace of Everhe could be found by the present researcher. However, some respondents said that Evrhe is still at Uruvwigbo – Uwherun.

(v). **Awoshi:** the origin of Awoshi is not clear; some said it originated in Urhoboland while others traced the origin to Calabar. It flourished in Urhobo for a long time before it declined in the manner of its predecessors.

Mediums in Urhobo are autonomous. They originate through possession by a fresh act of definition or through a physical manifestation of a spirit. The growth and the importance depend on the ability of the medium to satisfy the spiritual needs of the adherents. By the authority granted by the founder, some *Igbe* groups have extended their branches beyond Urhoboland to other parts of the country. The novices come from within and other parts of the country to practice the act of spiritualism under the principal medium. When they graduate, they are commissioned to open new braches in their towns or villages. They may carry the name of the founder and pay occasional visits to the parent *Igbe* when they are faced with problems which are above their comprehension.

In the same vein, the founder may make annual visits to the branches which, in the real sense, are autonomous. This visit is only a mark of solidarity and not as a head in the manner of papal ecclesiastical visits. The branches appoint their officers without reference to the parent body. The respect to the founder is no more than the one a primary school teacher would get from a former pupil who had become a medical doctor.

The development and growth of the medium is also significant. After the medium had acquired the skills, either through possession or by training, she starts the new unit. She signs, dances and predicts to people without invitation. The spirit is usually very potent at this stage. The accuracy of her predictions and efficacy of her prescriptions will attract a number of devotees. In the process, the *Igbe* will be established as an autonomous institution. From this humble beginning, novices would be trained who, in turn, would spread to other parts of Urhoboland. In this way many *Igbe* groups have developed in Urhobo.

Organizational structure of *Igbe*

The mediums have a well-defined organizational structure. The founder is usually the head. At his death, his son, relation or anybody so directed by the spirit becomes the head. If the new head becomes ineffective, the *Igbe* would decline and eventually give way to others. The following are the other principal officers of *Igbe*:

(i). Ilori: The *ilori* (leaders), are next in rank to the principal medium. The *ilori* are both men and women. Their main function is to assist the spiritual head. By the time they become *ilori*, they have developed to the stage when they could be possessed. Like the head, they could relay messages from the spirit world to members and clients who came to them. They prescribe solutions to attacks by evil spirits and ways of averting impending calamities. Some use medicines while others depend on "holy water", incense, scents and candles. The *ilori* are also responsible for the organization and the general welfare of the people by ensuring that the rules and taboos are kept.

The appointment of the *ilori* is done by the spirit in most cases. This is made known to the people by the frequency of the possession and the accuracy of predictions. As this becomes apparent, the leader announces the name of the *olori* (leader) and he/she joins other *ilori* (leaders). The successor is appointed in the same way. Ikogho-Ovu gave an example of a son who usurped the position of his father and imposed himself on the members. He died six months after his appointment. Since then the people fear to take up the responsibility when they are not "elected" by the spirit.

(ii). **Oniemo Ame** (mother of water). The medium is symbolically referred to as *ame* (water). She derives her spiritual power from water spirits. As the name implies, she plays the role of a mother (*oniemo*) to all members. She is constantly possessed and proffers immediate solutions to the problems of members.

(iii). **Oze or Owhame**: *Oze* in Urhobo language means basin and *owhame* is "carrier of water". Only women are appointed to this post. Her duty is to fetch the "holy water" from the stream. The appointment, like the previous ones, is made by the spirit. The mediums interviewed claimed that the "spiritual water" is charged with power, capable of healing all forms of sickness, and neutralizing the power of evil spirits and witches.

The writer witnessed an occasion when the *oze* went to the stream to fetch water. It was a colourful procession amidst music, singing and dancing. The *oze* led the procession and was followed by the head and then the *ilori* and *oniemo*. The drummers and members were in the middle and rear respectively. At the stream, the *oze* moved into the water, up to the waist level. She dipped the basin, *(oze)*, into the water and lifted it into her head. It was filled to the brim. She swayed left and right, and then turned to join other members. She led the procession back to the *Igbe* house. What surprised spectators most was the fact that in spite of her dancing, no water dripped out of the *oze*. This is absolutely impossible in normal circumstance.

Ikogho-Ovu narrated the story of an abortive outing at Ofuoma in Ughelli polity to emphasize the spiritual presence in the water. The *oze* had a grudge against the founder of the *Igbe* but did not confess before the annual feast started. On the fateful day, as usual, the procession started from the *ogwan* (hall) towards the stream amidst drumming, singing and dancing with the *oze* leading the group. Unknown to members, the *oze* menstruated just as they approached the stream. They should have returned if she had disclosed the unusual occurrence.

When they got to the stream, the *oze* entered and dipped the basin into the stream. All her attempts to bring the basin out of the water and lift it into her head failed. In spite of prayers, singing and dancing to the water spirit, the woman was unable to accomplish the task. In the process, one of the members was possessed and she relayed all that the *oze* had done to the astonishment of the members and spectators. They returned without fetching the water. When they got to the *ogwan*, the *oze* confessed and the necessary rituals were performed. Then the feast was rescheduled and the water was successfully fetched for the use of members.

(iv) **Akpine**: This is the office of the principal singer. The songs, according to Ikogho-Ovu, are dictated to the *akpine* by the spirit. The songs, which are usually short, come without conscious effort by the *akpine*. As she signs, other members join until they perfect the song.

Spirit possession in Urhoboland

Spirit possession that results in communication with spirit beings (*aruemre*), in the belief of the Urhobo, may occur in either of two forms. The first is involuntary or spontaneous possession while the second is induced or voluntary possession.

(a) Involuntary possession

This type of possession manifests during an ecstatic trance, especially during a public procession or when one is alone. Before the possession, the victim must have been called either in dreams or through physical manifestation of the spirit. At the early stage of the manifestation, the novice would ignore the call. Other subsequent calls would be relayed with a warning that if the novice fails to heed the call, she/he would be punished. Eventually, the punishment comes when the novice falls into a trance and she becomes unconscious. This could last for several days. In some abnormal cases, the victim could become insane for a time until the appropriate rituals are performed by an established medium.

A victim of spontaneous possession in the form of ecstatic trance was interviewed in one of the villages of Ewhu polity. She opted to be called Otiti. This woman was said to have received several calls by a water spirit to become a medium. She refused the calls and ignored the spirit. When the calls became very regular, the woman decided to join one of the Pentecostal churches. By this choice, Otiti thought she could overcome the power of the spirit by the use of prayers.

During one of the outings of the members of the church, Otiti fell in the course of the procession and became unconscious. All efforts by the Pastor of the church to exorcise the spirit failed. Other Clergy men who were invited could not perform the much anticipated miracle. Members of Otiti's family abandoned the Pastor and went to a diviner to find out the cause this ugly development. The diviner told them that Otiti had been called several times by a water spirit to become a medium but she rebuffed the calls. The present predicament of Otiti, according to the diviner, was her rudeness which has exasperated the spirit. The diviner proffered a solution: Otiti should be taken to an *Igbe* medium at Orogun where the necessary ceremonies would be performed to appease the spirit.

In compliance with the directive of the diviner, Otiti was taken to Orogun. The leader of the *Igbe* and her followers prayed, danced and sprayed "holy water" and scent on the victim. After a protracted bargain, the water spirit gave the conditions that must be fulfilled before Otiti would be admitted into its fold. These were quickly met and Otiti regained her consciousness. She narrated her experiences during the trance and asked for forgiveness. At the time of the interview, Otiti has one of the most potent and functional *Igbe* in Urhoboland. It must, however, be stated that the writer also interviewed some respondents who claimed that they were spontaneously called by spirits but they resisted. When the menacing actions of the spirit became unbearable, they converted to Christianity. Since then, they have never experienced the influence of the spirits.

The second form of spontaneous possession is by family or public appointment. According to a source at Okuama (one of the towns in Ewhu polity) a spectacular event happened when the father of one Mr. Ikokoyogo, who trained many mediums, died. It was assumed that the most potent medium would succeed the leader. This was, however, not the case; the spirit insisted that Mr. Ikokoyogo, the eldest son of the leader, should be the successor. Ikokoyogo refused the offer as he felt he was not powerful enough to hold the position. Soon members of his family and the adherents of the *Igbe* joined in the efforts to made Ikokoyogo the leader. One afternoon, Ikokoyogo was sitting with other members of the community in a public rest place called *ohwarha*. Suddenly, he shouted, "*Me sere, me sere, mi che se ruo-o*" (I refuse, I refuse, I cannot do it). He got up and his eyes became red. He jumped up and down repeatedly to the surprise of all present. As efforts were made to hold him, he turned towards the direction of the river, and in a matter of minutes, he jumped into the river and disappeared.

Immediately, a search party of expert divers started. For a whole day the search continued without success. A diviner was consulted and his prediction corroborated with that of the mediums that the spirit had taken him. There was the assurance that no harm would be done to him but certain rituals must be performed to ensure his quick release by the spirit. Accordingly, offerings were made to the spirit, and the search was abandoned. On the evening of the following day, Ikokoyogo was seen sitting on the brink of the river up-stream by women who were returning from their farms. A number of selected men, including the principal mediums, left for the place. Ikokoyogo was brought to town healthy, amidst singing and dancing.

As would be expected, Ikokoyogo narrated his ordeal with the spirit. He was taken by the spirit into the river. He was not drowned because he had acquired spiritual powers. For the time he stayed in the river, he neither ate nor drank water. He narrated that he was kept by the side of what looked like an evergreen tree with full foliage. Although he did not eat, he felt as if nothing was wrong. Occasionally, the spirit would return to warn him against his decision not to become the leader of the mediums. He consented and after a promise, the spirit held him in the right hand and led him to where he was seen by the search party.

(b) Induced possession

This is a possession that occurs with the express permission of the medium. Special pleas are made to the spirit to manifest and to fulfil specific conditions. In an interview with Ikogho-Ovu of Agbarha on 8/4/94 at Ughelli, he pointed out that possession is best induced through music, dancing and singing. In his view, any spirit possession which is induced by drugs, alcohol or magical means is not true possession. He emphasized that matured mediums do not need music, singing and dancing before they are possessed. The spirit comes at will to direct the medium on what should be done on daily basis.

The present writer was present in the annual festival of *Igbe-Uku-Ezene* of Orogun town. Several mediums were invited to take part in the ceremonies. Many people who had problems also attended so that their problems could be identified and possible solutions proffered. All the mediums were dressed in white robes except the *ilori* (leaders) and *ewhame* (water carriers). The *ewhame* wore skirts and exposed their breasts and bellies. All the mediums carried white fans made with leathers of cow and a mirror fixed in the middle. The principal singer (*akpine*) started the first song and members joined with music coming from the background. The dancing was systematic and marked with rhythmical movements of the fans up and down to the legs. The noise of the fans also produced a kind of music. Eventually, the head moved out of the hall into the open compound and other members followed. By the time the third song was over, many of the mediums have been possessed.

The act of possession starts when the medium fails to dance to the normal rhythm. After an uncontrollable trembling, the medium sways left and right and then starts to circle round. She starts to speak unintelligible languages in the form of ventriloquism. No sooner the first medium was possessed than others followed. At the climax of possession, the entire arena was disorganized with each medium expressing her act of possession in a definite manner. After about twenty minutes of this grand display, normalcy was restored with a change of the music beat. When the drumming eventually stopped, the chief medium started to call on those possessed to relay their messages from the spiritual realm. As they moved to the middle, they called out those who had messages from the spirit world. Several messages of success, failure and victory over witches and enemies were relayed to the astonishment of the spectators. One of the mediums called a man who was later identified as Akokpokpo and made the following declaration; "You married about four years ago. All your efforts to get an issue have so far failed. About a year ago, you lost money and property to armed robbers. The worst is yet to come; this year would be most troublesome. You shall lose your mother and immediate sister."

The medium asked Akpokpokpo whether what she said was true. The man answered in affirmative. Then Akpokpokpo requested to know what should be done to ameliorate the wrath of the evil forces. Several prescriptions were made including sacrifices and observances of some taboos. It was not possible to know whether the impending doom predicted was averted. However, what is significant is that the medium was able to tell the man what happened in the past.

Spirit possession is a reality in Urhoboland as we have shown. The mode of possession varies from on medium to the other. There are cases when some people are possessed only once in their life time and after they accomplished their mission, they are never possessed. There are also instances when some people are possessed by evil spirits in which case they become mad and after a protracted suffering they die. Such possessions are attributed to sinful indulgence by the victims.

Clairvoyance and society in Urhoboland

In the belief of the Urhobo, any successful enterprise of the living members of the community must receive the blessing of the ancestors. This is precisely where mediumship is given a position of honour within the religious structure. Mediumship is concerned with the explanation, prediction and control of space time events. In this capacity, mediums have made immense contributions towards the social development of the people.

The annual festivals are important social events in Urhobo communities. This is the period when all Urhobo sons and daughters, both home and abroad, congregate to re-enact the primordial mythologies and loyalty to the ancestors and constituted authority. Before the commencement of the festivals, the mediums are consulted to know the outcome. In some instances, they predict that the festival would be marred by sudden deaths, fighting or heavy rains. They do not only predict doom; in several occasions they give the go ahead. Even when problems are predicted, they provide the appropriate control mechanism. Throughout the period of the annual festivals, the mediums are always at alert to ensure that evil spirits and other forces are driven out of the community.

The psychological fears generated by the activities of witches and sorcerers constitute one of the greatest social problems in Urhoboland. It is the belief of the people that witches use their psychic or spiritual powers to punish members of the society. Apart from premature deaths, they are responsible for disasters, such as storms, heavy rains and protracted droughts, which result in large-scale destruction of property. .

The sorcerers, on the other hand, use medicine made from physical objects to punish their victims. These medicines are in the form of poisons which are added to food, gin or water. They also manipulate objects, which like magic, affect the victim. By these negative activities, witches and sorcerers are dreaded in Urhoboland. The mediums have helped to solve these psychological fears by either prescribing appropriate control mechanism or medicines. In this regard, several witches have been identified while others have been compelled to make voluntary confessions by the mediums.

In Urhoboland, the relevance of religious message depends on precise set of political and economic conditions under which it is given. Thus, when religious beliefs and practices are detached from both the political and other societal values, any interpretation of them is likely to be highly distorted. This was also the view of Durkheim (1961) when he states that any coherent society must rest on a set of moral beliefs which ground the political order on a transcendental basis. In this way, religion is a social evolution and as a society evolves her clan cults change. This is consequent on the fact that religion is a unified system of beliefs and practices by which individuals represent to themselves the society which they belong. In this perspective, religious forces are human forces as they come from the very depths of our being.

In Urhoboland, the kings and chiefs are assigned religious functions. By their activities in key political, social and economic life of the people, the religious ethos demands that their positions be legitimized by religion. It is the quest to achieve this objective that made the mediums very important in the political life of the people. The installation of the kings entails several rituals and religious observances. The mediums may be invited to confirm the choice by communicating the decisions of the people to the ancestors and other divinities of the community. It is only when the appointment is confirmed that the necessary machinery are set in motion for the coronation of the king.

In Urhobo traditional society, religion also plays a major role in the economic life of the society. Faith and work are in continuous tension with one another, thus the secular and the religious meaning of work are inseparable. Work, success and wealth are public visible signs of election, just as laziness, poverty and failure are visible signs of damnation by the divinities. The traditional religion of the Urhobo propounds an ideology of a unified and integrated community in which each member believes that he works for the benefit of all.

The economic sphere is not abstracted from the other realities; there is a sense in which the entire religious complex could be said to serve the economic advancement of the society. Viewed from this perspective, such concerns as search for good health, job opportunities, peaceful interactions and other related issues are aimed at enhancing the economic progress of the polity. In other words, the quest for achievements, success or other good things of life is concerned with economic development. These concerns, in the belief system of the Urhobo, are intrinsically interwoven with religion.

Mediumship is a veritable source of wealth to the devotees. It is speculated that the water spirits bestow wealth on the mediums. This could be in the form of success that they record in their various enterprises. For example, some of the devotees who are traders receive greater patronage than their counterparts in the same business. Others who are farmers have greater yield during the harvesting period. The most spectacular are the ones who receive direct gifts from the water spirits. It is believed that some of the mediums are in constant physical touch with the spirits and in the process they receive physical objects, such as jewelries and money from them.

The stability and progress of any economy depends, to a greater extent, on the physical health of the people. There is a common adage among the Urhobo which says that the first step to wealth is physical health. This implies that any successful undertaking requires good health and this in turn, produces a favourable atmosphere that enhances intellectual advancement. By their healing abilities, the mediums provide manpower for the economic advancement of the society. They do not only predict impending dooms, accidents, drought etc. that could disrupt the economic activities of the people but also proffer appropriate remedies. When the economy is declining, the mediums are consulted and in most cases, they direct the entire people of the polity to perform rituals of affliction. In the same vein, life crisis rituals are recommended to individuals by the mediums to improve their social and economic wellbeing.

In Urhobo traditional society, the success of man depends on the number of wives and children he is able to acquire. This is consequent on the fact that more hands are required in the farms to cultivate large expanse of land. The paradox is that in spite of the many wives and children, some people still fail to acquire the wealth that is desired. It is in this predicament that the role of mediums becomes mandatory. After they have consulted the spiritual world to know the cause of failure, they prepare medicines or recommend rituals that could enhance productivity.

In most cases, rituals in the form of *izobo* (offering) are prescribed by the mediums. The supplicant is told to collect a number of food items, such as rotten eggs, pieces of yam or plantain, oil, salt, cowries, coins etc. for the ritual which is performed either at *awharode* (bad bush or sacred grove) or at *aderha* (crossroad). The choice of the ritual elements is consequent on the belief of the people that when unwholesome items are sacrificed to evil spirits, they keep out of human habitation. By these rituals, the mediums have made great contributions to the economic progress of the people. In the first place, ill-fated destinies have been altered to become more productive and also, the evil activities of witches and sorcerers have been checked.

The good aspects of mediumship notwithstanding, some fake ones have done incalculable damage to the social, political and economic advancement of the people. False predictions by some mediums have resulted in the disintegration of families and caused social and political instability. Elderly males and females are usually the victims of false predictions. In several occasions, they have been accused of witchcraft and are, therefore, held responsible for premature deaths and general decline in the economic activities of the people. For this reason, some people have left their aged mothers and fathers to die so that they could live in peace. When the anticipated death fails to materialize, they resort to violent attacks; the suspected victims are either strangled to death or killed in most brutal manner.

The problems brought to the mediums are always attributed to witches and evil spirits. The psychology is that nothing happens without a cause. Many people have been accused of witchcraft even when there is no empirical proof to substantiate the claim. To be on the safer side, many people have traveled out of the villages for fear of being accused. In some cases, the young and old who have been accused of witchcraft in the villages go to the cities which provide safe haven for them. Law enforcement agents are always available in the urban centres to protect them. There are others who convert to Christianity to consolidate their safety, and eventual burial when they die.

The result is that the farmlands have been abandoned and this scenario has resulted in shortage of the traditional food items which require more hands to produce. The social dimension is that as the people go into the urban centres the rural areas are depopulated whereas the cities are overpopulated. The effect of the rural drift is that most of those who migrate to the cities are jobless. They do not have sound education to give them gainful employment. In this predicament, many of them resort to stealing and other unlawful ways of ensuring their survival. The good ones among them engage in menial jobs, such as street trading and touting for drivers of commercial vehicles.

Another negative effect of the activities of the mediums is their attitude towards both traditional and orthodox healing methods. Some of the mediums are vehemently opposed to the use of orthodox as well as traditional medicines. They recommend the use of *orhe* (kaolin), scents, olive oil and prayers. As a result of this development, many people who should have been saved in public hospital have died in the hands of the mediums. For the mediums, no diagnosis is necessary; all forms of sicknesses are attributed to evil forces or the contravention of natural laws. In their judgment, solution to all human problems lies in the ability of man to propitiate the powers that are believed to be responsible for the malady.

There are some other ways in which the prescriptions of the mediums adversely affect the economic wellbeing of some individuals as well as the general public. Some people have been told to leave their jobs for fear of being killed by witches and sorcerers. This has created serious problem to some skilled workers who spent money and time learning their jobs only to be told that they would die if they continued with the jobs. In some areas, certain food items have been proscribed by the mediums, while some farmers have been told not to cultivate certain crops. In the same vein, some fertile lands have been abandoned as they are designated the homes of evil spirits.

In spite of the negative impacts examined above, mediumship is still a potent part of Urhobo traditional religion. Several efforts are being made to check the activities of the quacks among them. Those known to be fake mediums do not receive patronage. They may succeed at the initial stage but at the end, they are either driven out of the village or their halls *(egwan)* are destroyed by irate members of the community.

Conclusion

This work sets to throw insights into the roles of clairvoyants in Urhobo traditional religion. The paper established that the traditional religion of the Urhobo explains to men and women the discrepancies in their fates with respect to suffering, success, illness, inequality and bad fortune. Success in life is anchored on the good disposition of God and the deities towards the affairs of men, while failure or misfortune is predestined or as a result of punishment from the evil spirits. The Urhobo believe that the way to success is to be at peace with the spiritual powers. It is the quest for this ideal that has given the mediums their prominence in Urhobo society.

Mediumship is a viable media for the explanation, prediction and control of space-time events. The *emraro* have consistently helped to direct the people on the observance of the religious ethos and the societal norms. This has evolved over the years an egalitarian society in which human dignity is respected by both rulers and subjects. The result is that everybody considers himself as good as everyone else and demands a voice in the affairs of the polity.

Works cited

Awolalu, J.O. & Dopamu, P.A, West *African Traditional Religion* Ibadan: Onibonoje Press, 1976.
Bouquet, A.C. *Comparative Religion,* Harmondsworth: Penguin Books, 1971.
Durkheim, E., *The Elementary Forms of Religious Life* (trans. Free Press 1961.
Mbiti, J.S. *African Religions and Philosophy,* London: Heinemann 1969.
Parrinder, G., *West African Religion,* London: Epworth Press 1975.
Robertson, R. (ed.) *Sociology of Religion,* Harmondsworth: Penguin Books Ltd. 1969.
Smart, N., *The Religious Experience of Mankind,* Glasgow: William Collins Sons & Co. Ltd. 1969.

Select bibliography

Abd 'Al-Ati, H., *Islam in Focus*, Lagos I.P.B., n'd.
Abimbola, W., *Ifa An Exposition of Ifa Literary Corpus*, Ibadan: 1976.
Adebonojo, B.O. *Itan Ido Ijebu*, Ikeja, John West Publications Ltd., 1990.
Adepegba, C.O. *Yoruba Metal Sculpture*, Ibadan, Ibadan University Press 1991.
Adogbo, M.P. & Ojo, E.C., *Research Methods in the Humanities*, Lagos: Malthouse Press Ltd., 2003.
Adogbo, M.P., "The Spirit World of African Peoples" in Erivwo, S.U. & Adogbo, M.P., *Contemporary Essays in the Study of Religions*, Lagos: Fairs & Exhibitions Nig. Ltd., 2000.
Afonja, S., Olu-Pearce, T, (eds.), *Social Change in Nigeria*, London: Longman, 1986.
Ahmad, G., *The Philosophy of The Teachings of Islam*, London: Ahmadiyya Centenary Publications, 1979.
Ahmad, T., "Revelation, Rationality, Knowledge and Truth," *Islam International Publications*, London: Tilford, Survey, 1998.
Ajayi, J.F.A., *Christian Missions in Nigeria 1841 – 1891*, Ibadan: Longman, 1977.
Ajayi, J.F.A., *Christian Missions in Nigeria*, 1841-1891, Longmans, 1965
Akinjogbin I. A. & Ayandele, E. A. "Yoruba-land up to 1800" in Obaro Ikime (ed.). *Groundwork of Nigeria History*, Ibadan, Heinemann & Historical Society of Nigeria, 1980.
Ali, M., *The Religion of Islam*, New Delhi: Taj. Co.1986.
Alward, S., *African Christian Theology*, London: Geoffrey Chapman, 1975.
Amponsah, K., *Topics on West African Traditional Religion*, Vol. 1, Ghana Adwinsa, 1977
Aronson, L. "Ijebu Yoruba Aso Olona – A contextual and Historical Overview" *African Arts* (XXV) 3, July 1992.
Avoseh, T.O. *A short History of Epe*, Parochial Committee, St Micheal's Anglican Church, 1960.
Awolalu O. J "Ayelala – A Guardian of Social Morality," *Orita – Ibadan Journal of Religious Studies* (11) 2, Dec. 1968.
Awolalu O. J "The Interaction of Religions in Nigeria" *Orita – Ibadan Journal of Religious Studies , (XV)* 1, 1983.
Awolalu O. J *Yoruba Beliefs and Sacrificial Rites*, London, Longman, 1979.
Awolalu, J.O. & Dopamu, P.A, West *African Traditional Religion* Ibadan: Onibonoje

Press, 1976.
Awolalu, J.O. & Dopamu, P.A. *West African Traditional Religion*, Ibadan: Onibonoje Press 1979.
Awolalu, J.O. & Dopamu, P.A., *West African Traditional Religion*, Ibadan: Onibonoje Press, 1979.
Ayandele, E. A. *The Ijebu of Yorubaland: 1850-1950: Politics, Economy and Society*, Ibadan, Heinemann, 1992.
Ayandele, E.A., *Holy Johnson: Pioneer of African Nationalism*, 1836-1917, Frank Cass Co. Ltd., 1970.
Ayandele, E.A., *The Ijebu of Yorubaland, 1850-1950: Politics, Economy and Society*, Ibadan: Heinemann Educational Books Nig. Plc. 1992.
Ayandele, E.A., *The Missionary Impact on Modern Nigeria, 1842-1914*, London: Longman, 1962.
Aziz-us Samad U, *The Great Religions of the World*, Darūl Kutūb Lahore, 1976.
Bakker, J., *Prosperity and the Coming Apocalypse*, Benin: Joint Hairs Pub. Nig. Ltd., 1998.
Balogun I.A.B., "Utilizing Religion for Peaceful Unity and Progress in Nigeria," Ilorin, Univ.of Lectures, Notes 1981
Balogun, S. A. "History of Islam up to 1800" O. Ikime (ed), *Groundwork of Nigerian History*, Ibadan, Heineman for the Historical Society of Nigeria, 1980.
Bane, J. *Catholic Pioneers in West Africa*, Dublin: Clonmore & Reynolds, 1957.
Barnhouse, D. C., *God's Glory*, Michigan: Wm. B. Eerdmans Publishing Company, 1964.
Barrett, C.K., Paul's Speech in the Areopagus, *New Testament Christianity for Africa and the World*, London: SPCK, 1985.
Bascom, W.R., *Ifa Divination, communication between Gods and men in West Africa*, Bloomington: Indiana Univ. Press, 1959.
Baxter, J. S., *The Strategic Grasp of the Bible*, Michigan: Zondervan Publishing House, 1974.
Berger, P., *The Sacred Canopy*, New York, Double Day Press, 1969
Berkhof, L., *Systematic Theology*, Edinburgh: The Banner of Truth Trust, 1981.
Bertocci, P.A., *Religion As a Creative Insecurity*, New York, Assoc. Press, 1958.
Bettenson, H.(ed.) *Early Christian Church*, Oxford: University Press, 1963.
Boice, J.M., *Foundation of the Christian Faith*, England: Inter Varsity Press, 1981.
Borchert, O., *The Original Jesus*. London: Pickering & Inglis Ltd., 1968.
Bornkamm, G. *Jesus of Nazareth*, London: Hodder & Stoughton, 1960.
Bornkamm,G., *Paul*. London, Hodder & Stoughton, 1871.
Bouquet, A.C. *Comparative Religion*, Harmondsworth: Penguin Books, 1971.
Bourgeois, Jean-Louis "The History of Great Mosques of Djenne" *African Arts* (XX) 3. 1987
Bradbury, R.E., *The Benin Kingdom and the Edo-speaking Peoples Peoples of South Western Nigeria*, London: Int. African Institute, 1970.
Bravmann, R. A. *Islam and Tribal Art in West Africa*, London, Cambridge University Press, 1974.
Brown, C., (ed.), *The New International Dictionary of New Testament Theology*, Michigan: Zondervan Publishing House, Three Volumes, 1982.
Bruce, F.F., *Jesus and the Christian Origins outside the New Testament*, London: Holder & Stoughton, 1974.
C.M.S. G3/A3/04, Journal Extracts for the Half Year Ending, June, 1887.

C.M.S. Report, 1912-1913, West Equatorial Africa, (also,1915-1916; 1921-1922).
Capps, W., *Ways of Understanding Religion*, New York, Macmillan, 1972.
Carman, J.B., "Religion as a Problem in Christian Thought" in D.C. Dawe & Carman (eds.), *Christian Faith in Plural World*, New York: Orbits Books, 1978.
Clarke, P.B., *West Africa and Islam*, London, Edward Arnold, 1982.
Conner, W. T., *The Gospel of Redemption*. Nashville: Broadman Press, 1945.
Conton, W.F., *West Africa in History, Vol. 1, before 1800*, London: George Allen & Unwin Ltd., 1965.
Dike, K.O., Origins *of the Niger Mission*, 1814-1891, Ibadan: U.P., 1957.
Dillon, R.J. & J. A. Fitzmyer, Acts of the Apostles. *The Jerome Biblical Commentary*, New York, Geoffrey Chapman, 1974.
Doi, A.R., *Islam in Nigeria*, Zaria: Gaskiya Corp. Ltd., 1984.
Durkheim, E., *The Elementary Forms of Religious Life* (trans. Free Press 1961.
Eades J. S. *The Yoruba Today*, Cambridge, Cambridge University Press, 1980.
Edersheim, A., *The Life and Times of Jesus the Messiah*. New York: Longman's, Green, & Co., Volumes I & II, 1917.
Eichrod, W., *Theology of the Old Testament*, Vol. I, London: SCM. Press, 1975.
Ejenobo, D. T., *Jesus Christ Our Saviour*. Warri: Jonokase Publishing House, 2001.
Eliade, M. (ed), *The Encyclopedia of Religions*, New York, Macmillan, 1984.
Ellis, J. & Johnson, J., *The Missionary Visits to Ijebu Country 1892,* Ibadan: Daystar Press, 1974.
Emovon, O., "Ominigbon Divination" in *Nigeria Magazine* No. 151, 1984.
Engineer, A.A., *The Islamic State*, New Delhi: Ulkaa Publishing House, 1980.
Eniola, S.O., "Religious Crisis in Nigeria: Causes and Effects," Unilorin, 1990.
Erivwo, S.U & Adogbo, M.P. (eds.), *Contemporary Essays in The Study of Religion,* Fairs and Exhibitions Nig. Ltd., Lagos, 2000
Erivwo, S.U., *Traditional Religion and Christianity in Nigeria: The Urhobo People,* Ekpoma: Bendel State University, 1991.
Erivwo, S.U., "Christianity in Urhoboland," Ph.D. *Thesis*, University of Ibadan, 1972.
Erivwo, S.U., "Epha: Divination System among the Urhobo of the Niger Delta," *African Notes* Vol. VII, No. 1, 1979.
Erivwo, S.U., "Traditional Religion and Christianity among the Urhobo" in Ikenga-Metuh, E., *The Gods in Retreat,* Enugu: Fourth Dimension Pub., 1986.
Erivwo, S.U., *A History of Christianity in Nigeria: The Urhobo, The Isoko and The Itsekiri,* Ibadan: Daystar, 1979.
Erivwo, S.U.,"The Delay of the Evangelisation of the Western Delta of Nigeria," *West Africa Religion,* Nsukka, Department of Religion, vol. 17, 2, 1978
Ezeanya, S.N., A Critical Review of Ancestral Cults in Nigeria, *Ife Journal of Religions,* Vol. 1, December 1980.
Ezzati A. *An introduction to the History of the Spread of Islam*, Lagos, Islamic Publication Bureau, 1979.
Fage, J.D., *Introduction to the History of West Africa*, Cambridge: University Press, 1961.
Fajana A. and Biggs, B. J, *Nigeria in History*, Ibadan, Longman, 1964.
Falusi G. K, Lecture Note to Master's Students, May 1987.
Farid, G., (ed.). *The Holy Qur'an,* Eng. Transl. And Commentary, Rhwah The Oriental and Religious Publishing Corporation Ltd., 1969.
Floyd, V. F., *A New Testament History,* London: SCM. Press Ltd., 1977.
Forster, W.P., "Pre-twentieth Century Isoko: It's Foundation and Later Growth" in

Benneth, N.R., (ed.) *African Historical Studies*, Vol. II, No. 2, 1969.

Gbadamosi, G. "Odu Imale: Islam in *Ifa* Divination and the case of Predestined Muslims," *Journal of the Historical Society of Nigeria*, (8) 4, June 1977.

Guillame, A., *Traditions of Islam* Oxford: Clarendon Press, 1924.

Guthrie, D., et al., *The New Bible Commentary Revised*, Inter Varsity Press, 1970.

Guthrie, D., *New Testament Introduction*, England, Inter Varsity Press, 1968.

Gwakkin, R.I., Early *Church History to AD. 313*, 2Vols, Macmillan, 1927.

Haykal, M., *The Life of Muhammad*, Transl. I.R.A. al. Faruqi, North American Trust Publications, 1976.

Hubbard, J.W., *The Sobo of the Niger Delta*, Zaria: Gaskiya Corporation, 1948.

Idowu, E. B. *Olodumare –God in Yoruba belief*, London, Longman, 1962.

Idowu, E.B "The Challenge of Witchcraft" *Orita, Ibadan Journal of Religious Studies*, Vol. IV, No. 1, June, 1970.

Idowu, E.B.,*African Traditional: A Definition*, London: S. C. M., 1969.

Ifesieh, E.I., The Concept of Chineke as Reflected in Igbo Names and Proverbs: *Communic Viatorun*, No. XXVI, 1983.

Ije, Prof. 165 Vol. II, *Annual Report for 1932*, also 916, *Diary Ijebu Ode, 24 April, 1907*

Ikenga-Metuh, E., *Comparative Studies on African Traditional Religions*, Onitsha: Imico Press, 1992.

Ikime, O., *The Isoko People: A Historical Survey*, Ibadan: U.P., 1975.

Ikime, O., "The Coming of the C.M.S. into the Itsekiri, Urhobo and Isoko Country," *Nigeria Magazine*, No. 86, 1965.

Ikime, O., *Merchant Prince of the Niger Delta*, Heinemann, 1968.

Jewitt, D., "Report to the Synod" 1931, (unpublished MS. n. d.)

Jung, *et al.* (eds.); *Relations Among Religions Today*, London, 1963.

Kee, H.C. & F. W. Young, *The Living World of the New Testament*, London, Longman & Todd, 1974.

Kee, H.C. & Young, F.W., *The Living World of the New Testament*, London: Dalton, Longman & Todd, 1960.

Kelly, J.N.D., *Early Christian Doctrine*, London: Adam & Charles Black, 1968.

Krass, A.C., *Go . . . And Make Disciples*, London: SPCK, 1974.

Kwesi, A. D., *The Story of the Early Church*, London: Darton, Longman & Todd, 1977.

Latourette, K.S., *A History of Christianity*, Eyre & Spottiswoode, 1964.

Law, R. "Early European Sources Relating To The Kingdom of Ijebu (1500 – 1700): A Critical Survey," *History in Africa*, 13, 1986.

Lemu, A., "The Quranic Basis of Ethical Revolution". Conference Papers on Religion and Ethical Revolution in Nigeria; Dept. of Religious Studies, University of Ibadan, April 1983.

Lloyd, P. C. "Osifekunde of Ijebu" in Philip D. Curtin's *Africa Remembered - Narratives by West Africans from the Era of the Slave Trade*, Madison, The University of Wisconsin Press, 1967.

Makozi, A.O., & G. J. Afolabi Ojo (Ed); *The History of the Catholic Church in Nigeria*, Lagos: Macmillan, 1985.

Mala, B. & Oseni, Z.I., (eds.), *Religion, Peace and Unity in Nigeria*, Ibadan: NASR, 1984.

Mannan, M.A., *Islamic Economics, Theory and Practice*, Sh. Muhammad Ashraf, Lahore, Pakistan, 1970.

Marshall, L.M., *The Challenge of New Testament Ethics*, London, Macmillan, 1966.

Matthews, W.R., *God in Christian Thought and Experience*, Digswell Place; James Nisbet & Comp. Ltd., 1963.

Mbiti, J.S. *African Religions and Philosophy*, London: Heinemann 1969.
McKenzie, J.L., *Dictionary of the Bible*, New York, Geoffrey Chapman, 1968.
Montgomery, W. *What is Islam?* London, Longman, 1979.
Mullins, E. Y., *The Christian Religion In Its Doctrinal Expression*. Valley Forge: Judson Press, 1974.
Mume, J.O., *Confession of the Wizard of Igbinse* (Ughelli: Jom Nature Cure Centre, Agbarho): 1972,
Nabofa, M.Y "A Survey of Urhobo Traditional Religion" *The Urhobo People*, Ibadan, Heinemann 1981.
Nabofa, M.Y "The Symbolism of Obo: The Urhobo Altar of Hand" *Owu: Port Harcourt Journal of Humanistic Studies,* Vol. 1, No. 1, June,1994.
Nabofa, M.Y., "Erhi: The Urhobo Concepts of the Human Double and the Paradox of Self-Predestination in Urhobo Religion", Ph.D. Thesis 1978.
Niger Mission, G. 3. A3/012: Protector to Editor, *C.M.S. Gazette*, 29th April, 1911, (also, A3/013, 1913; 1914).
Obanta Newsday (4) 1, Jan-March, 1999.
Odumuyiwa, E.A., "A Century of Christianity in Remoland", *M.A. Thesis*, University of Ife, Ile-Ife, 1982.
Odunmuyiwa, E. A. A History of the Anglican Church in Ijebuland: 1892-1984 – A Sociological Analysis', Ph.D. Thesis, 1987.
Ogunkoya, T.O. "The Early History of Ijebu," *Journal of Historical Society of Nigeria* (1) 1, Dec 1956.
Oladimeji, T. A. G. "The Essence of Dwellers of Heaven: A search for new functions and Forms for Ibadan Masquerades" in *JONART – A Journal of Humanities* (St. Andrews College of Education, Oyo) (1) 2, June 1995.
Olayiwola, D.O., "Incultural Theology: A Nigerian Pentecostal Perspective", in Olayiwola, D.O. (ed.), *Contextualization of Christianity in Nigeria*, Lagos: Derib Books Ltd., 2002.
Ononeme, F.E., "The Anglican Evangelistical Band in Isoko Local Government Area of Bendel State of Nigeria," (unpublished Long Essay, University of Ibadan, 1978).
Opoku, K.A., *West African Traditional Religion,* FEP Int. Private Ltd., 1978.
Parrinder, A.G., *African Mythology*, London: 1967.
Parrinder, A.G., *West African Religion*, London: Epworth Press, 1961.
Parrinder, G. *The World's Living Religions,* London, Pan Bks., 1974.
Peek, P.M., "The Founding of the Isoko Clan of Uzere" (unpublished typescript, 1966).
Pfeffer, L., *Church and State and Freedom*, Beacon Press, Boston, 1967.
Raji, M.G.A., *Background to Islamic Culture*, A.B.U. Press, Zaria, 1991.
Robertson, R. (ed.) *Sociology of Religion*, Harmondsworth: Penguin Books Ltd. 1969.
Ryder, A.F.C., "Missionary Activities in the Kingdom of Warri to the early Nineteenth Century," *Journal of the Historical Society of Nigeria*, Vol.II, I, 1960.
Seriki, I. A. A. Islam Among the Egba and Ijebu Peoples (1841-1982) Ph.D. Thesis, University of Ibadan, Ibadan, 1986.
Shorter, A. *African Christian Theology*, London: Geoffrey Chapman, 1975.
Siddiqi, M.I., *Asharah Mubash-Sharah,* Lahore, (n.p.), 1989.
Smart, N. "Worldviews: An Inventory" in *Worldviews: Cross Cultural Explorations of Human Beliefs*, New York: Charles Scribner's Sons Publishers, 1983.
Smart, N., *The Religious Experience of Mankind*, Glasgow: William Collins Sons & Co.

Ltd. 1969.

Smith, D.E. (ed), *Religion, Politics and Social Change in the Third World.* New York, Free Press, 1971.

Smith, R. S. *Kingdoms of The Yorubas,* London, Methuen and Co Ltd., 1976

Stott, J., *Men With a Message.* England: Evangelical Literature Trust, 1994.

The Church Missionary Outlook II, 1974.

Thompson, F.C. (ed.), *The Thompson Chain-Reference Bible, New International Version,* Michigan, Zondervan, 2000.

Ubrurhe, J.O. "Urhobo Cosmology: A key to Understanding Urhobo Art" in, Ubrurhe, J. O. (ed.), *African Beliefs and Philosophy* Warri: International Publishers, 1992.

Ubrurhe, J.O., "A Functionalist Approach to the study of Taboos: A Case Study of Urhobo Traditional Society", Unpublished Master's Thesis, UNN, 1986.

Ukuanu, M.O.U., *A Short History of St. Michael's Anglican Church, Otie,* Oleh: Mercury Printing Press, 1970.

Uyeri, J.E., "Development of Education in Isoko, 1910-1960," (unpublished M.A. Thesis, University of Ibadan, 1977).

Vogel, S.M., Baule: *African Art Western Eyes.* New Haven, Yale University, 1997,

Walker, W., *A History of the Christian Church, Edinburgh,* T. T. Clark, 1968.

Watt, W. M. "Some Problems Before West African Islam" in *The Islamic Quarterly – A Review of Islamic Culture* (IV) 1, April 1958.

Wessels, A. *A Modern Arabic to Biography, of Muhammad, A Critical Study of M.H. Haykal's Yayat Muhammad,* Lei den, E.J. Brill, 1972.

X Leon-Duffour, *Dictionary of the New Testament,* London, Geoffrey Chapman 1980.

Index

Abacha, Sani; 4
Abd 'Al-Ati, H.; 103
Abimbola, W.; 137
Abimbola, Wande; 134
Abogunrin, S.O.; 15
Adamolekun, T.; 15
Adebonojo, B.O. ; 105, 116
Adeboye, Pastor; 3
Adepegba, C.O. ; 116
Adesola, J.A., 85
Adogbo, M.P. & Ojo, E.C., ; 137
Afonja, S.; 103
African Christian theology, 44
African religions and philosophy, 44, 151
African traditional religion, 103
African wisdom and the recovery of the earth, 15
Agbebi, Mojola; 83
Agberia, J. T.; 121
Ahmad, G.; 103
Ahmad, T.; 103
Aitken, Rev. J.D.; 67
Ajayi, J.F.A; 55, 75
Ajowhomu, Isaiah; 65
Akande, Bisi; 15
Akinjogbin I. A. & Ayandele, E. A. ; 116
Ali, M.; 103
Alimi, Mallam; 107

Alward, S.; 44
Amponsah, K.; 55
Apena, Venerable B.P.; 72, 75
Aquinas, Thomas; 14
Aronson, L. 105, 117
Avoseh, T.O. ; 117
Awokoya, Stephen Oluwole; 86
Awolalu, J.O. & Dopamu, P.A.; 44, 137, 151
Awolalu, J.O.; 44, 108, 117, 123, 151
Awoniyi, Senator Sunday; 3
Ayandele, E.A, 75, 78, 83, 87, 105, 108, 116, 117
Aziz-us Samad U.; 103
Bakker, J.; 87
Balogun Atambala, 80, 107
Balogun I.A.B.; 103
Balogun Oderinlo, 107
Balogun, S. A. ; 117
Bane, J. ; 75
Banjo, S.A.; 86
Barnhouse, D. C.; 31
Barrett, C.K.; 55
Bascom, W.R.; 134, 137
Baxter, J. S.; 31
Bello, Sultan; 109
Benin Kingdom and the Edo-speaking, 137
Berger, P., ; 103
Berkhof, Louis; 19, 31

Bertocci, P.A.; 103
Bettenson, H.; 44
Blyden, Edward Wilmot; 83
Boice, J.M.; 55
Borchert, O.; 31
Bornkamm, G.; 44, 45, 47, 48, 51, 55
Bouquet, A.C. ; 151
Bourgeois, Jean-Louis; 117
Bradbury, R.E.; 137
Bravmann, R. A. ; 117
Brown, C.; 31
Bruce, F.F.; 44
Bryant, M.D.; 15
Capps, W., ; 103
Carman, J.B.; 44
Catholic pioneers in West Africa; 75
Challenge of New Testament ethics, 55
Challenge of religious studies, 15
Odutola, Chief Timothy Adeola; 78
Christ Apostolic Church, 81
Christian inferences from the Resurrection narratives; 40
Christian Missions in Nigeria, 55, 75
Christian Resurrection and the challenges of the African traditional cosmologies; 41
Christianity in Urhoboland, 75
Clarke, P.B.; 103
Coming of the C.M.S, 75
Comparison of the religious life of the Athenians and Africans; 51
Concept of *Chineke*, 55
Conner, W. T.; 31
Conton, W.F., ; 117
Critical Evaluation of the Resurrection and Appearances; 38
Crowther, Bishop Ajayi; 59
Curtin, Philip D. ; 117
dan Fodio, Uthman; 107, 116
Danfulani, U.H.D.; 15
Dawe, D.C; 44
Delay of the Evangelisation of the Western Delta of Nigeria, 55

Development of Education in Isoko, 75
Dike, K.O, 75
Dillon, R.J. & J. A. Fitzmyer; 55
Dillon, R.J.; 47
Divination System among the Urhobo of the Niger Delta; 137
Divine Favour Weekend Crusade; 3
Doi, A.R.; 103
Durkheim, E.; 151
Eades J. S. ; 117
Early Christian Church, Oxford; 44
Edersheim, A.; 31
Egburie, Phillip Akpona; 72
Eichrod, W.; 44
Ejenobo, D.T.; 19, 31
Elementary forms of religious life, 151
Eliade, M. ; 103
Ellis, J. & Johnson, J. ; 87
Emovon, O.; 137
Encyclopaedia of Religions, 103
Eniola, S. O.; 89, 103
Erivwo, S.U & Adogbo, M.P. ; 103
Erivwo, S.U.; 55, 75, 137
Ezeanya, S.N.; 55
Ezekwesili, Rev. E.; 72
Ezzati A. ; 117
Fage, J.D. ; 117
Fajana A. and Biggs, B. J. ; 117
Falode, Revd. Canon; 81
Falusi G. K, 55
Farid, G. ; 103
Fitzmyer, J.A.; 47, 50
Floyd, V. F, 55
Forster, W.P., 75
Foundation of the Christian Faith, England, 55
Founding of the Isoko Clan of Uzere, 75
Garbutt, Rev.; 72
Garrard, Rev; 62
Gbadamosi, G. ; 107, 117
Gladstone, William; 14
Gollmer, Revd. C.A.; 81
Great religions of the world, 103

Index

Greek Concept of Divine Men; 24
Guillame, A.; 103
Guthrie, D. ; 55
Gwakkin, R.I.; 44
Gwamna, J.D.; 15
Haastrup, Ademuyiwa; 80
Hawarden, 14
Haykal, M.; 103
History of Christianity in Nigeria, 55
History of the Catholic Church in Nigeria, 56
Holy Johnson: pioneer of African nationalism, 75
Howkins, K.G.; 15
Hubbard, J.W, 75
Huxley, J.S.; 15
Ibrahim, J.; 4, 15
Idamarhare, A. O.; 45
Idowu, E.B.; 15, 55, 103, 117, 137
Idowu, Professor E. B.; 1
Ifa Divination, communication between Gods and men in West Africa, 137
Ifesieh, E.I.; 55
Ije, Prof. ; 87
Ikenga-Metuh, E.; 137
Ikenne, 78
Ikime, O. ; 75
Imo, C.O.; 15
International Association for Mission Studies, 11
International Association for the History of Religions, 11
International Congress of Christians and Jews, 11
International Society for New Testament Studies, 11
Islamic Economics, theory and practice; 103
Jehwe, M.O.; 140
Jesus and the Christian Origins outside the New Testament, 44
Jesus the Messiah: Son of Man and Son of God, 19
Jesus the Son of God; 23

Jesus the Son of Man; 21
Jewitt, D.; 75
Haastrup, Joseph Pythagoras; 80
Jung, *et al.* (eds.); 103
Kalu, O.U.; 15
Kee, H.C. & Young, F.W.; 31, 44, 55
Kee, Howard Clark; 52
Kelly, J.N.D.; 39, 44
Krass, A.C.; 87
Küng, H.; 15
Kwesi, A. D. ; 52, 55
Lasbery, Bishop; 72
Latourette, K.S, 75
Law, R. ; 117
Lemu, A.; 103
Leon-Dulfour, 45
Life of Muhammad, 103
Lloyd, P. C. ; 117
Makozi, A.O., & G. J. Afolabi Ojo ; 56
Mala, B. & Oseni, Z.I.; 103
Mannan, M.A.; 103
Manus, C.U.; 15
Mariere, M.E; 140
Marshall, L.M.; 55
Mary Magdalene, 34, 38
Maslow, A.H.; 16
Matthews, W.R.; 44
Mbiti, J.S.; 44, 137, 151
McKenzie, J.L.; 56
Men with a Message, 31
Merchant Prince of the Niger Delta, 75
Messianic Son of God in Judaism; 24
Metuh, E.E.; 16
Missionary impact on modern Nigeria, 87
Missionary visits to Ijebu Country 1892; 86
Montgomery, W. ; 103
Muhammad Abduh, 101
Muhammad, modern Arabic to biography of 104
Mullins, E. Y.; 19, 31
Mume, J.O.; 137
Nabofa, M.Y.; 137

New Bible Commentary Revised, 55
Njoroge, N.; 16
Obasanjo, Olusegun; 3, 11, 13
Oduduwa, 108
Odufuwa, J.J.; 85
Odumuyiwa, Prof E.A.; 79, 82, 87, 105, 109, 117
Odutola, Rt. Revd. Solomon O.; 86
Odutola, Timothy Adeola; 78
Ogbu, Prof.; 4
Ogundana, Bishop; 82
Ogunkoya, T.O. ; 105, 109, 117
Ojo, A.; 16
Oladimeji, T. A. G.; 105, 117
Olayiwola, D.O.; 77, 87
Olu-Pearce, T.; 103
Omako, Opelomo; 72
Omoyajowo, Revd. Professor J.A.; 83
Onibere S. G. A., 59
Ononeme, F.E.; , 75
Onwu, N.; 16
Opoku, K.A.; 137
Origins of the Niger Mission, 75
Oseruvwoja, M. ; 140
Oyegunsen, Daddy Joseph; 81
Parrinder, A.G. ; 103, 117, 137, 151
Paul's Address at Areopagus in African context; 45-55
Peek, P.M., 75
Pfeffer, L. ; 103
Philosophy of the teachings of Islam, 103
Politics of religion in Nigeria, 15
Promise and Ministry of the Holy Spirit, 16
Prosperity and the Coming Apocalypse,, 86
Pursuit of divine learning, 14
Quranic basis of ethical revolution, 103
Raji, M.G.A.; 104
Relations among religions today, 103
Religion and democracy in Nigeria, 15
Religion and human values, 13
Religion as a creative insecurity, 103

Religion of Islam, 103
Religion without revelation, 15
Religion, peace and unity in Nigeria, 103
Religious experience of mankind, Glasgow, 151
Religious human rights, 6
Revelation, rationality, knowledge and truth, 103
Ricoeur, Paul; 9
Robertson, R. ; 151
Ryder, A.F.C.; 76
Sacred canopy, 103
Sangotoyinbo, 83
Schmidt, R.; 4, 16
Seriki, 105
Seriki, I. A. A. ; 117
Shorter, A.; 44
Siddiqi, M.I. ; 104
Sierra Leone, 107
Smart, N. ; 137, 151
Smith, D.E. ; 104
Smith, R. S. ; 117
Sobo of the Niger Delta, 75
Social change in Nigeria, 103
Son of Man and Son of God: the African perspective; 29
Spirit World of African Peoples, 137
spread of Islam in Nigeria: the case of Ijebuland, 105
St Deiniol's Library, 14
Story of the Early Church, 55
Stott, J.; 31
Strategic grasp of the Bible, 31
Takaya, B.J.; 16
Theology of the Old Testament, 44
Thompson, F.C, 56
Tugwell, Bishop; 59
Ubrurhe, J.O. ; 137
Ukuanu, M.O.U.; 76
Uyeri, J.E.; 76
Vishigh, I.R.; 16
Vogel, Susan M.; 132, 138
Walker, W.; 56
Watt, W. M. ; 117.

Ways of understanding religion, 103
Wessels, A. ; 104
West Africa and Islam, 103
Wiredu, Kwesi; 9

Wittgenstein, L.; 16
World's living religions, 103
X Leon-Duffour, 56.
Young, Franklin W. ; 52

www.ingramcontent.com/pod-product-compliance
Lightning Source LLC
Chambersburg PA
CBHW021408290426
44108CB00010B/434